GoLive™ 5.0 For Du...

CW00857961

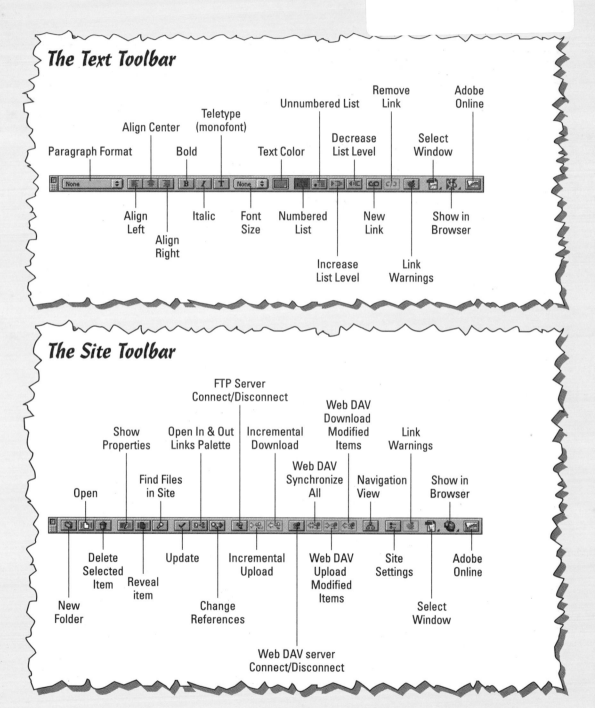

The Text Toolbar

- Paragraph Format
- Align Center
- Teletype (monofont)
- Bold
- Text Color
- Unnumbered List
- Decrease List Level
- Remove Link
- Select Window
- Adobe Online
- Align Left
- Align Right
- Italic
- Font Size
- Numbered List
- Increase List Level
- New Link
- Link Warnings
- Show in Browser

The Site Toolbar

- FTP Server Connect/Disconnect
- Show Properties
- Open In & Out Links Palette
- Incremental Download
- Web DAV Download Modified Items
- Link Warnings
- Find Files in Site
- Web DAV Synchronize All
- Navigation View
- Show in Browser
- Open
- Delete Selected Item
- Reveal item
- Update
- Incremental Upload
- Web DAV Upload Modified Items
- Site Settings
- Adobe Online
- New Folder
- Change References
- Select Window
- Web DAV server Connect/Disconnect

GoLive™ 5.0 For Dummies®

Cheat Sheet

Shortcut Keys in GoLive 5

Windows keys	Mac keys	What it does
Ctrl+B	⌘+B	Opens a directory and the file you choose will be the linked file
Ctrl+Alt+F	Option+⌘+F	Lets you edit font sets
Shift+Alt+Ctrl+I	Shift+Option+⌘+I	Shows document statistics
Alt+Ctrl+Y	Option+⌘+Y	Displays Site settings when in the Site window
Alt+Ctrl+L	Option+⌘+L	Removes link from selected linked text or graphic.
Shift+Ctrl+G	Shift+⌘+G	Left aligns text
Shift+Ctrl+M	Shift+⌘+M	Center aligns text
Shift+Ctrl+R	Shift+⌘+R	Right aligns text
Shift+Alt+Ctrl+ K	Shift+Option+⌘+ K	Displays all keyboard shortcuts

The Color Palette

True Web
(Web Safe)

New Site
Colors

Greyscale   HSV

CMYK

RGB   System

Index   Named
Web Colors

The Objects Palette

Basic   Head   Site Extras

Smart   Frames   Quicktime

Forms   Site   Custom

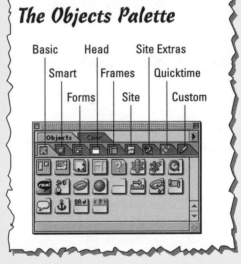

Copyright © 2000 IDG Books Worldwide, Inc.
All rights reserved.

Cheat Sheet $2.95 value. Item xxxx-x.

For more information about IDG Books,
call 1-800-762-2974.

For Dummies®: Bestselling Book Series for Beginners

GoLive™ 5

FOR

DUMMIES®

by Bill Sanders

IDG Books Worldwide, Inc.
An International Data Group Company

Foster City, CA ◆ Chicago, IL ◆ Indianapolis, IN ◆ New York, NY

GoLive™ 5 For Dummies®

Published by
IDG Books Worldwide, Inc.
An International Data Group Company
919 E. Hillsdale Blvd.
Suite 400
Foster City, CA 94404
www.idgbooks.com (IDG Books Worldwide Web Site)
www.dummies.com (Dummies Press Web Site)

Library of Congress Control Number: 00-101257

ISBN: 0-7645-0687-0

Printed in the United States of America

10 9 8 7 6 5 4 3 2 1

1B/RY/QY/QQ/IN

Distributed in the United States by IDG Books Worldwide, Inc.

Distributed by CDG Books Canada Inc. for Canada; by Transworld Publishers Limited in the United Kingdom; by IDG Norge Books for Norway; by IDG Sweden Books for Sweden; by IDG Books Australia Publishing Corporation Pty. Ltd. for Australia and New Zealand; by TransQuest Publishers Pte Ltd. for Singapore, Malaysia, Thailand, Indonesia, and Hong Kong; by Gotop Information Inc. for Taiwan; by ICG Muse, Inc. for Japan; by Intersoft for South Africa; by Eyrolles for France; by International Thomson Publishing for Germany, Austria and Switzerland; by Distribuidora Cuspide for Argentina; by LR International for Brazil; by Galileo Libros for Chile; by Ediciones ZETA S.C.R. Ltda. for Peru; by WS Computer Publishing Corporation, Inc., for the Philippines; by Contemporanea de Ediciones for Venezuela; by Express Computer Distributors for the Caribbean and West Indies; by Micronesia Media Distributor, Inc. for Micronesia; by Chips Computadoras S.A. de C.V. for Mexico; by Editorial Norma de Panama S.A. for Panama; by American Bookshops for Finland.

For general information on IDG Books Worldwide's books in the U.S., please call our Consumer Customer Service department at 800-762-2974. For reseller information, including discounts and premium sales, please call our Reseller Customer Service department at 800-434-3422.

For information on where to purchase IDG Books Worldwide's books outside the U.S., please contact our International Sales department at 317-596-5530 or fax 317-572-4002.

For consumer information on foreign language translations, please contact our Customer Service department at 1-800-434-3422, fax 317-572-4002, or e-mail rights@idgbooks.com.

For information on licensing foreign or domestic rights, please phone +1-650-653-7098.

For sales inquiries and special prices for bulk quantities, please contact our Order Services department at 800-434-3422 or write to the address above.

For information on using IDG Books Worldwide's books in the classroom or for ordering examination copies, please contact our Educational Sales department at 800-434-2086 or fax 317-572-4005.

For press review copies, author interviews, or other publicity information, please contact our Public Relations department at 650-653-7000 or fax 650-653-7500.

For authorization to photocopy items for corporate, personal, or educational use, please contact Copyright Clearance Center, 222 Rosewood Drive, Danvers, MA 01923, or fax 978-750-4470.

About the Author

Bill Sanders has written more than 30 computer-related books, including his most recent, *Creating Learning-Centered Courses for the World Wide Web*. He has worked with the Web since its inception and developed sites with virtually every component in Web pages. Currently he is a professor in the Interactive Information Technology program at the University of Hartford.

ABOUT IDG BOOKS WORLDWIDE

Welcome to the world of IDG Books Worldwide.

IDG Books Worldwide, Inc., is a subsidiary of International Data Group, the world's largest publisher of computer-related information and the leading global provider of information services on information technology. IDG was founded more than 30 years ago by Patrick J. McGovern and now employs more than 9,000 people worldwide. IDG publishes more than 290 computer publications in over 75 countries. More than 90 million people read one or more IDG publications each month.

Launched in 1990, IDG Books Worldwide is today the #1 publisher of best-selling computer books in the United States. We are proud to have received eight awards from the Computer Press Association in recognition of editorial excellence and three from Computer Currents' First Annual Readers' Choice Awards. Our best-selling ...For Dummies® series has more than 50 million copies in print with translations in 31 languages. IDG Books Worldwide, through a joint venture with IDG's Hi-Tech Beijing, became the first U.S. publisher to publish a computer book in the People's Republic of China. In record time, IDG Books Worldwide has become the first choice for millions of readers around the world who want to learn how to better manage their businesses.

Our mission is simple: Every one of our books is designed to bring extra value and skill-building instructions to the reader. Our books are written by experts who understand and care about our readers. The knowledge base of our editorial staff comes from years of experience in publishing, education, and journalism — experience we use to produce books to carry us into the new millennium. In short, we care about books, so we attract the best people. We devote special attention to details such as audience, interior design, use of icons, and illustrations. And because we use an efficient process of authoring, editing, and desktop publishing our books electronically, we can spend more time ensuring superior content and less time on the technicalities of making books.

You can count on our commitment to deliver high-quality books at competitive prices on topics you want to read about. At IDG Books Worldwide, we continue in the IDG tradition of delivering quality for more than 30 years. You'll find no better book on a subject than one from IDG Books Worldwide.

John J. Kilcullen

John Kilcullen
Chairman and CEO
IDG Books Worldwide, Inc.

Eighth Annual
Computer Press
Awards ≥1992

Ninth Annual
Computer Press
Awards ≥1993

Tenth Annual
Computer Press
Awards ≥1994

Eleventh Annual
Computer Press
Awards ≥1995

IDG is the world's leading IT media, research and exposition company. Founded in 1964, IDG had 1997 revenues of $2.05 billion and has more than 9,000 employees worldwide. IDG offers the widest range of media options that reach IT buyers in 75 countries representing 95% of worldwide IT spending. IDG's diverse product and services portfolio spans six key areas including print publishing, online publishing, expositions and conferences, market research, education and training, and global marketing services. More than 90 million people read one or more of IDG's 290 magazines and newspapers, including IDG's leading global brands — Computerworld, PC World, Network World, Macworld and the Channel World family of publications. IDG Books Worldwide is one of the fastest-growing computer book publishers in the world, with more than 700 titles in 36 languages. The "...For Dummies®" series alone has more than 50 million copies in print. IDG offers online users the largest network of technology-specific Web sites around the world through IDG.net (http://www.idg.net), which comprises more than 225 targeted Web sites in 55 countries worldwide. International Data Corporation (IDC) is the world's largest provider of information technology data, analysis and consulting, with research centers in over 41 countries and more than 400 research analysts worldwide. IDG World Expo is a leading producer of more than 168 globally branded conferences and expositions in 35 countries including E3 (Electronic Entertainment Expo), Macworld Expo, ComNet, Windows World Expo, ICE (Internet Commerce Expo), Agenda, DEMO, and Spotlight. IDG's training subsidiary, ExecuTrain, is the world's largest computer training company, with more than 230 locations worldwide and 785 training courses. IDG Marketing Services helps industry-leading IT companies build international brand recognition by developing global integrated marketing programs via IDG's print, online and exposition products worldwide. Further information about the company can be found at www.idg.com.

1/26/00

Author's Acknowledgments

Many talented people from both sides of the Atlantic from Adobe Systems provided unselfish help throughout the Beta tests of GoLive 5. Just a few with whom I was in contact literally every day of the week include John Kranz, Lance Lewis, Kim Platt, Adam Pratt, and Jens C. Neffe. Other software engineers at Adobe System worked to enhance GoLive 5 in every way imaginable (and some unimaginable).

In the Adobe Beta group, everyone shared their insights, and to all of them, I am most grateful. A truly international group spanned the globe from Tokyo to Switzerland in a cooperative effort to make GoLive 5 the best Web site development tool on earth. Especially selfless in their help were Glenn Fleishman (glennf.com) who provided invaluable insights into WebDAV and Oliver Zahorka who set up the WebDAV for testing and refining GoLive 5.

At the University of Hartford, I had good support from Dave Demers, Karen Barrett, and Steve Misovich. Good knowledge and software support goes a long way. Also, many conversations with Laura Spitz, a talented designer, has taught me a lot about Web design and was most helpful in the chapter on design.

Mike Roney and Paul Levesque of IDG Books saw the book through from concept to completion, providing every type of help along the way. Margo Hutchinson of Waterside Productions was instrumental in getting the project off the ground.

Like all authors who hunker away in solitude, a patient and encouraging spouse is invaluable, and in this respect, I am fortunate indeed. My wife Delia was a pillar of support and understanding. Our dog Bogee would periodically take me away from the keyboard and out for a walk, and his total lack of understanding about deadlines and work schedules was a blessing indeed.

Publisher's Acknowledgments

We're proud of this book; please register your comments through our IDG Books Worldwide Online Registration Form located at http://my2cents.dummies.com.

Some of the people who helped bring this book to market include the following:

Acquisitions, Editorial, and Media Development

Project Editor: Paul Levesque

Acquisitions Editor: Michael Roney

Copy Editors: Bill Barton, Christine Berman

Proof Editor: Jill Mazurczyk

Technical Editor: Lee Musick

Editorial Manager: Leah Cameron

Editorial Assistant: Seth Kerney

Production

Project Coordinator: Amanda Foxworth

Layout and Graphics: Amy Adrian, Joe Bucki, Jason Guy, LeAndra Johnson, Tracy K. Oliver, Jacque Schneider, Brian Torwelle, Erin Zeltner

Proofreaders: Charles Spencer, York Production Services, Inc.

Indexer: York Production Services, Inc.

General and Administrative

IDG Books Worldwide, Inc.: John Kilcullen, CEO

IDG Books Technology Publishing Group: Richard Swadley, Senior Vice President and Publisher; Walter R. Bruce III, Vice President and Publisher; Joseph Wikert, Vice President and Publisher; Mary Bednarek, Vice President and Director, Product Development; Andy Cummings, Publishing Director, General User Group; Mary C. Corder, Editorial Director; Barry Pruett, Publishing Director

IDG Books Consumer Publishing Group: Roland Elgey, Senior Vice President and Publisher; Kathleen A. Welton, Vice President and Publisher; Kevin Thornton, Acquisitions Manager; Kristin A. Cocks, Editorial Director

IDG Books Internet Publishing Group: Brenda McLaughlin, Senior Vice President and Publisher; Sofia Marchant, Online Marketing Manager

IDG Books Production for Branded Press: Debbie Stailey, Director of Production; Cindy L. Phipps, Manager of Project Coordination, Production Proofreading, and Indexing; Tony Augsburger, Manager of Prepress, Reprints, and Systems; Shelley Lea, Supervisor of Graphics and Design; Debbie J. Gates, Production Systems Specialist; Steve Arany, Associate Automation Supervisor; Robert Springer, Supervisor of Proofreading; Trudy Coler, Page Layout Manager; Kathie Schutte, Senior Page Layout Supervisor; Janet Seib, Associate Page Layout Supervisor; Michael Sullivan, Production Supervisor

Packaging and Book Design: Patty Page, Manager, Promotions Marketing

◆

The publisher would like to give special thanks to Patrick J. McGovern, without whom this book would not have been possible.

◆

Contents at a Glance

Cartoons at a Glance

By Rich Tennant

page 151

page 237

page 351

page 299

Fax: 978-546-7747
E-mail: richtennant@the5thwave.com
World Wide Web: www.the5thwave.com

Table of Contents

Part II: Looking Good — Designs That Delight 151

Chapter 7: Color Me Web! 153

Getting a Mix of Color 153
Tickled #FFC0CB: Color on the Web 155
   Practicing safe Web-page coloring! 155
Coloring Text by Using the Color Well 157
Matching Your Web Page to Your Graphics 158
   Customizing your color scheme 160
   Transferring color schemes from outside sources 161
Storing a Color Set in the Site Window 163
Using Site Colors to Paint Your Pages 165
Setting the Tone with Background Color 166
Keeping Up Your Background Image 167

Chapter 8: How to Flaunt a Form: Buttons, Boxes, and Lists 169

The Line Forms at the Right 169
An Entire Palette of Forms 171
The User Gets a Word In 173
   Name, please: The Text Field element 174
   Adding values 175
   Text fields in a single-form container 176
   Text Area elements 177
   Focus in elements! 179
Click Here: Check Boxes and Radio Buttons 181
   Adding radio buttons to your page 181
   Placing check boxes on your page 183
   Labeling your radio buttons and check boxes 185
Making the Buttons Behave 185
Working with Lists and Menus 188
   Using the list box 188
   Popups and URL Popups 191

Chapter 9: The Right Frame of Mind 195

Defining Frame Elements 195
Why Frames? 196
Setting Up Your Frame Set 197
Loading the Frame Set 198
Naming the Frames 199
   Fine-tuning a frame 200
   Tweaking the frame size and placement 201
Adjusting the Frame Set 202
Navigating with Frames 204
   Linking to frames within a frame set 205
   A frame menu 207
Adding Frames 211

Introduction

*E*very time I turn around, I see more great tools for creating Web pages and Web sites. At the same time, World Wide Web art and technology advance at a rate that's astounding. A few years ago, people were impressed by animated images bouncing up and down on their page or happily blinking text. But now, Web pages and sites are castles of art and design with liquid pages that respond to your touch and remember your name.

Welcome to *GoLive 5 For Dummies!* Anyone from a novice to a professional designer can use this book to create great-looking, sophisticated sites. Want to learn how to use GoLive 5 without a degree in computer science? This is the book for you. You get what you need, when and where you need and want it. In no time you'll be creating sites that you never thought you could create. You might even start your own business on the Web.

If you've ever wondered how the Web designers accomplish these major feats, let me give a tip: *Do not look at the source code.* Both Netscape Navigator and Internet Explorer have source code views built into their browsers, and when you look at the code — a mass of JavaScript, Cascading Style Sheet tags, calls to .swf files, maybe some applets, plus mind-boggling loads of HTML — it can be scary.

I'll let you in on a secret. The designer didn't put in all that code. She may have tweaked it a little, but you can bet your neighbor's dog that she used a page development tool. It wasn't some little freeware tool she downloaded from the Web. It was a full tilt boogey — a site-crunching, code-making, image-enhancing, big, bad site development tool.

Now here's the best part. If that tool was *Adobe GoLive 5,* she didn't have to spend a lot of time on the great-looking site. She may have had to patiently consider a navigation system, with a lot of help from GoLive 5's design planning tools, and she had to develop and gather images and content. However, once those chores were done, all the pieces were organized, updated, optimized, and synchronized by GoLive 5. Those really cool rollovers, the integrated color scheme, and the nifty floating boxes were all coded, loaded, and floated by GoLive 5.

At this point, the only question should be, "How can I learn to use GoLive 5?"

About This Book

This book is a user's book. By that, I mean that you don't curl up in bed with it like you would with a copy of Dickens' *Great Expectations.* You use this book with Adobe GoLive 5 loaded on your computer and ready to go. You can use the book to find out about GoLive 5 from scratch, or you can use it as a reference when you want to look up stuff on the fly. Keep it handy and flag those sections that you use a lot.

Each chapter deals with a logical chunk of GoLive 5. If you want, you can read the book from beginning to end, but (unlike your high school English teacher) I'm not telling you that you have to. If you want to find out about a certain aspect of GoLive 5, you can flip to a chapter to immediately see a list of what the chapter covers. You don't have to read the previous chapters, either. If you want to find out how GoLive 5 deals with frames, just go to the appropriate chapter and follow the guides. Like I said, this is a *user's book.* So use it.

How to Use This Book

You may have noticed the detailed Table of Contents and Index in this book. They're tools to be used. Typically, when you want to know something about GoLive 5, you don't expect to pick up the book and begin on page one for a topic covered on page 253. You look up the chapter or a key word in the index and then go directly to the part you want.

You can take or leave the tips, warnings, and technical explanations, but you'll probably find them useful. Here's a tip you can take or leave: Go down to your office supply store and get a set of those sticky tabs you can put in your book. Use a different color for each topic that interests you. That way you can quickly look up information that you've tagged. (See? You can take it or leave it, but there it is.)

The book has detailed instructions on how to get something done with GoLive 5. At times, the instructions may appear to use material from previous chapters or even previous sections of the book that you know well. However, that's the whole point. You don't have to carefully read Chapter 1 before you can use the information in Chapter 7. Usually, I give you more than one way to perform a function with GoLive. For example, to put a graphic image on a page, I tell you to drag it from the Site window, place it with the Point-and-Shoot tool, or use the Browse window. Likewise, I give you both the menu path to a tool *and* the keyboard shortcut just in case you prefer using the keyboard.

The book contains some HTML and JavaScript code (but not a great deal of it) that you can put in yourself. GoLive generates the great bulk of the code in a GoLive 5 page. What little code there is looks like the following:

```
function goFigure() {
        var
        taxrate=parseFloat(document.calculate.tax.value);
        var
        ship=parseFloat(document.calculate.shipping.value
        );
        var
        stuff=parseFloat(document.calculate.item.value);
        var combine=(stuff + ship +(taxrate * stuff));
        document.calculate.total.value=combine;
        }
```

So, although there isn't much code, what there is clearly stands out. And as with the rest of the book, you use just what you need. (You don't need to program a single line of code to use GoLive 5, but if you like to add your own code, it's easy to do.)

What You Don't Need to Read

If you don't have access to and never plan on using WebDAV with GoLive, don't feel obligated to read the material on WebDAV. On the other hand, if you bought this book because it does cover using GoLive with WebDAV, just read the material on WebDAV and nothing else. There's probably a lot more information here than you want to know about, and that's fine. A book's value is measured by what you *do* get from it; not by what you didn't want to waste time reading. So read what you need — from cover to cover or just those parts when and if they help you get done what you need done. In addition, if the paragraphs marked by those little Technical Stuff icons start to give you a headache, skip those, too.

Foolish Assumptions

I assume that you know how to install GoLive 5 into your computer and how to use either the Windows or Macintosh operating systems to launch a program. I assume that you are *not* a computer programmer, you *do* know what the World Wide Web is, and you have used an Internet browser such as Internet Explorer or Netscape Navigator. You don't have to know how to create Web pages; I just assume that you know what a Web page is when you see one. Otherwise, this book assumes you want to find out how to use GoLive, and little more.

How This Book Is Organized

This book is arranged into five parts. Each part organizes related chapters based either on the level of complexity or common elements. The chapters' order within each part is not as important as the order of sections within each chapter. Some features require foundational knowledge. Chapter 1 is important if you're new to GoLive 5 because it introduces the way you use GoLive 5 as a tool. You'll see that the user interface (UI for the totally cool) is unique compared to other applications you may have used. However, each chapter is self-contained, and you can use the chapters and sections to get just what you need when you need it.

Part I: Ready, Set, GoLive 5!

These first chapters give you a running start with GoLive 5 by showing you how to use the key tools and letting you jump right in and use them. This part assumes very little and even guides you through some design tips. It also pops the hood on HTML and lets you know what's going on behind the scenes just in case you want to tweak some code.

Part II: Looking Good — Designs That Delight

This part brings together key elements of Web pages and GoLive 5. You find out how to enhance your Web pages and site by using key Web page elements including forms, frames, and style sheets. In this part of the book, you find the next level of Web site authoring beyond the basics of both GoLive 5 and creating Web pages and sites.

Part III: A Site for Sore Eyes: Care, Feeding, and Organization of Web Sites

Part III shows you how to develop, design, and maintain your Web presence at the site level and how to use common components throughout a Web site. By using components, stationeries, and templates, you can create a design once and use it lots. Not only can you discover ways to organize your site, you can also find and incorporate some features in FTP and WebDAV that you may not have realized existed.

Part IV: Swinging Pages — Tapping the Power within GoLive 5

Here's where the fun is. In this section, you find all those neat and crazy special effects from bouncing buttons to movies on the Web. Part IV introduces all of GoLive's action objects both in Dynamic HTML and on plain old pages that come alive with actions. The QuickTime movie editor is a whole major application unto itself. Keep your pages looking cutting-edge with the information in these chapters. (You'll also keep yourself up way past your bedtime.)

Part V: The Part of Tens

If you want a summary of the most important things to keep in mind when designing Web pages with GoLive 5, this is the place to be. In three concise chapters, you get my ten best design tips for Web pages and sites, the ten best features of GoLive 5, and the ten *worst* and most common mistakes found in Web pages.

Icons Used in This Book

When writing this book, I'd come to a section and think, "Hey, the reader could use this tip. I use it all the time." Keep your eyes open for these helpful hints that can save you time and effort.

When a quirky little step or feature that's easy to overlook crops up, I put in a reminder. (These reminders were usually a result of my forgetting to do something and figuring that you could use the same reminder.)

The technical stuff comes under the category, "Just thought you might want to know why." Most of the technical stuff I mention in *GoLive 5 For Dummies* concerns peculiarities with code, the different browsers, and something about the Web or Internet. If you come across a technical note, you can take it or leave it. Whatever you do, though, don't get all tangled up in or worried about the technical stuff. You really don't have to know this stuff to use GoLive 5. But if you're the kind who's got to know the details, some of the technical stuff might help you understand why certain features of your Web page or site work they way they do.

Warnings are just what they claim to be. They warn you that if you do certain things, you might run into unwanted consequences. For example, Internet Explorer uses Marquees and Netscape Navigator does not. So you will be warned of what to expect if one browser or the other views your page.

Where to Go from Here

Crank up your computer, open up *GoLive 5 For Dummies,* and start having some fun with your Web pages. Get your bookmarks, yellow marker, and all the stuff you want to make this book work for you. There's no time like the present to put together the finest Web site the world will ever see!

Part I
Ready, Set, GoLive 5!

The 5th Wave
By Rich Tennant

©RICHTENNANT

"I'm gonna have a little trouble with this 'Full Moon' icon on our new Web page."

In this part . . .

Get ready to jump into the turbocharged, silicon-guzzling, big, bad mother of all Web site-building tools — GoLive 5. In no time at all you'll be leaving those Web page tinkerers in the dust as you charge ahead with untold power and tools to crank out red hot sites and sizzling Web pages. With more tips on design than your mother gave you on your first date, you'll quickly tap in to the secrets of creating good-looking pages on budget and on time. You'll even understand enough HTML to drop the jaws of the pocket-protector crowd. So what are you waiting for? Get going with GoLive 5!

This first part of this book shows you how GoLive 5 uses a system of toolbars, palettes, inspectors, menus, and windows to help you put together great sites with ease. As soon as you're familiar with the individual elements of GoLive 5, you're off and running to create your own pages and sites. Along the way, I let you in on the secrets of good Web site design (my own personal bag of tricks for making your sites stand out as clear and good-looking while avoiding the most common pitfalls that come from ignoring design precepts). I also show you how to use GoLive 5's visual navigation tools and palettes to ensure that visitors to your site find what you want them to find. To end things with a bang, Part I concludes with a quick and clear tour of HTML which emphasizes how to use and edit HTML tags with GoLive's Source and Outline views.

Chapter 1

Going Places with GoLive 5

*Y*ou've seen the Web, and now you want to become a part of it. No tool's better for getting you there looking smart and looking good than the powerful GoLive 5 program. GoLive 5 enables you to express yourself, sell your products, or get across your point with far more pizzazz than does the standard, plain-vanilla, static text and graphics that you often see on the Web, set up as they usually are in a rigid, default HTML arrangement of spots and spaces. GoLive 5 makes your pages stand out and get the kind of attention that you seek from Web surfers all around the globe.

You probably know what a Web page looks like on your own computer and in your favorite browser, but GoLive helps you make your Web pages look exactly the way that you want on all different kinds of computers, monitors, and versions of browsers. GoLive 5 helps you develop not only a Web page but also entire Web sites of different pages that all link together, making the entire site look easy and, well, just plain *cool* to use.

GoLive 5 is smart enough to write your code, place your pictures, and even show you how your site looks on someone else's favorite monitor and computer (so that Windows users can see how it looks on a Mac and vice versa) and in any browser — whether a visitor's using Netscape Communicator or Microsoft Internet Explorer. GoLive 5 is smart, experienced (hey — this version's GoLive's fifth time out after all), and intuitively easy to use. It helps you avoid common mistakes in creating Web sites and has power to spare for even the most elaborate Web-slinging tasks. So whether you're making pages for the folks back in Kankakee or way off in Katmandu, GoLive 5 gets you going on the World Wide Web fast — and with plenty of class!

What's Up, Document Window?

To start using GoLive 5, just double-click the GoLive 5 icon on your desktop to launch the application or use your computer's file-opening menus. After you launch GoLive 5, the big, gray rectangle that you first see on-screen is the *Document window.* (Think of a Document window as a canvas on which you paint your creation.) Here's where you bring together the graphics, texts, movies, links, and all the other parts of your Web page. After you're inside a Document window, you can use any of six different views to create (as well as keep tabs on) your ever-evolving Web site. (For the curious out there, the official names of these views are *Layout, Frame Layout, Source, Outline, Preview,* and *Frame Preview.*) Each view has its own tab sitting along the top of the Document window, and you can easily toggle back and forth between views simply by selecting the appropriate tab. You get a chance to see what each view can do for you in the following sections of this chapter.

Layout view: intuitive creations

You end up spending most of your time in *Layout view* while creating your Web pages. That's because Layout view is *the* place to go to drag graphics into position, write text, and add on all manner of goodies that you simply *must* have on your Web page. Figure 1-1 shows the blank slate on which you create your masterpiece.

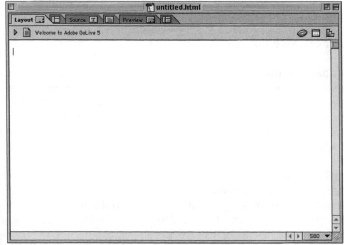

Figure 1-1:
You perform most of your Web-construction work in GoLive 5's Layout view.

After you first fire up GoLive 5, the program provides you with a new, untitled page in the Layout view, similar to the one in Figure 1-1, unless you change your Preferences to start out in some other view. (As you first start using GoLive 5, however, you're probably best off leaving the Preferences in their default configurations.) Although the little icons along the top of the Document window in Layout view have important functions, you don't need most of them to get going. Keep the majority of them on your mental back burner for now. You get the opportunity to become better acquainted with those features soon.

One tiny box that you see in Layout view, however, may prove useful now. The box in the lower-right corner displays the size value of the window in monitors of different sizes. Big deal, you may say, and in most cases you're probably right to remain unimpressed. But if you've invested in one of those big-screen monitors and create your Web site with such a big monitor in mind, you may end up frustrating a lot of folks: Those visitors with less-endowed monitors may experience difficulty viewing the length and breadth of your Web site on their tiny screens. You can plan for this situation, how-ever, by creating your Web pages for a monitor size that those viewing your Web site are most likely to use. To change the monitor size settings, click the arrow next to the number appearing in the box to open the Window-Size pop-up menu, as shown in Figure 1-2. Then select the setting for the monitor size that you want. A setting of 580, for example, is appropriate for a 14-inch moni-tor, which is the most common size of monitor out there. For viewing on a 17-inch monitor, the menu shows you that 780 is the right choice.

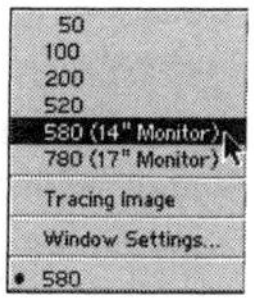

Figure 1-2:
GoLive
enables you
to create
pages for
different-
sized
monitors
in the
Window-
Size pop-up
menu.

You may also change the setting by dragging the lower right-hand corner of the screen, as shown in Figure 1-3. You can make the document screen virtu-ally any size that you want by dragging the corner. This feature may prove helpful in creating pages that can fit into frame windows of different sizes than those selected sizes that you find in the Window-Size menu.

Figure 1-3:
You can
make fine
adjustments
to the size of
the moni-
tor's viewing
area by
dragging the
lower-right
corner of
the screen.

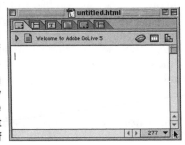

The other views

After you familiarize yourself with the Layout view, you can take a quick look at the other views available to you from the Document window. The following list summarizes the basics of each of these other views (which I discuss in greater detail in later chapters):

- ✔ **Frame Layout view:** Use the *Frame Layout view* if you want to view and organize all icons of the pages in a frameset at the same time. (A *frameset* shows several Web pages on the same screen organized into sections known as *frames*.) Unlike in the Layout view, you don't use the Frame Layout view for actually editing pages — it merely shows you which pages are in a certain frameset. (Chapter 9 tells you all about frames.)

- ✔ **Source view:** Use the *Source view* if you want to see and edit the source code for the items that you add to a Web page. This view is very useful if you need to do a little code tweaking — you don't need to open a separate editor just to add a little HTML or JavaScript of your own. (Chapter 6 shows you how to use the Source view and fine-tune your HTML.)

- ✔ **Outline view:** The *Outline view* is similar in appearance to the Source view except that it includes a structural view of your source code — that is, you can see the hierarchy of the blocks of HTML and JavaScript code. If you view a Web page in Outline view, you can easily insert the cool styles that you create (and just as easily insert text) right into the code windows in the Outline view. (Chapter 6 explains how to use this unique GoLive 5 feature.)

- ✔ **Preview view:** Use the *Preview view* to take a peek at your page in a simu-lated browser. Get to know this feature, because you're going to use it a lot.

✔ **Frame Preview view:** Use the *Frame Preview view* to preview any of your Web pages in a frameset. You see all the pages in the frameset as they appear in the browser. (***Note:*** Only the Macintosh has the Frame Preview view. Windows computers view both frame and nonframe pages in the Preview view.)

To save some of your computer's memory, just use the Preview view instead of keeping a browser open to check how your page looks. Often, you need to keep several applications open as you develop a Web page — for example, a graphics program or a word processor — and these programs all take up memory. As a bonus, you can simulate in Preview view just how your page appears in different browsers on different computers, so you're not stuck just knowing how it looks in your own browser.

Le Menu du Jour

What's up with all those menus? As you do in just about every other application in Windows or on the Mac, you see plenty of menus in GoLive 5 (see Figure 1-4). Most of the work that you do in the program, however, involves its various inspectors, toolbars, controllers, and palettes. The menus contain many features that are also on the support windows, bars, and palettes, and until you're comfortable using the other GoLive 5 support elements, the menus serve as a handy source for tools. As you use the support windows and bars more and more, however, you become less dependent on the menus — and accomplish your work a lot faster to boot.

Figure 1-4:
The
GoLive 5
main
menu bar.

🍎 File Edit Type Special Site Design Movie Window Help

You also find a lot of the less-often-used features, gadgets, and goodies in the menus, where they don't get in the way of your work area. The Special menu, for example, contains a Toggle Binary option that's not usually at the top of most Web designer's lists of most-used features. (Toggle Binary switches between unary tags and binary tags in the Outline view.) If you need to toggle a binary, however, it's right there on the menu waiting for you — thankfully out the way whenever you don't need it.

As soon as you can, you want to break the menu habit. In GoLive 5, you quickly find that using the windows, toolbars, and palettes that the program provides is a lot quicker than using menus. But if old habits die hard, you don't need to tangle yourself all up by *not* using the menus either — at least for now.

The GoLive Objects Palette — at Your Fingertips

You can access several different windows from the Window menu on the GoLive 5 menu bar. The Objects-palette window (or just *Objects palette*), with its nine different tabs, is one of the more useful of these windows, because it's like a toolkit from which you can choose various tools to use in creating your Web page. Each tab offers several icons that you can use in creating the Web page, and you can drag each icon from the Objects palette onto the Layout view, which makes the task of getting exactly the tool that you need for your page quite easy indeed. I suggest that you use the Basic tab of the Objects palette to start off, as shown in Figure 1-5.

Forms   Site Extras

Head

Smart   Frames |Quicktime

Figure 1-5: Basic| Site   Custom

The GoLive 5 Objects palette is a handy window full of tools that you can use in creating your Web page.

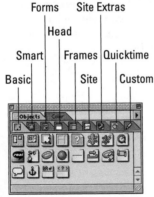

The general model for creating a Web page in GoLive 5 is simply to drag materials (or icons) from the Objects palette over to the Layout view, just as you drag stones across a field to use in building that neighborly stone fence. The

Objects palette thus provides you with a handy, intuitive tool for building your Web pages. The following list describes all the tabs of the Objects palette, from left to right, and tells you what you can do on each tab:

- ✔ **Basic:** Use this tab to add general icons that you use on several different kinds of Web pages. The Basic tab includes familiar objects such as tables and horizontal lines. But these Basic objects also include place-holders for SWF (Shockwave) files, a grid, and floating boxes, among other objects. (Shockwave runs animated movies made with Macromedia Flash and Adobe LiveMotion.)

- ✔ **Smart:** The Smart tab contains a number of different kinds of objects that easily perform some of the more complex Web-design tasks. You can drag and drop a *Rollover object,* for example, to instantly set up a Rollover button. Other smart objects include PhotoShop and LiveMotion objects that you can link and update in Adobe applications by the same name. Chapter 14 shows how to use smart objects.

- ✔ **Forms:** Forms in Web pages include different kinds of objects that you use to get information from your visitors. Use this tab to access several different Web forms, such as text areas, buttons, check boxes, and menus that you can add to your pages to enable the user to respond to information on the page. (Chapter 8 tells you all about using forms on your Web page.)

- ✔ **Head:** Use the Head tab for creating special code (such as JavaScript functions) that goes in the Head section of an HTML page. (The Head section loads before the body of your page and can store important functions and information about your page.) You can put information about your site that helps search engines find your Web pages by using Meta tags in the Head section, and GoLive 5 provides a handy Meta icon for you to drag and drop in the page's head. Chapter 6 explains how.

- ✔ **Frames:** You use the Frames tag for creating framesets. The process is very simple on this tab: Just drag and drop the frame arrangement that you want from the tab to your Web page. (Chapter 9 acquaints you with this innovative and simple process for creating framesets.)

- ✔ **Site:** The Site tab enables you to add icons that you use in the Site window. (The Site window enables you to see all the other Web pages, graphics files, and other media files that make up your Web site.) You can drag and drop font sets or color schemes from this tab for use throughout your entire site. You can also drag blank pages to add to the site from this tab. And you can find new design elements in the Design Section and Design Group for sketching out site design for GoLive 5 on the Site tab. (Chapter 11 covers all the details for this tab.)

✔ **Site Extras:** Use this tab to retrieve your own site extras that you create in the Site window. You can create and drag templates and components from this tab to your Web page. (*Components* are reusable page elements that do something for a Web page, such as an image map that you want to use for navigation on different pages in your site.) After you create a cool design and devise components for it once, you can use the same design and components over and over again simply by dragging them from this page. (Chapter 12 shows how to create templates and components and then use them in your Web pages.)

✔ **QuickTime:** Lights! Camera! Action! You can use this tab to direct your own movies in QuickTime, the video-compression software that enables you to create and view movies on the Web by using either a Windows or Mac computer. GoLive 5 enables you to actually edit QuickTime movies with some great special effects. (Chapter 15 shows you how to put your movies in the biggest theater around — the World Wide Web.)

✔ **Custom:** You can create an object on one Web page, drag it to the Custom tab, and then use it on another Web page. That process saves you from needing to reinvent the wheel every time that you create a page. (Chapter 12 tells you about creating custom objects.)

A (Web-Safe) Rainbow at Your Fingertips

You may notice that the Color palette lives in the same window as the Objects palette. The GoLive 5 *Color palette* also features nine different tabs; each represents a different way to look at colors and describes the number of colors available to you for different projects, including ones that you make yourself. Tab 7 (the seventh from the left) contains *Web-safe colors* (or colors that appear the same on all monitors — a full 216 of them). Throughout this book, I generally stick with Web-safe colors, because the use of other color sets runs the risk of creating a set of colors that look ugly on different monitors. Drag colors from the Color palette's preview pane to an object or an object's color well. Or you can just click the many different context sensitive color wells that appear when you select an object that can be colored. The Color palette jumps to the screen and by selecting the color on the palette, as soon as the color well fills with the desired color, the object gets colored too. Figure 1-6 shows the Web-safe tab in the Color palette.

Grayscale   System

CMYK   True Web (Web Safe)

Index   Named Web Colors

Figure 1-6:
You use
the Color
palette to
easily
change the
colors of
bacgrounds
and fonts
on your
Web page.

RGB HSV   New Site Colors

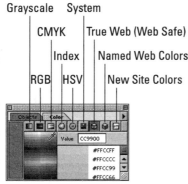

Your GoLive desktop can become crowded with all the windows that you open on-screen to help create Web sites and pages. By pressing Control-Click on the top bars of the palettes and windows you can *dock* these features (move them to the side or bottom of the screen to appear as tabs). Windows dock at the bottom of the screen and palettes dock at the side of the screen, as do toolbars.

The Seven Faces of the Toolbar

The GoLive 5 toolbar is *context sensitive,* meaning that the toolbar changes with what you're working on. (The toolbar's very smart and knows exactly what you're doing at any given moment.) The toolbar serves as a handy bar of buttons that enable you to access specific GoLive 5 features quickly. Figures 1-7, 1-8, and 1-9 show three of GoLive 5's different toolbars, all of which I describe in the following sections.

The Text toolbar

If you're placing text on your Layout page, you see the *Text toolbar* (refer to Figure 1-7). (Oh, and his friends, by the way, call him "Tex.") This toolbar provides quick access to several text-formatting tools *and* the Link and Delete-Link buttons. Believe me, using the Text toolbar is a lot faster than fishing through menus to find the formatting options that you need.

Figure 1-7:
The Text
toolbar
provides
several text
options that
you can
access right
on your
GoLive 5
desktop.

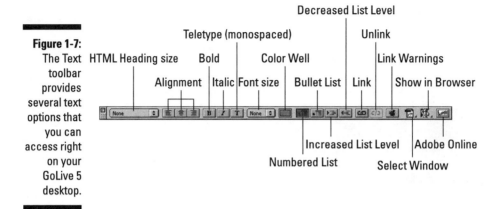

Decreased List Level

Teletype (monospaced)   Unlink

HTML Heading size   Bold   Color Well   Link Warnings

Alignment   Italic Font size   Bullet List   Link   Show in Browser

Increased List Level   Adobe Online

Numbered List   Select Window

The Objects toolbar

In working with *objects* in the GoLive grid, such as graphics and text-layout boxes, you use the *Objects toolbar* (see Figure 1-8). In Chapter 3, you find out all about the grid and how it makes placing objects on the page as simple as pie — and that includes adding text-layout boxes so that you can place text anywhere that you want on-screen. After you select an object, you can quickly type information about object sizes and positions in the toolbar's text boxes or click buttons on the toolbar to designate what you want the object to do without needing to fish through menus to obtain the same results. Just click the appropriate buttons on the Objects toolbar, for example, for quick alignments of selected objects.

Figure 1-8:
The Objects
toolbar
includes
text boxes
that you use
for entering
object
sizes and
positions
along with
buttons for
positioning
objects on
the page.

Object sizes   Object positions

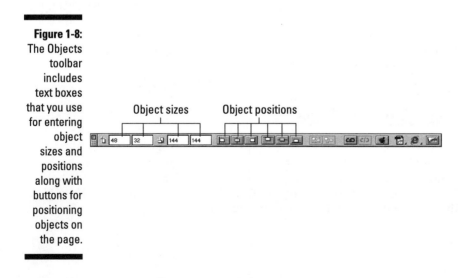

The Site toolbar

In thinking about GoLive 5, the first thing that you must do is to get beyond thinking only about individual Web pages; the beauty of GoLive 5 is that it makes tying all your Web *pages* together into a true Web *site* extremely easy. And one of the tools that GoLive provides to help you do so is the *Site toolbar*.

After you select the Site window, the Site toolbar appears on-screen (see Figure 1-9). This toolbar provides you with easy access to the different options available in the Site window and its accompanying windows and tools. Select a file in the Site window and click, for example, the Page button to open it, the Trash button to delete it, or one of the other buttons on the bar to obtain information easily. (The third button from the right, for example, toggles between the Site and your Document window, enabling you to easily switch between the Layout view of a page and one providing specific information about that page within the overall Web site — such as where it lies relative to all the other pages in the site. Click the second-to-last button on the right, and you can view any file in the Site window within the browser of your choice.)

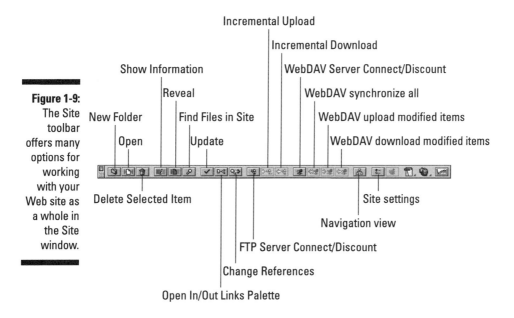

Figure 1-9:
The Site toolbar offers many options for working with your Web site as a whole in the Site window.

The Style Sheet toolbar

You don't find much to look at on the *Style Sheet toolbar*, but it does serve a useful purpose (see Figure 1-10). This toolbar appears whenever you work with *Cascading Style Sheets* (CSS), a neat feature that enables you to impose a certain style or formatting uniformly on selected items on your Web page. The little staircase-shaped button in the upper right corner of the Document Window opens the CSS interface. (The Style Sheet toolbar pops up again when I discuss Cascading Style Sheets in more detail in Chapter 10.)

New Class

New Tag

New ID

New Item

Duplicate

Figure 1-10:
The Style
Sheet
toolbar
appears
when you
open the
Cascading
Style Sheet
interface.

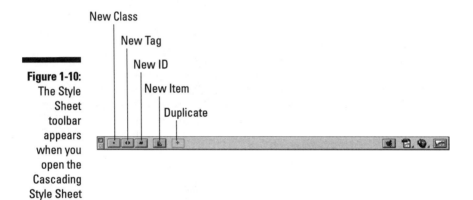

The Outline toolbar

As you're working in Outline view, you discover that the available toolbar buttons become pretty sparse as well — but still, the *Outline toolbar's* got just what you need (see Figure 1-11). A single click of a button on this toolbar enables you to insert special code for Active Server Pages and XML, add comments to your HTML code (so that you can remember later what you want it to do), and insert text. (Chapter 6 tells all about using the Outline view and its toolbar as well as HTML tags.)

New HTML Tag

New HTML Attribute

New HTML Text

New HTML Comment

New Custom Tag

Toggle Binary

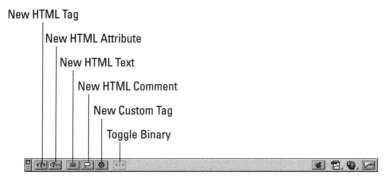

Figure 1-11:
As you're
working in
the Outline
view, the
Outline
toolbar
helps you to
add code to
your Web
page.

The Navigation and Design toolbars

A new feature in GoLive 5 is the *Design feature.* In creating a site design,
you're creating an organization and navigation system for your site. The organization of a site is how the pages are to be grouped and ordered, and the
navigation considerations refer to how the groups are to be linked. Before
you start making a set of Web pages, you need to get an idea of how your Web
site is going to look. Imagine that you have little cutout cardboard squares for
each page that you can lay on top of a table and organize with pieces of yarn
indicating links. In the Design and Navigation windows, that's exactly what
you do — set up a design and navigation system to see the relationship
between all your pages. Naturally, the toolbars for these windows are going
to appear very similar, although with some key differences (three buttons on
the Design toolbar let you check the design for bugs and put or remove the
design from the site window), as you can see in Figure 1-12 (Navigation) and
Figure 1-13 (Design). Chapter 11 covers using the site design tools.

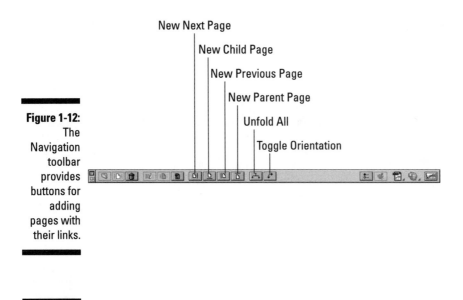

New Next Page

New Child Page

New Previous Page

New Parent Page

Unfold All

Toggle Orientation

Figure 1-12:
The Navigation toolbar provides buttons for adding pages with their links.

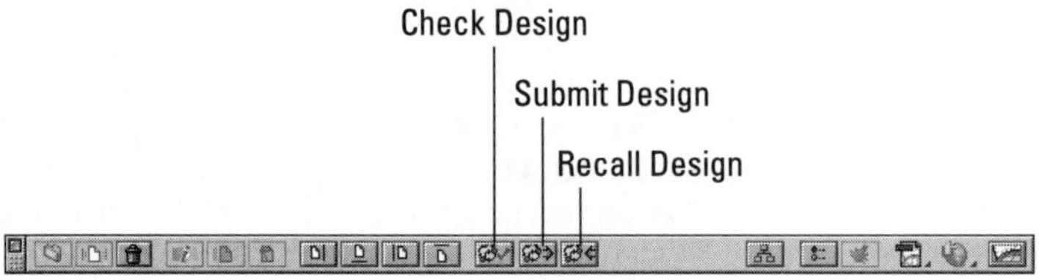

Figure 1-13:
The Design toolbar is very similar to the Navigation toolbar except that it features a Toggle button to take you to the Navigation view and three buttons that you can use for turning designs into sites.

Check Design

Submit Design

Recall Design

One browser at a time on your toolbar

The sharp-eyed among you may notice that some of the GoLive 5 toolbars feature a different button at the far right. In GoLive 5, you can select how many — and which — browsers launch after you click this last button. Unless, however, you have lots and lots of memory (*DRAM memory*, that is — the kind that your computer has only after you turn it on), launching more than one browser at a time is expensive in terms of memory use and may even result in lockups. If you have enough memory, however, and routinely examining your pages in multiple browsers is critical to you, you're likely to find this feature very handy. To make changes, just choose Edit⇨Preferences from the menu bar and click the Browsers icon in the left pane of the Preferences window that appears. In the Browser Selection window that appears on the right, select which browser you want to use as your primary one. (GoLive automatically searches your computer for browsers and then brings them into the Browser Selection window.) The checked browser's icon appears on the toolbar as a button. If you don't want either as the primary browser, remove the check mark from both browsers; a Globe button then appears with a drop-down list menu that enables you to select either one. (If you select both in the Preferences window, you also see the Globe button instead of either Browser button.)

Keeping Everything in Site

Even if you plan to create only a single-page Web site, the *Site window* in GoLive 5 is likely to quickly become one of your favorites. You can quickly create a site by selecting File⇨New Site⇨ Blank from the menu bar and saving it in a folder on your computer. You are given a new page named "index.html" with the site. From the Files tab in the Site window, you can open that page into a Document window by double-clicking it. The Site window shows you everything that you need for your site in six different tabs (or *views,* a term I will use interchangeably), and it makes creating sites very easy. You can drag your files from anywhere on your computer onto the Files tab of the Site window, for example, and a copy of that file goes into the root folder for the site. The Files tab shows the root folder for your site, including folders within the root folder. Figure 1-14 shows the Files tab of the Site window for a typical Web site that you can create in GoLive 5. All the different media appear together in a single Media folder, and you can easily see each page of the site within the window.

You can move back and forth between the Site and Document windows by clicking the third button from the right on the toolbar. If you're in the Site window, the button for the Document window appears on the toolbar, and if you're in the Document window, the Site window button appears. Play around with switching back and forth to accustom yourself to this simple switch. You're going to be switching back and forth a lot before you're through creating your site.

Figure 1-14:
The Files
view of the
Site window
shows you
all the files
associated
with the
site.

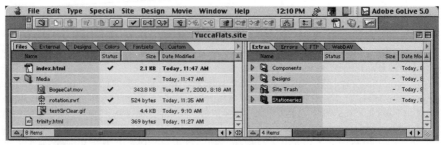

Switching between the Site window and the Document window makes organizing your site much easier, because you can see where everything is and obtain a better overall sense of where your work lies in the context of the site. So as you're working on a page, you're likely not only to be looking at all the pages and media that you need for the current page, but also those for the entire site.

Files view

The first tab in the Site window opens a window displaying all the files in your site — the *Files view* (refer to Figure 1-14). This handy overview enables you to know whether all your files are in place and whether they're working right. Different symbols in the Status column show you either that something's wrong with a file (in which case you see a big, green bug) or that your files are doing well (a check mark designating this status appears). You use the right frame of the window for adding components or stationeries — either those that you store from previous sites or new ones that you develop for use in future sites. (*Stationeries* are pages that you use as templates and *components* are reusable page elements — I explain both in detail in Chapter 14.) You can also toss an unwanted file into the Site Trash folder in the right frame.

The External view

Open up the External view by selecting the External tab on the Site window. Ever see a link to a Web page or an e-mail that you want to put on one of your Web pages? All you need do is to drag a *URL* (a link to an external Web address) from a browser page to the External view of the Site window, and GoLive 5 stores that link there. Then you can select text or an image and easily link it to that URL or e-mail address. The Site window's External view makes life easy, because you can use your browser to surf throughout the World Wide Web, drag all kinds of links and e-mail addresses into your Site window, and then use those links and addresses whenever you need them. (Chapter 11 explains how to use the External view and bring in all the e-mail and Web site addresses you want.)

The Designs view

The Designs tab gives you access to the Designs view, a new feature in GoLive 5. In the Designs view of the Site window, all you see is a list of designs (see Figure 1-15), but from this view you can launch your own site design windows. Think of the Designs view as a place where you can try on all different types of designs and then store them. Then, after you decide that you're ready to make a design choice, you go into this view and select the one that best fits the needs of your site. Designs can be stored and when submitted they become part of your site window. You can try out several designs and then submit the one you like best. Part of the design preview process includes inserting potential links between pages for a navigation overview. (Chapters 4 and 11 show how GoLive 5 handles both site design and navigation planning.)

Figure 1-15:
The Designs view is the storage shed for all the site designs that you may want to use for your site.

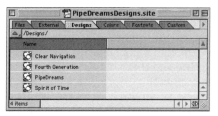

The Colors view

A good Web site displays a set of colors that go well together. You can easily keep such a set of colors consistent by dragging all the colors that you use on your site from the Color palette to the *Colors view* of the Site window. (Access the Colors view by selecting the middle tab in the Site window, as shown in Figure 1-16.) After you move a specific set of colors to the Site window's Colors view, the Color palette places those same colors together as a set on the Color palette's own Site tab (the tab farthest to the right). You can then access just the set of colors that you need from either the Colors view of the Site Window or the Site tab of the Color palette. (Chapters 7 and 11 tell you a lot more about colors and using colors in the Site window.)

Figure 1-16:
The Colors view provides a way for you to put together a complimentary set of colors and reduce the possibility of ending up with colors that clash on your site.

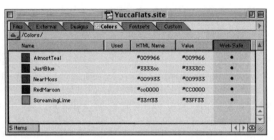

The Fontsets view

The *Fontsets view,* accessed by selecting the second tab from the right in the Site window, helps you set up the *fonts* (type styles) for your Web site (see Figure 1-17). GoLive 5 provides you with several different ways to put font sets onto the Fontsets tab. Give the font set a name, and you can then drag it from here to text on any page in the site that you want. (This process also is easier than wading through the menus to perform the same task.) As with everything else in GoLive 5, the Site window's Fontsets view makes the job of creating a great Web site that much easier. (Chapter 11 provides more details on how to get your font set and site together and the different ways to go about it.)

Figure 1-17:
The Fontsets view provides easy access to the fonts that you want to use in your Web site.

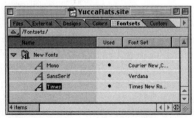

The Custom view

The final tab on the Site window is the Custom view (see Figure 1-18). Whenever you develop anything on a page that is so cool that you want it on several pages in the site, just drag it to the Custom view. You can drag everything from text to loaded Shockwave files to the Custom view. When you need any of the objects stashed in the Custom tab on one of the other pages in your site, just drag it from the Custom view to your page. (I like to think of the Custom view as my attic where all sorts of odds and ends can be stored until I need them — even if I never actually use them.)

Figure 1-18: The Custom view shows the different objects collected that can be placed on other pages in the site.

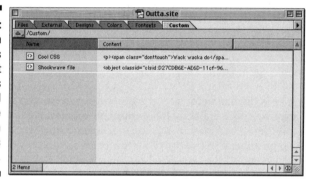

Inspector GoLive, at Your Service

As you work on different parts of your Web page or Web site, GoLive 5's context-sensitive *Inspector* is always at your side. You soon discover that the Inspector is a bit of a chameleon, however, changing disguises as Inspector Clouseau does, as the need arises. Happily, the Inspector's changeable nature saves you from spending a lot of time fumbling through menus looking for what you need, because it always pulls the context-appropriate rabbit out of its hat just at the time that you need it the most.

You can summon the Inspector to your side (on-screen, of course) by choosing Window⇨Inspector from the GoLive 5 menu bar. Depending on what you're doing at the time that you access the Inspector, different Inspectors arrive on-screen. If you're working with text, a *Text Inspector* arrives, but if you're selecting an image, the Inspector takes on the guise of *Image Inspector* (see Figure 1-19). Using the Inspector really isn't all that complex; just remember that it changes its persona on-screen, depending on what you're doing with your Web page or site at any given time. After you entice the Inspector on-screen, you don't need to call for a different Inspector if you decide to start working with some other component of your site. The versatile Inspector changes its identity automatically as you change tasks.

Watch the toolbar as the Inspector changes. Often, the toolbar changes at the same time, depending on what you're doing.

The *View Controller* is the Inspector's roommate — they live in the same window. The View Controller is handy for setting the appearance of your Web page in the Layout view (see Figure 1-20). You can control how the page is going to look before you examine it in the Preview view or in a browser. You can establish the type of browser and the type of computer on which you want to view your pages in as you're working on them. You can set all links to appear as they do after someone visits them, for example, instead of how they look before a user clicks them. If your browser displays a purple background color for a page and your links on that page also appear in purple after you click them, they become invisible if you view them in that browser. The View Controller enables you look at your page as it appears under different circumstances so that you aren't unpleasantly surprised as you view it in a certain browser.

Context what?

I bandy about the term *context-sensitive* throughout this chapter, so providing a little clarification here may help you to understand just what I mean by it. Something that's context-sensitive is like a really smart carpenter's assistant; if you're nailing a board, the assistant knows to hand you a hammer and nails; if you need to cut some wood, however, your assistant hands you a saw. The Inspector that I describe in the accompanying section is similar to such a smart assistant in that it gives you exactly what you need when you need it. Having such a capability makes a lot of sense if you're working on different parts of a Web page or site. If, for example, you select text that you indicate you want to use as a link (which you do by clicking the Link button on the toolbar), the Text Inspector's Link tab provides you with all the tools that you need for finding the page to which you want to link. If you're working on a graphic, however, you need to inspect different things, and so the Image Inspector provides a different set of windows and buttons that you need for that purpose.

Figure 1-20:
The View Controller provides you with many options for changing the appearance of objects appear.

The Rest of the Cast

The windows that you use the most are the Document window, the Site window, the Objects and Color palettes, and the Inspector. After you set up the View Controller, you use it only occasionally. Several more windows and their palettes, however, are available for specialized tasks that I can best explain as you explore the tasks that they perform in subsequent chapters. Not giving them at least some introduction here would, however, be impolite. So the following list offers a brief introduction for the rest of the windows and palettes that you find in GoLive 5. (GoLive 5 groups its palettes by the windows in which they live.) The palettes are all found in the Window menu bar and below are grouped by the palette window in which they reside. Most of the following palettes also have a counterpart in the Inspector, who dons the appropriate face to work with the palette and object you select. (The following groupings have no intuitive or inherent combinations. They are simply grouped that way in palette pack windows. Each palette has its own tab, but they are always referenced as *palettes* in GoLive 5.)

Transform, Align, and Tracing Image palettes

- *Transform:* The Transform palette helps change an object's configuration, most notably it's size.

- *Align:* You use the Align palette to arrange objects on your Document or Design windows.

- *Tracing Image:* You can use this palette to trace images from Photoshop in the predesign stages of your Web-page layout. You can see what it looks like on your page with other elements before you settle on using it.

Floating Boxes, Table, and Actions palettes

- *Floating Boxes:* You can use the Floating Boxes palette to control floating boxes in GoLive5 on your Web page. Floating boxes can move around a page when you apply an action to them. (See Actions below.)

- *Table:* You can set your tables and style them easily by using GoLive 5's new features on its Table palette.

- *Actions:* The Actions palette enables you to generate JavaScript to make your objects come alive. (These are the kinds of actions that make floating boxes fly around the page.) Just add the action that you want, and GoLive 5 does the rest.

In & Out Links, Site Navigator, Source Code palettes

- *In & Out Links:* The In & Out Links palette shows you the links for selected objects on your page.

- *Site Navigator:* This little palette provides a thumbnail view of the Navigation Links or Design window icons and controls the size of the page icons in both the Navigation Links or Design windows. (Powerful little guy!)

- *Source Code:* Whenever you make a change in the Layout view, the source code (HTML, JavaScript) appears in the Source Code palette. You make fine adjustments in one and view the changes in the other.

Markup Tree, History palettes

- *Markup Tree:* If you select different elements on your Web page, the Markup Tree palette shows the hierarchical position of the objects that you select. You can see the object's position relative to other objects such as tables, links, and images that may be on the same page.

- *History:* The History palette is so cool, you're going to use it all the time. Each time that you do something in creating a page or site, GoLive 5 records that action in the History palette. If you make an error — or several, as I do — you need a way to undo the mess. Just select the point in the palette's history list where things were going right, and the History palette discreetly removes anything that may have been added after that point.

Just Point and Shoot Me

One of my favorite features of GoLive 5 is the *Point-and-Shoot button* — the little spiral or squiggle icons that you see in the context-sensitive Inspectors. By dragging a pointer line from one of these buttons to a file, a graphic, or some other object on the page, you can easily and intuitively create a link to or place that object on a Web page. Figure 1-21 shows how an image icon from the Object palette links to a graphic in the Site window. (Not only are the buttons and their pull-lines intuitive to use, but they look pretty cool as well.)

Throughout the book, you find Point-and-Shoot buttons in different places besides the Inspector. If you use Point-and-Shoot buttons, all the links relate to the root (site) folder. So whenever you see the little corkscrew button, you can point, pull, and shoot your way through page design as long as you have placed your pages and media in the root folder. (You know they're in the root folder if they are listed in the Files view in the Site window.)

Point-and-shoot line.

Point-and-shoot button. | File view of site Window.

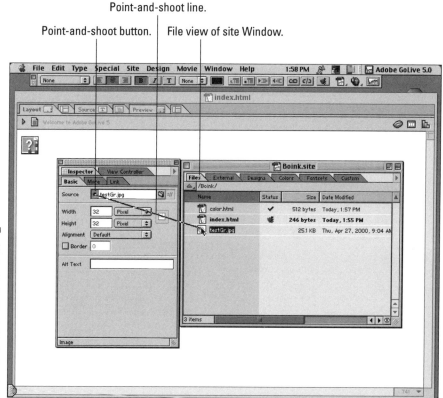

Figure 1-21:
The context-sensitive Inspector shows a Point-and-Shoot button whenever you need it.

Chapter 2

Just Do It — Creating Your First GoLive 5 Page

· ·

In This Chapter

▶ Establishing a Web site

▶ Placing text, graphics, and links on a page

▶ Checking the view in the View Controller and Preview view

▶ Saving Web pages and sites

· ·

You can best think of GoLive 5 as both a site tool and a Web-page tool. (The site is the overall environment for the different Web pages that make up that site.) To most effectively use the program to create a user-friendly Web site, I suggest that you put yourself in the shoes (or, perhaps, the mouse) of the person who's going to use your site. Consider how to set up the site so that users can best navigate it, while making sure all the pages combine — or integrate — into a cohesive whole. Think of yourself as conducting an orchestra of Web pages instead of just creating single pages that you get around to organizing some time down the road.

As they were developing GoLive 5, its creators had *you* in mind as a Web-site developer. So instead of just handing you a tool for creating one page at a time, the program provides you with a tool that you can use to create an entire Web site. GoLive 5, therefore, enables you not only to create single pages more easily than you can in other site-building programs, but also to integrate those pages into a cohesive whole. Later, after you put your Web site on a server, you can see just how well all the parts work together. Even during the development phase of your site, GoLive 5 helps you keep all your pages, media, and links working together as a unit. If you take full advantage of the site-development elements of GoLive 5, you can watch your sites bloom right before your eyes.

Ladies and Gentlemen, Set Your Sites!

After you first turn on GoLive 5, an untitled page appears on-screen, displaying a perky message in the upper left-hand corner of the window: `Welcome to GoLive 5`. A single blank page is fine if you just need one page for a Web site, but you're better off if you begin with an entire new site rather than just a new page. Why, you may ask? Because GoLive 5 prides itself on being a Web-*site* development tool and not just a Web-*page* development tool. (I told you so!) Most of the really neat features of GoLive 5, therefore, come into play only if you orchestrate a number of Web pages together into a true Web site. To take full advantage of such features, you want to close the blank page that GoLive 5 offers you on startup and get into a site frame of mind.

To begin working on your first Web site in GoLive 5, just follow these steps:

1. **Choose File⇨Close from the menu bar (or press Ctrl+W in Windows or Cmd-W on the Mac) to close the blank page that appears on-screen after you start GoLive 5.**

   You can also click the Close icon on the blank page — the little box that you see in the top right-hand corner of your screen in Windows and in the top left-hand corner on Macintosh computers. (Don't worry — you get a new page with your new site.)

2. **Choose File⇨New Site⇨Blank from the menu bar.**

   The Create New Site dialog box appears. In this dialog box, a list shows the files in the current folder or desktop.

3. **Enter a name for your site in the New Site Name text box and make sure that the Create Folder check box contains a checkmark.**

   Use a one-word name such as **HereNow.** You want to leave the checkmark in the Create New Folder check box so that you keep everything for your site together in one place. The following list describes what GoLive 5 generates after you create a new site and a new folder using the name *HereNow*.

   The HereNow folder contains the following items:

   > HereNow (the name of a second folder inside the site folder; the second folder is the one that you eventually place on a server)

   > HereNow.site (an icon for launching your site so that you can work on it in GoLive 5)

   > HereNow Backup.site icon (your life raft)

   > HereNow.data (a folder where GoLive 5 stores the information that it uses in generating sites)

Be careful not to confuse the folder named "Site folder" and the folder inside simply named "Site." GoLive 5 adds the word "folder" to the outermost folder.

Later on, you may want to put your site (HereNow) onto a server, and servers can get cranky about folder names. Servers don't care about upper- and lowercase letters, but they do care about spaces and special characters. So play things safe and just use a single word for your folder's name — one without any special characters such as & or #. Figure 2-1 shows how you want the name for your new site to look.

Figure 2-1:
Use the
Create New
Site dialog
box to
create a
new folder
on the
desktop and
enter a site
name
for your
GoLive 5
Web site.

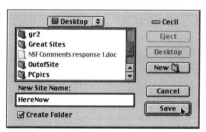

4. **Select the Desktop as your *workspace* — the folder/directory in which you do the work — and click Open.**

   GoLive 5 generates a folder with the name HereNow Folder (or whatever name you use) on the desktop. On both the Mac and in Windows you want to use your desktop area to work in and then store your Web site folder off the desktop to make room for the next project.

5. **Double-click the new folder on the desktop to open it.**

   In the example, double-click the folder called HereNow Folder.

6. **Within the folder, launch the site by double-clicking the site icon (the one with the SITE extension).**

   You see, for example, a file with the name HereNow.site. GoLive 5 automatically generates a page with the name *index.html* within the site. Your first Site window now appears, as shown in Figure 2-2. (You're looking at the Site window in the Files view.)

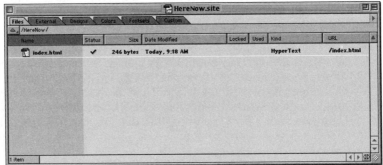

Servers usually use the name index.html as the home page in a directory. The
server automatically loads index.html if you provide no file name in the URL
directory. If you type www.interqualcom.com/Fred/, for example, and the
server uses index.html (or index.htm) as the default directory page, the
index file for the directory Fred appears. Your server may, of course, use
another default home-page name, such as welcome.html, or some other name
that the server administrator dreams up. If index.html isn't an appropriate
name for your own home page, however, just change it. You don't hurt GoLive
5's feelings at all by doing so. (You can change the default name by choosing
Edit⇨Preferences⇨Site from the menu bar.)

To give yourself something on which to work, go ahead and open index.html
by double-clicking the file icon in the Site window that you open at the end of
the preceding steps. You now see a blank page in the Layout view with
another Welcome to GoLive 5 greeting next to the Page icon in the upper-
left corner. The first thing that you want to do is to change this "name" to
reflect the page's actual title by following these steps:

1. **Select the text that you want to change on the new page.**

   In this example, you want to change Welcome to GoLive 5 to an actual
   title for the page, so you select that text.

2. **Type another title for your page.**

   You can name your page anything that you want — such as **My Home
   Page, Bob's House of Fun,** or (my personal favorite) **Lint Recycling.** As
   you type, the new title replaces the selected text.

3. **Press Return (on the Mac) or Enter (in Windows).**

   That's it. Your index.html page now has a unique title (and maybe even
   one that's a bit too unique, depending on the nature of your own sense
   of humor!).

You can, of course, start GoLive 5 by clicking the icon for an associated file from the desktop or in a file folder. You're far better off, however, if you open the Site window first. (You open the Site window by double-clicking the icon for a site file instead of the icon for a page file.) If you open the Site window, you can immediately view all the other files associated with the site — including graphics, HTML files, and any other files that you may decide to attach to a page. (Notice in Figure 2-3 the difference between the icons that GoLive 5 uses for files and sites.) Just remember that, if you see the partial globe on the icon, it means that you want the whole enchilada — the site.

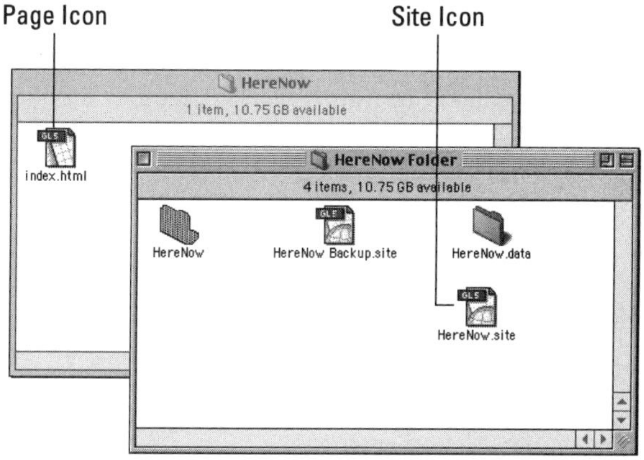

Page Icon   Site Icon

Figure 2-3:
Their
distinctive
icons
identify
GoLive 5's
site and
HTML page
files.

Before getting to work on a Web page, you not only need stuff to put on your page, but you also need to get your stuff neatly in order (at least, relatively so). If you want to make additional pages part of the site, put them in a nicely labeled folder somewhere convenient on your computer. (I like keeping things that I need right on my desktop). Do the same to all the Flash, LiveMotion, and QuickTime movies, animated GIFs, audio files, and any other kinds of media you may want to add to your Web site. (Chapters 14 and 15 provide lots of detail on creating and embedding these files in your Web pages, but for now, just know they have a good home.) Simply gather similar items together, just as Noah did for his ark, storing text files in one folder, audio files in another, and graphics files in another. You can use any name that you want for the individual folders, but the important thing is to get everything together before going any farther. Then you can simply drop any file or folder that you need for your site into the Site window you create by clicking and dragging those items from the desktop or folder right into the Site window.

You jump back and forth between your Site window and Layout page quite often in developing your Web site, which may become confusing at times. Don't forget that dragging files or folders into the Site window effectively copies them into your site folder, providing you with a nice, central location where you can keep all your file and folder ducks in a row. After you get them in the Site window, you can easily keep an eye on individual files, folders, and even the contents of folders.

It's All Text, Graphics, and Links

After you load your Site window with the pages and the media that you want to use on your site, you're all set to put the parts together by entering text, placing graphics and making links. The following sections tell you how to do just that. And don't forget! Open your site first. You can use the index.html page from the site for learning how to use the page tools.

Entering text

Entering text in GoLive 5 is simply a matter of clicking the arrow at the top of the page area in the Layout view and starting to write. As soon as the cursor's in position, an *I-beam cursor* replaces the arrow pointer, and you know that you're ready to start typing. The I-beam defaults to the upper and left of the page relative to whatever else is on your page. After you enter the text, you can perform most basic formatting and all coloring tasks by using the toolbar or the Color palette. More elaborate formatting, however, requires the use of GoLive 5's menus and other guises of the Inspector, as I discuss in Chapter 1.

Make sure that you use only the Layout view for entering text; if you try to type text in Preview view, for example, nothing appears on-screen. (For more information on the various views at your disposal, refer back to Chapter 1.)

Using the toolbar to format text

What kinds of makeovers can you achieve by using the toolbar? Take a close look at Figures 2-4 and 2-5 and see what a little magic can do. By employing that same bit of magic, you, too, can now take any mousy bit of text and transform it by changing the font size, the paragraph alignment, and the font style. Look closely at Figure 2-5 and you can see the technical tricks behind this formatting magic: The buttons for Center alignment, Bold typeface, and Size 6 fonts (*not* six points or pixels) are selected on the toolbar.

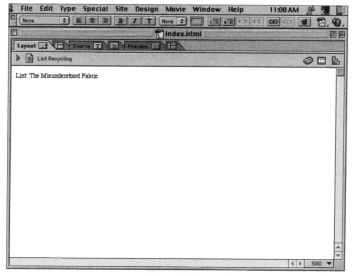

Figure 2-4:
Plain-vanilla
text in
GoLive 5's
Layout view.

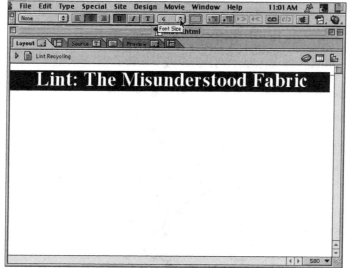

Figure 2-5:
Clicking
your
selections
on the
GoLive 5
toolbar
provides
your text
with basic
formatting.

Your toolbar offers the following format selections, from left to right:

✔ **Paragraph Format:** Use this set of six drop-down headings selections to change font sizes for page and section titles. Header 1 is the largest, and Header 6 is the smallest.

- ✔ **Alignment (Left, Center,** and **Right):** The three alignment buttons place text where you need it relative to the page margins. You generally center page headings and left-align most text; anything that you need to put off to the side you right-align — for example, numbers, dates, and mother-in-laws.

- ✔ **Bold, Italic,** or **Monospace (T) font styles:** You can use these buttons to set your type styles to your liking. Be careful about using italics, however, because italic type can prove hard to read in smaller sizes. (By the way, the *T* on the monospace button stands for *Teletype* — use that wisdom the next time you're stuck for something to offer the conversation.)

- ✔ **Font size:** You set font sizes to one of the seven standard HTML sizes and not in standard point measures. The 7 selection represents the largest and 1 represents the smallest — just the opposite of the HTML heading sizes. You can use the font size selections to create large caps to kick off a paragraph or just to adjust the overall font size to enable an easier reading of your messages.

- ✔ **Text Color well:** The text color well is a handy device for adding color to your text. When it is selected (clicked *once*), it automatically brings up the Color Palette, and it transforms any selected text to the color you click in the Color palette.

- ✔ **Numbered list:** You can order your sequences by using a numbered list. After you click this button and create the initial paragraph, the numbered-list function automatically numbers sequential paragraphs. This feature comes in handy, for example, in explaining a sequence of steps that you use in dancing the rumba.

- ✔ **Bulleted list:** If list elements fall in no specific order, you can use a bulleted list (like this one). Bullets are good for listing major points that you want to emphasize on a page.

- ✔ **Increase or Decrease list level:** You can use these handy tools for indenting lists further to provide different levels — as you find in an outline. You can also use the same tools for indenting even blocks of text displaying no list properties. Indented blocks of text serve to break up long streams of text and make the page more interesting.

Coloring text

You can brighten things up a bit by adding color to the text that you add to your page. First, select the text by clicking and dragging across it with your mouse. Then click the Text Color well on the toolbar or choose Window➪Color from GoLive 5's menu bar. The Color palette dialog box appears, offering a rainbow's worth of colors from which to choose. You select from nine different collections of colors and different ways to bring up a color. With the Text Color well selected, all you need to do is to click any color in the Color palette, and as soon as you see the color in the Text Color well, you text has been transformed to that color. If you want to take things a little slower and view the color in the preview pane of the Color palette first, don't click the Text Color well on the toolbar. Just click any color in the Color palette to bring it into the preview pane, then take a good, long look at it. If that color satisfies you, click and drag it from the preview pane to the selected text. Presto, change-o — your text becomes the selected color.

You must *first* select a block of text before trying to add color. (Don't try to select a color first and then the text — it doesn't work.)

Formatting from the menu bar

Because you want to spend most of your time on the desktop and not riffling through menus, you use the toolbar for the bulk of your formatting. Some formatting items in the menus, however, aren't available on the toolbar, so you need to know how to use the menus for formatting, too. You can perform a task as basic as selecting a font for your text, for example, only from the menu bar. And if you want to use Underline, Superscript, Subscript or the ever-annoying Blink format, you must use the Type menu to access these features.

To prevent user madness, try to avoid using the Blink style. (It's a style that makes text continuously blink on an off with the effect of distracting the viewer from whatever message you may have on your page.) Early amateur designers of Web pages often used this odious style because it was a style not available on paper. If you simply *must* use it, do so on a site that you design specifically to annoy your enemies. (Of course, you're certain to try it out now just to see what's so annoying about Blink.)

Choosing a font is easy. Just follow these steps:

1. **Select the text that you want to style by pressing and holding the mouse button while dragging the pointer over the text.**

2. **Choose Type⇨Font from the menu bar and then, in the Font submenu that appears, drag the mouse pointer over the font that you want and release the mouse button.**

   Each font name is highlighted as you drag the mouse over it. So make sure that the font style you want is highlighted before you release the mouse button. (The first time that you select a font, you see only a limited list of fonts available.)

If you don't see the font that you want in the Font submenu, GoLive 5 enables you to add fonts and font sets of your own liking. To do so, follow these steps:

1. **Select the text that you want to style, as I describe in Step 1 of the preceding steps.**

   You can too easily go through all the work to set up a special font style and then realize that you didn't select the text that you want to style. D'oh!

2. **Choose Type⇨Font⇨Edit Font Sets from the menu bar.**

   The Font Set Editor appears, displaying three panes. The pane on the left is for selecting changes that you want to make to the default font sets or just for the page. The middle pane is for font sets, and the right is the one that you use for selecting fonts. As you're just acquainting yourself with the Font Set Editor, you want to select Page in the pane on the far left.

3. **Click the New button in the center pane of the Font Set Editor.**

   The words New Font appear in both the center and right panes.

4. **In the rightmost pane, click the arrows next to the text box where** New Font **appears in a window near the bottom of the dialog box to view a selection of fonts.**

   Select any font that you want from the drop-down list in the Font Set Editor's right window, but remember that an unusual font may not appear on someone else's computer. Palatino, for example, is a fairly common serif font. If George, in Wallaby Gulch, Australia, doesn't have Palatino on his computer, however, you have no way of telling what George is going to see. In GoLive 5, fortunately, all you need to do is to select another font from the list that then appears in place of the primary font if the primary font isn't on a computer that someone uses to view your Web page. Times, for example, is a common serif font on virtually every computer. To add Times to the Palatino font set just click the font drop-down list again and select Times. In the right window, you see both Palatino and Times, but in the Font Set window, you see only Palatino, which means that both fonts are in the set. If a particular computer can't view Palatino, therefore, GoLive 5 uses Times instead.

5. **Click OK and you're done.**

After you create a new font set, it appears in the initial set of fonts in the Fonts submenu of the Type menu, and you don't need to go through the process again.

Here's a way to get a desired font without going through the font menus every time you want to use a certain font in your text. After you have all the fonts that you plan to use on a page, you can copy and paste a font from any of the text on the page. Select a piece of text with the desired font from the page. Choose Edit⇨Copy from the menu bar and then choose Edit⇨Paste. After you paste the text, backspace over the existing text and start typing in the font style of the text you just backspaced over. By using this method, you can save the time of going through the menu sequence. You can change the size if you want without losing the font settings, too.

Adding a graphic

As is true of everything else in GoLive 5, adding a graphic is intuitive and simple. The following steps describe how to add graphics to your page:

1. **Choose Window⇨Objects from the menu bar.**

   The Objects palette appears.

2. **Click the Basic tab (the first tab on the left), if necessary.**

   The Basic tab is the default tab, so it's probably already selected — but if you've been experimenting with the Objects palette, just make sure that it's currently set on the Basic tab of the Objects palette.

3. **From the Basic tab of the Objects palette, drag the Image icon (the one displaying the question mark) onto the page where you want it to go, as shown in Figure 2-6.**

Figure 2-6:
A place-holder icon that you drag from the Objects palette sets the initial placement of images on your Web page.

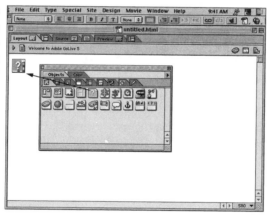

4. **Select the Image icon on the page by clicking it and then choose Window⇨Inspector from the menu bar to open your Inspector window (if it's not open already).**

   The Inspector window opens as (or changes into) the Image Inspector.

5. **Click the Select Window button on the toolbar (the third button from the right) to toggle the Site window to the front and then move the Site window so that you can view both the Site window and the Layout view.**

   Aligning the two windows just right so that one doesn't cover up crucial parts of the other can prove a little tricky. You may need to change the window sizes so that you can see everything. (Scooting around windows is a talent that you acquire after working with them for a while.)

6. **In the Basic tab of the Image Inspector palette, place the pointer on the Point-and-Shoot button (the one to the far left of the Browse button) and drag the point-and-shoot line to the image in the Site window that you want to appear on your page, as shown in Figure 2-7.**

   The image that you indicate in the Site window replaces the Image icon placeholder on your page. (Notice the arrangement of the windows for this point-and-shoot operation.) As a further reminder, be sure that the image is in the Site window and it's one of the Web supported formats (JPEG, PNG, or GIF).

Figure 2-7:
Dragging a line from the Image Inspector's Point-and-Shoot button to an image in the Site window replaces the placeholder icon on your page with the actual image that you want to appear there.

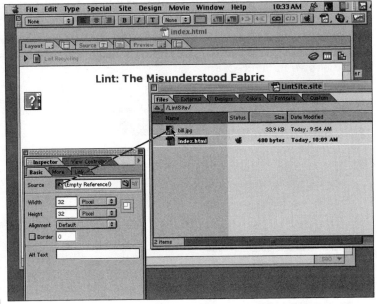

 After you click the Point-and-Shoot button on the Image Inspector, you can switch between the Site window and the Document window by pulling the point-and-shoot line from the Point-and-Shoot button to the Select Window button on the toolbar (the third button from the right). This action brings the Site window to the front so that you can select a file or link without needing to stop and rearrange your windows. Remember to keep holding the mouse button until after you select the image that you want from the Site window. After you finish placing your graphic, just click anywhere on the Layout page to bring it to the front. The Site window then sits hidden behind the Layout page until you need it again.

Drag and drop till you drop

You can also drag and drop a graphic right from its source onto a page. In fact, you don't even need to use the graphic placeholder (the Image icon) from the Objects palette in most cases. All you do is to the select the graphic from the Site window — or even from any other folder containing graphics — and drag and drop it where you want it to go. As you do in all drag and drop operations, you simply select the graphic file and then, holding the mouse button, move the pointer to the position you want on the page. Finally, just release the mouse button and your graphic's in place. By using this method, however, you don't get to use the Point-and-Shoot button; nor is the Browse folder available in the Inspector to help you find a graphic you didn't place in your site's root folder.

You can save a step by dragging a graphic directly from your Site window to your Web page, but you need to be careful. If you nicely organize all your graphics in your Site window, dragging them onto the page directly without using the Image-icon placeholder doesn't present a problem. If you just start dragging media files from all your computer's folders and disks directly onto your Web page, however, you're likely to end up with bad links between the page and some of the graphics. So if you decide to use the drag-and-drop method with media files, limit it to only those that reside in your Site window. Figure 2-8 shows a situation in which you have a potential mess on your hands.

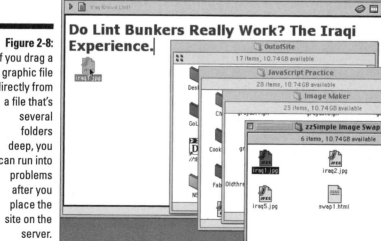

Figure 2-8: If you drag a graphic file directly from a file that's several folders deep, you can run into problems after you place the site on the server.

In Figure 2-8, the route from graphic to source begins with a folder by the name of OutofSite and continues through the folders JavaScript Practice, Image Maker, and zzSimple Image Swap to the file iraq1.jpg. If you drag the image directly onto the Web page through that route, all those folders and the disk must also be on the server for the operation to work and the image to appear on your page online. To put the situation in technical terms, *that ain't gonna happen!* Unless you plan to turn your trusty PC into a server, putting a copy of the file into your Site window and then performing your drag-and-drop procedure is a lot smarter way to go.

Although arranging everything neatly in the Files view of your Site window before you start cranking out Web pages is a good idea, GoLive 5 has a heart for those of you who post signs proclaiming, "Neatness is a sign of insanity." Chapter 11 shows you how to use the Clean Up Site command that collects the stray files you place in pages residing in your root site. For the time being, however, to quote Mom, "Clean up your site!"

Arranging text around your graphic

After you place your graphic on your page, you must decide where to place your text relative to the image. In GoLive 5, you handle such image/text issues by using a drop-down list in the Image Inspector. You need to select the image first and then open the Inspector by choosing Window➪Inspector from the menu bar. (Remember that the Inspector is context-sensitive and changes to the Image Inspector after you select an image or image icon.) Click the Alignment drop-down list box and select the alignment that you want from the list that appears, as shown in Figure 2-9. A black bullet appears next to the alignment that you select after you choose it.

Figure 2-9: The Alignment list in the Image Inspector aligns the currently selected image.

Image formats the Web likes

In creating pages for the Web, your choice of formats for graphics files is a bit limited, at least at the time of this writing. (You can always hope for rapid advances in the near future, I suppose). The formats that you can now use on a Web page are as the following list describes:

- ✔ *GIF* (Graphics Interchange Format), including GIF89a for transparent images and animated GIFs.
- ✔ *JPEG* (Joint Photographic Experts Group), including progressive JPEG.
- ✔ *PNG* (Portable Network Graphics).

If your favorite graphic isn't in one of these formats, you can transform it easily enough by using any of several graphic programs. Adobe's ImageReady is a great one to use to get your graphics ready for the Web. Similarly, you can use FireWorks, PhotoShop, Illustrator, and FreeHand to load your graphic file and then save it as a GIF, JPEG, or PNG file.

Making a link

Links (or *hyperlinks*) connect your Web page to the following different elements:

- ✔ Another Web page.
- ✔ A resource (a file that you can download).
- ✔ An e-mail address.
- ✔ An anchor (a target on a Web page to which a link can connect you).

For the sake of convenience, I refer to links to pages on your site (those that you view in the Site window) as *internal links* and links to other sites as *external links*. To set the stage for either an internal or external link, you first need to add a *destination page* to the site. Then you need to add some more text to your main page and format it so that it can act as the link to your destination page. You don't need to add much text; in fact, a single word or short phrase can act as the link. The following sections explain the process in greater detail.

Adding a page to your site

You use both the Site window and the Objects palette to add a page to your site. To do so, follow these steps:

1. **Open your Site window by clicking the Site button on the toolbar or by choosing File➪Open➪*Sitename* from the menu bar or by pressing Ctrl+O (in Windows) or Cmd-O (on the Mac).**

   The Site window appears, showing you the pages, files, and folders associated with your site.

2. **Choose Window➪Objects from the menu bar to open the Objects palette and then click the Site tab (the sixth tab from the left on the Objects palette).**

   The Site tab of the Objects palette displays a number of icons associated with different site tasks.

3. **Select the Generic Page icon (the first icon from the left in the top row) and drag it to your Site window, as shown in Figure 2-10.**

   This action adds a New Page icon with the name untitled.html to your site.

4. **Rename the new page by first selecting the page icon's title in the Site window and then typing a new name to replace the existing name.**

   I suggest that you choose a name that's both short and informative. Doing so helps you farther down the road, because the page name then gives you a clear idea of what's actually on the page. Take a look at the Status column next to the list of files, folders, and pages in your Site window. A yellow triangle in the Status column means that you haven't done any work on the page yet. (It's a blank page.) As soon as you do some work on the page and save it, the triangle changes to a check mark.

Figure 2-10:
Drag the Generic Page icon from the Site tab in the Objects palette to the Site window to add a new blank page to your site.

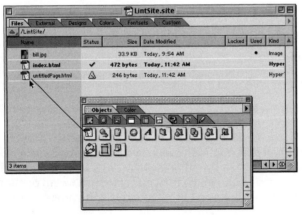

Hooking up to your site pages

After you have a page in your site to which you want to link, you can make the actual link in several ways. I recommend that you use the point-and-shoot technique — the same one that I use in the section "Adding a graphic," earlier in this chapter, to select an image for the site. To make a link by using this method, follow these steps:

1. **Select the text for the link in the Document window's Layout view.**

   If your Document window is behind the Site window, just click the third button from the right on the toolbar to toggle it to the front and select the Layout view.

2. **Click the Link button on the toolbar (the sixth button from the right — the one displaying two chain links), as shown in Figure 2-11.**

3. **Choose Window⇨Inspector from the menu bar to open the Inspector (which automatically opens as the Text Inspector after you select text), select the Point-and-Shoot button in the Link tab of Text Inspector, and drag the point-and-shoot line to the file in your Site window that you want to serve as your link.**

   Remember — if you can't see the Site window, you can just drag the point-and-shoot line to the Site button on your toolbar to toggle the Site window into view. As you're dragging the point-and-shoot line to the file, a green bug image appears in the status line of the Site window next to the page containing the link. After you select the file and release the point-and-shoot line, the bug disappears. The bug's telling you that a link from that page currently has no target. After you select the target, no problem remains to bug the bug, so it flies away into cyberhibernation.

Your selected text now appears on the page underlined and in the correct link color. GoLive 5's default link color is blue, but you can change the default color by clicking the Page icon in the upper-left corner of the Layout page, right under the text reading Layout (on the Layout tab). Use the Color palette (which you access by choosing Windows⇨Color from the menu bar) to choose a new link color and then drag that color to the Link, Visited Link, and Active Link Color windows that appear in the Page Inspector. (Surprise! After you click the Page icon, the Inspector opens to its Page tab, becoming — ta daaa! — the Page Inspector.)

Figure 2-11:
Use the Link button on the toolbar to convert selected text into a link on your Web page and the Unlink button to remove the link.

Link

Unlink

The Unlink button on the toolbar (fifth from the left) is very useful, too. If you accidentally set up the wrong link or you want to change a link, just select the text of the link and click the Unlink button. If you don't unlink a link before you change it to unlinked text, the correct Inspector may not appear.

Connections to the whole wide world

If you want to link your page to an external file, you need to know the *URL* (*U*niform *R*esource *L*ocator — the Web address) of the file. The steps that you take are similar to those for linking to a file on your own site, but you must add the step of typing in the URL. Follow these steps:

1. **Choose Window⇨Inspector from the menu bar.**

   The Inspector appears on-screen.

2. **Select the text for the link.**

   After you select text, the Inspector automatically becomes the Text Inspector.

3. **Click the Link button on the toolbar.**

4. **In the Text Inspector, type the entire URL in the URL text box.**

   In the Text Inspector's text window, you see the phrase (Empty Reference!). You type your URL over the Empty Reference!. Make sure that you start off the address with **http://**. The browser doesn't need to think as much if you include **http://**, and GoLive thinks it's a bug if the http:// part is missing on an external link.

Use Ctrl+Alt in Windows or Option-Cmd on your Mac when you click the Browse button and a much larger window opens to place your URL. It's also a good idea to copy and paste a URL into the URL window so you make sure you have the address just right.

Controlling the View: Looking Before You Leap

If Web page designers had a Web fairy godmother, they'd all wish for the same thing — page consistency in different browsers and computer platforms. The next best thing to pixie dust, however, is GoLive 5's View Controller and Preview views.

Using the View Controller

After you finish creating a Web page, you're all set to look at it. It looks fine in the GoLive 5 Layout view, but before you do anything else, you need to look at it from different perspectives. You want to make sure that what you create on a Macintosh looks good on a Windows PC and vice versa. In addition, you may want to see how the page looks in different browsers. GoLive 5 offers you a designer's dream in the View Controller. It enables you to view a page as it appears on different computers using different browsers and even different versions of browsers. (The View Controller is the Inspector's roommate — they live in the same window.) To use the View Controller to look at your pages from many perspectives, follow these steps:

1. **In the Layout view, choose Window⇨View Controller.**

    The View Controller appears on-screen. (Of course, if you're already using the Inspector, you can just click the View Controller tab to bring that aspect of the Inspector to the front.)

2. **In the area where you see** `Root CSS`, **open the drop-down list and select the type of computer (Mac or Windows) on which you want to view the page and the type and version of browser for that computer.**

    After you set the View Controller for the type of computer and browser through which you want to view the page, both the Layout view and Preview views provide images of how the page looks on that respective computer and browser. Figure 2-12 shows a page on a Mac disguised as a Windows PC that's looking at the page while using Version 4 of Internet Explorer.

Figure 2-12:
The View Controller enables you to view your page from different computers and browsers while you're working on the page.

You may face serious design consequences for your creations on different platforms. What may look great on a Macintosh can look simply awful on a Windows PC. The fonts look big and bulky and the alignment is different. Similarly, if you do your designing on a Windows PC, the guy looking at your page with a strawberry-colored iMac may see itty-bitty fonts and poor alignment. Hence, try out your page on more than one platform and browser preview before you declare it a done deal.

Using Preview view

Besides looking at your page in the Layout view from the perspective of different computers and browsers, you also want to use the Preview view to look at your pages before saving final versions. Some of the work that you do in the Layout view uses tools, such as the grid, that don't appear on-screen if you view the page in a browser. (I discuss the grid in Chapter 3.) You want to use the Preview view, therefore, to examine these pages to see how they look after they're on the Web.

As I note in Chapter 1, the Windows and Mac versions of GoLive 5 are different in that the Macintosh version offers two Preview views and the Windows version only one. (See Figures 2-13 and 2-14, showing the different tabs in the Document windows.) The only difference is that, after you begin working with frames in Chapter 9, Mac users need to select the Frames Preview view, while Windows users can view both frame and nonframe pages by using the same Preview view.

To preview your page, follow these steps:

1. **Select File ⇨New or Ctrl+N in Windows or Cmd-N on a Mac to create a new page in the Layout view of the Document window.**

   A new page appears. Go ahead and write text on it or put an image on it just so that you have something to look at.

2. **Select the Preview tab in the Document window.**

   Your page now appears as it does in a browser. (Try some different views by using the View Controller that I describe in the preceding section.)

If you're tight on computer memory (and who isn't with 15 other applications open at the same time), using the Preview view enables you to save some good old RAM (what memory the computer can keep in its head at the same time). You don't need to open a browser application (or even two browsers, just to be on the safe side). You can see what the browser sees right there in the Preview view.

Figure 2-13:
The
Macintosh
Document
window has
an extra
Preview
view for
Frames —
the tab on
the far right.

Figure 2-14:
The
Windows
Document
window has
a single
Preview
view for
looking at
pages with
and without
frames.

Saving Your Page

Saving your page isn't exactly rocket science, but you must do it right. As is the case with everything else on computers, until you save your page, it exists in an electronic silicon dream. As soon you turn off your computer, the dream is gone unless you save it first — and so is all your work. Save often and save backups of your pages. After you save your pages and create folders for them, you need to remain aware of some important guidelines.

Because you're building a Web site and not just a Web page, you need to save *both* the site and the page. To do so, follow these steps:

1. **In the Document window, choose File⇨Save or press Ctrl+S (in Windows) or Cmd-S (on the Mac).**

   While in the Document window, you save only the page on which you're currently working. If you have other pages open, you need to save them separately.

2. **Switch to the Site window by selecting the Select Window button on the toolbar (third from the right.)**

   You are switched to the Site window. If a piece of the Site window is in view while you're in the Document window, you can switch by clicking on the visible portion of the Site window.

3. **In the Site window, choose File➪Save or press Ctrl+S (in Windows) or Cmd-S (on the Mac).**

   Changes that you make in the Site window may include saving several different Web pages. If you save a new page to the site, that action changes the site, and so you must save these changes as well.

As I said, it's not rocket science, but you do need to remember to save your pages. Fortunately, GoLive 5 helps you remember by presenting you with a dialog box that asks you whether you want to save your pages or site before you quit the program — just in case you forget.

In the past, you faced severe limits on what you could name your files and folders. Spaces between words weren't possible, and you could use only eight characters in a file name — and you had all those extension names to remember. Well, guess what? Remembering some of those old habits is probably still a good idea. Unlike personal computers, some servers are very fussy about names. (Remember that Web pages eventually go onto servers.) Following are a few guidelines to follow in naming your files and folders.

✔ Don't put spaces between words. Lint Pages isn't a good name for a file or folder that's going on a server, but LintPages or Lint_Pages is fine.

✔ Be as descriptive as possible in your file names. IndustrialLint.html is clearer than InLi.html. (Besides, *InLI* may be an abbreviation for *In line* or *Inter Lingo* or anything else.)

✔ Keep your file names relatively short. Some servers limit the number of characters they accept in a file name.

✔ Don't use characters such as @#$%^&*. Invariably, the server has special meanings for those characters. (The server may think that you're offending its dear old mother.)

✔ If you rename a file, make sure that you have GoLive 5 update any links involving that file. If you make a name change to a file with a link, a number of dialog boxes appear and ask whether you want to update the links. Make sure that you always say, "You're darn tootin' I do." (Either that or click OK.)

Chapter 3

Worth a Second Look

· ·

In This Chapter

▶ Creating clear pages that make your point

▶ Using the GoLive 5 grid to make design easy

▶ Constructing pages with balance and alignment

· ·

*N*oticing what's wrong with something is often easier than pointing out what's right. That's because, if something's wrong, the parts are incongruent — like a traffic accident or a sliver in your finger. If nothing's wrong, nothing's there to notice. Often, *beautiful is invisible* because nothing's jarring the senses. Everything flows as it does in nature. Other times, the designer wants to jar the senses, but he does so in a way that engages and intrigues rather than annoys or repels the viewer. On viewing good Web design, the viewer wants to see more but perhaps can't explain exactly why. ("I think it's cool.")

A good-looking Web page, however, doesn't happen by accident or chance but because the Web-page designer knows what she's doing. In some part, this ability to create such a page comes from an artistic talent on the part of the designer, but more often, it's simply the result of lots of hard work and an understanding of certain principals of design. Most of these design principles are common to both paper and Web pages, but some are unique to designing Web pages. This chapter covers the principles of good Web-page development and then shows you how using GoLive 5's grid feature makes applying such principles simple.

Talent borrows; genius steals!

In working to make a page look good, the best place to start is with good-looking pages. That's how professional graphic artists start. Design is a skill and talent that you develop over years of study and practice, and most people who want to create a Web page don't have that kind of background. To find out a great deal about what makes a good-looking Web page, however, you can explore the Web for award-winning designs — or just for designs that appeal to you. Study the way the various parts go together and why the pages and sites appeal to you as they do. Then adopt those elements that you find most attractive for your own Web pages. A good place to start such a search online is at www.killersites.com. David Siegel provides a wealth of tips and examples of well-designed sites. Click on his 'Design Tip' link in his core page to see what the pros consider in making a Web site. Take a look, too, at the site of talented designer Hillman Curtis at www.hillmancurtis.com/. For other links to good designers and cool sites, check out www.adobe.com — GoLive 5's hometown.

Design Tips to Get the Right Kind of Attention

Design is half *not doing the wrong thing* and half *doing the right thing.* This section provides tips on doing a little of both. Certain design tenets that you can follow by way of a set of rules can prove extremely useful for novice designers. The guides of mature design reflect a corpus of knowledge developed over centuries of design development in everything from architecture to book design. The rules have been extrapolated and modified from examples and design theory. Experienced designers not only know these rules, but they also know how and when to bend and break them and still come up with a good design. Even the most experienced and creative designers, however, consider a number of guidelines before plunging ahead. Furthermore, although typography and graphic design enjoy rich histories, Web design is a little different from other types of design, so a good deal of experimentation and innovation often is in order — while you still keep older design guides in mind.

Communication

A Web page is a means of communication. As is true in all communication, you have *senders* and *receivers.* Even if the Web page includes feedback forms for Web viewers to fill in, to take advantage of the forms those viewers must first understand the message you're sending that tells them to fill in the form. This point is important to remember, because you must always consider the people who are meant to understand any message that you send.

Audience: To whom exactly are you talking in that manner?

Whenever I visit Mexico or Spain, I try to speak Spanish. Now, my Spanish may bring tears to the eyes of native speakers, but I'm communicating my respect for the culture and customs. Sending a message is easy, but for the person on the other end to understand or even read the message may prove more difficult. Because Web pages are messages, your first consideration is to find out everything that you can about your audience. If your audience consists of members of your flower club or business organization, you probably know a good deal about their interests already. If, however, you're trying to create a Web page for a new audience about whom you know little, you need to take some time to find out something about them. If you want people to understand you, consider the following tips:

- ✔ Avoid (as you would the plague and taxes) anything that your audience dislikes. Young adolescent audiences don't want you to preach to them, and hobby groups don't like people making their hobbies the butt of jokes. (Seriously, folks, the teddy bear collectors take umbrage with anyone who thinks that collecting teddy bears is silly — and the same goes for the Barbie Doll enthusiasts.)

- ✔ Provide the audience with an incentive for looking at your page. Among the most common incentives that you see on the Web are free downloads. (Adobe, at `www.adobe.com`, for example, provides free trial downloads of its software.) Other incentives include daily information about a topic (as at `www.weather.com`), something fun, such as a daily fortune (check out `www.excite.com`), or interesting graphics and photos (as you find at `www.eyewire.com`). Ask yourself the following question: "What incentives attract me?" The chances are good that those same incentives attract others who have the same area of interest.

- ✔ Take a look at some books on the topics of marketing and advertising. Web sites hardly represent the dawn of the concept of attracting people to an idea, service, or product. Many of the classic books on marketing and advertising offer great information. (You may not believe how corny some of that advice on advertising and promotion seems today — but it still applies.) So head for your library, bookstore, or online sources and see what you can find.

- ✔ Look at trade publications for your target audience. You can't perhaps launch a full-scale marketing survey, but you can find plenty of information about every conceivable audience you can imagine in both online and paper publications. Many trade publications also conduct marketing surveys for their readers that can give you just the information you need. *The Industry Standard,* for example, features lots of articles about e-commerce in both magazine form and online.

✔ Talk to people in your target audience and then, listen, listen, and listen. If you have a client who wants you to sell her product or service, listen to what she tells you. Sit in on chat rooms online that discuss a particular hobby, service, or product. Sign up for an online discussion group with a focus on your target audience's interests. You can ask questions and get the information that you need. Good designers are good listeners.

You may even consider creating different Web pages for the same message. Suppose, for example, that you receive an e-mail list for readers of an adventurer's magazine, the audience of which is mostly male. At the same time, you obtain another e-mail list of readers of a woman's magazine. Your job, by the way, is to sell travel packages to Timbuktu — not an easy task. (Well, at least you didn't get Afghanistan or Burbank.) Women designers need to ask men what could possibly interest them in a trip to Timbuktu, and men need to ask women the same question. You're dealing with two different audiences here, and one's from Mars while the other's from Venus — so your work's cut out for you.

Figure 3-1 shows a Web site design for the readers of the men's adventure magazine. A Web page that wants to attract male adventure-magazine readers considers what such readers may do or want to do. The page in Figure 3-1 combines text, graphics, and color to kindle in the mind a trip that's risky but worth it. In the text, words such as *adventurous* and *dare* are prominent, implying the conquering of a challenge. The graphic shows a skyline with many openings for exploration but without a known inner side. It also displays a fortress-like appearance — shades of the French Foreign Legion. I use the GoLive 5 color palette to select FireBrick (a terra-cotta red) as a color — not only to complement the image, but also to characterize the desert setting of Timbuktu.

Figure 3-1:
The type of Web page that you may design particularly for men.

A female audience may have different interests. Selling a place such as Timbuktu can prove a challenge at best, even to a gung-ho bunch of men looking for new adventure. Women's interest, however, may lie in different types of challenges and desires. A Web page that you want to appeal to women, therefore, may take an entirely different approach. Figure 3-2 shows what may seem to appear as an entirely different location, but it's still just Timbuktu. First, I change the spelling to *Tombouctou* — the French spelling and the one that you find on most contemporary maps. The art-nouveau graphic font elicits a feminine style (see the accompanying sidebar). Finally, the exotic Islamic architecture unique to the city provides an invitation for women travelers in that it's less forbidding than the fortress-like image that I use for the men. The many windows create more of a bazaar atmosphere, where shopping is a distinct possibility. Even the French spelling of the city makes it appear, quite by design, less a remote rat hole than an inviting destination.

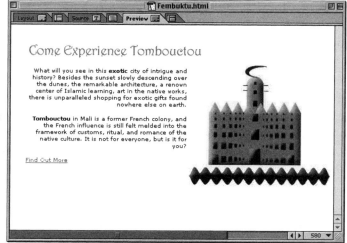

Figure 3-2: This Web page offers a more feminine invitation to Timbuktu.

Good Information at Spook Central: For a good source of basic information and maps of just any place on earth, check out the CIA's home page at `www.cia.gov`. Major demographic information is extensive there, and the simple maps provide a good overview of a country and its neighbors. And because this site represents the taxpayer's dollars at work, the graphic maps are public domain, so you can freely use them on your own Web site. Just go to the site and, from the CIA home page, click Publications & Reports ☞ The World Fact Book ☞ Reference Maps. Then click the link for the map that you want.

Funny fonts for effective results

In Figure 3-2, I use the Harrington font to spell *Tombouctou;* this font isn't likely to reside on all the computers that may view this page. Instead of using a text font, therefore, I create the header by using a graphic font (or just "graphic" because that's what it really is in GoLive) and then insert it in the page by using GoLive 5. Graphic fonts take up more memory, but if you require a certain look and feel to communicate the spirit of a page, such a font's worth the extra memory that you use. (While you're thinking about it, look also at the art-deco font that I use in Figure 3-13, later in this chapter. It, too, is a graphic font.)

Inserting graphic fonts uses exactly the same steps that I describe in Chapter 2 for placing graphic images on your Web pages. You need a graphic program such as Photoshop, CorelDraw, Fireworks, or some other graphic application that includes a text-writing module. Save the graphic text as either a GIF or JPG file and then put it where you want it on your Web page. Using the GoLive 5 grid that I describe in the section "Putting Your Objects on the GoLive 5 Grid," later in this chapter, makes placement simple and precise.

On a clear day, you can see my Web page

Another key design consideration for Web pages is *clarity.* Whenever people visit your Web page, you want them to see clearly what your page is all about and how to get more information. After all, how can a muddled page that's difficult to understand attract people? The KISS (*Keep It Short and Simple*) advice *generally* applies to Web pages — and almost always to the first page. Figure 3-3, for example, shows a very clear, simple, and complete message for its viewers. The page may be a bit minimalist for some, but the page that you see in GoLive 5's Preview view in this figure clearly shows *and* distinguishes these choices for the viewer. The page announces its options, presents a picture of each one, and provides a message telling the viewer what to do. Even if the viewer arrives at the page by mistake, what he sees on-screen is clear enough to suggest to him that he needs to click the Back key on his browser and browse elsewhere.

Simple and clear, however, doesn't need to mean *uninteresting.* After all, to a person who wants information about either pottery or plants, what this page offers is clearly interesting. If a page is unclear because it's attempting to appear interesting and clever, a visitor is more likely to skip it than view it. The design here is clean, however, offering no distracting elements, and so the viewer knows exactly what's what.

 In using graphic images on a Web page, you need to remain aware that a few large images work better than several small ones. Two tricks can help you make your page look better if you're using a pair of images as clickable links: Make sure that both images share at least one common dimension and then place both images within the same grid on your page. (The second part of this chapter explains using the GoLive 5 grid.) In Figure 3-3, for example, I make sure that the vertical heights of the two images are nearly identical You can make them pixel identical by matching the image size in Adobe Photoshop. You don't need to give all your images identical dimensions on all sides, however, because doing so requires too much cropping or distortion of the images. If, however, the vertical sizes are the same (or the horizontal sizes, depending on placement), this similarity helps reinforce the clarity of your message.

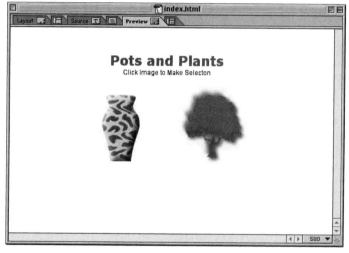

Figure 3-3:
Web pages
need to
provide the
viewer with
a clear
choice and
directions
on what
to do.

A more complex page than that shown in Figure 3-3 can also be clear. Clarity in design relates more to the viewer's ability to understand what's on a page than to how much information is on that page. The clearer a page is, the more quickly a viewer knows how to access more information or use the information on the page. Well-organized images and text can be clear — even if they're relatively small and abundant in number. You can find good examples of clear but fairly complex pages at the Web sites of most online retailers. Outpost.com, at `www.outpost.com`, for example, uses a clear home page containing a great deal of information. Right in the center of the page you see listings for eight big categories: Computers & Software, Electronics, Cameras, Games, Business Traveler, Innovations, Business Shopping and Gift Shopping. Each main category offers several examples immediately below it to give the reader a better idea of what sort of items the category describes. Surrounding the center of the page, you see several special promotions and other information about online shopping at the Web site. Excellent organization — primarily in the form of a clear focal point right in the center of the page — keeps the entire page clear and functional, however, despite all the information that you find on it.

Where am I now? Am I on the same planet?

Ever since the great Ralph Waldo Emerson penned the lines, "A foolish consistency is the hobgoblin of little minds, adored by little statesmen and philosophers and divines," many have believed that something is inherently wrong with consistency. Well, plenty's wrong with *foolish* consistency, because it's blind to change and misuse — a common problem of many Web pages. An *intuitive* consistency, however, is an elegant thing and a delight to the viewer. Good Web-page design incorporates intuitive consistency in laying out a common theme that pulls together all the pages in a Web site. At all times, the Web surfer is in a familiar place, knows where she is, where she's been, and what to do next. As the viewer explores the site, she's never lost, because a consistent look and feel tells her that she's still in the same site, and a consistent navigation system enables her to easily know where she wants to go next on the site.

Your navigation system needs a common and familiar look and feel. The viewer also needs to know where she is and where she can go at all times. One navigation scheme is to set up a central or core page that shows where everything is, along with a set of icons as a common set of tools to point the viewer in the right direction. Figure 3-4, for example, shows a *core page* with a collection of icons that indicate the places on the site that you can visit. The arrow icons link to the six connected topics, and the Exit button takes the viewer out of the site. The user immediately sees where she can go from this perspective. Figure 3-5 shows another page from the same site — but notice that the icons in use along the top of this page are identical to the ones that you find on the core page. By using a common set of icons throughout your site, you provide a consistent guide to the viewer and thus ensure that a viewer can navigate through your site with confidence. Don't forget that the more at home a viewer feels in your site, the more likely she is to return to check out your Web site again.

Clear to the core

One design strategy that David Siegel suggests in *Creating Killer Web Sites, 2nd Edition,* is to design your pages around a *core* rather than a home page. The core page usually is not the first page the viewer encounters but rather one that she finds by going down various paths that entice the viewer to seek more information about the site. Figure 3-4 shows a typical core page, where the Web surfer gets an overview of the site. Each page displays a clear label, with an icon next to the page indicating order and the option of a direct jump. Subsequent pages always provide a way back to the core and an escape hatch (Exit) so that the viewer doesn't feel lost or trapped in a site.

The arrow navigation system points to the next and previous pages by using an icon containing an X to mark the current page, as shown in Figure 3-5. As the viewer goes from page to page, the arrows show the page's position relative to the other pages in the site or subsection. Left-pointing arrows indicate previous pages in a sequence, and right-pointing arrows suggest future pages. If the viewer ever gets lost or wants to see a page out of sequence, all he needs to do is to jump to the core to find exactly where he wants to go and make a direct jump.

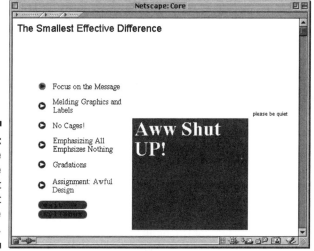

Figure 3-4:
A core page shows the viewer what to expect at the Web site.

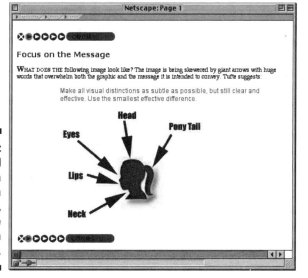

Figure 3-5:
Internal pages in a site offer a common, intuitive navigation system.

The best test of success for a good navigation system is whether the user can intuitively *sense* what to do next to get anywhere on your site. Getting someone else to try out your navigation system before you post it to your Web site is always a good idea. Don't tell your tester what to do; just ask him to look at your site and tell you what he thinks. Watch to see whether he navigates the site the way that you expect. A *consistent* navigation system means that a visitor needs to figure out the system only once. An *inconsistent* one requires a visitor to figure out each different navigation system that you set up on a site.

So recruit someone to test-drive your Web site *before* you post it. If you do, you can ask questions and make adjustments while you still have time. If you wait until your site is up on the server, strangers using your site aren't going to ask you how to navigate. They just give up and go somewhere else.

Put Your Objects on the GoLive 5 Grid

In Chapter 1 (as I describe the Objects toolbar), I make a reference to the GoLive 5 *grid* and do so again in Chapter 2, while discussing the Preview view. This section shows you how to use this great tool in setting up your pages.

Having all the best design principles down pat doesn't help much if you don't have a way to cleanly and efficiently carry out what you want to do. Transforming a great idea into something that actually runs on a Web browser isn't always easy. One of the major challenges for anyone putting a Web page together, for example, involves making the text and graphics behave on the page itself. Getting the different parts of the page to go right where she wants in HTML is often a nightmare for the designer. Fortunately, an easy way to lay out your page is available — simply use a piece of graph paper and clippings of graphics and text and links. (Links? You know — *hyperlinks.*)

I highly recommend such a low-tech beginning to the Web-layout process: Get hold of a nice piece of graph paper (or regular paper, if you haven't kept graph paper in the house since high school) and sketch out a rough plan showing exactly where you want to place the text, graphics and links on your Web page. After you get a pretty good idea of where you want things to lie on the page, you can go ahead and transplant your design from low-tech paper to high-tech electronic format. The following section shows you how to do so.

Grab the grid!

The *grid* feature of GoLive 5 puts a nice set of horizontal and vertical lines onto your computer screen, enabling you to easily line up the elements of your Web page just right. As you place an object, such as a graphic, in the grid, it snaps into place right where you place it. Accessing the grid in Layout view is as simple as using the grid to create your Web page. Just follow these steps:

1. **Open GoLive 5 (if it's not already open) and open a new site and new page by double-clicking the Index page in the Site window — or simply open GoLive 5 and use the blank page that appears.**

   A new blank page appears in Layout view. (Chapter 2 provides more details on how to open a site and a page if you need to review the page and site opening process.)

2. **From the Layout view, choose Window⇨Objects from the main menu bar.**

   The Objects palette appears, displaying its nine handy tabs. The default view shows the contents of the first tab, which is known as the *Basic tab*.

   If you aren't doing so already, keep the Objects palette and the Inspector open and nearby. If you have a lot of palettes open at the same time, the screen can get pretty crowded, but keeping these key windows open is easier than running back to the Window menus every time that you need one of them. You can minimize palettes that you use less often.

3. **Click the Layout Grid icon (the first icon in the first row of the Basic tab of the Palette) to select it and then drag it onto your blank page.**

   A square grid pattern appears in the upper left-hand corner of the page.

4. **Use your mouse to pull one of the corners or sides of the grid to resize the grid until it covers the entire page.**

   The grid expands to cover your entire page. The grid pattern changes to show the number of horizontal and vertical lines that you specify.

5. **Open the Inspector by choosing Window⇨Inspector or undock it by clicking the Inspector tab at the side of the screen.**

   The Inspector shows the dimensions of the grid. For a 14-inch monitor setting, the grid is about 580 by 330 — that's 580 pixels wide and 330 pixels high. You can change the size by changing the values directly in the Width and Height text boxes of the Inspector.

Figure 3-6 shows an example of what you see in the Inspector after dragging the grid to fill the screen. Notice that other options in the Inspector enable you to specify the size of the grid boxes or add a background color. Such fancy features aren't necessarily important for someone just wanting a few simple lines as an aid to keeping Web page elements nicely in line on the page.

Figure 3-6:
The
Inspector
helps you
set up a grid
on your
Web page in
the Layout
view.

After you set up the grid, you can drag and drop text and graphics right onto the page where you want them to go — and they snap right into place. The following sections show you exactly how to accomplish these tasks.

Getting your words down pat

Entering text into a Web page by using the grid involves more than just inserting your cursor somewhere on the page and then typing away. You first must set up a special area (known as a *Layout Text Box* in GoLive 5) on your Web page and then type text into it. The Layout Text Box is actually a great help for Web-page designers, because it enables you to determine exactly where to place text on the page. To add a Layout Text Box to your page, follow these steps:

1. **Choose Window➪Objects to open your Objects palette (if it's not open and selected already).**

   The (by now familiar) Objects palette appears, displaying the contents of the Basic tab.

2. **Click to select the Layout Text Box icon (the second icon from the left on the first row of the Object palette's Basic tab) and drag and drop it onto the grid where you want it to go on your Web page.**

   A Layout Text Box now appears on your Web page. Notice, too, that the toolbar changes to the Objects toolbar.

3. **After adding a Layout Text Box to the Layout page on the grid, type any text that you want into the Layout Text Box and then resize the text box and its text by dragging the corners and sides, as shown in Figure 3-7.**

   A made-to-order text box, complete with scintillating prose, now graces your Web page. Resizing the Layout Text Box simply tidies up the page and gives you more room to add new objects. If you want to add new text to the box later, the Layout Text Box automatically grows to accommodate the new text.

4. **Select the text in the Layout Text Box as you would any other text on the page and apply the desired format.**

   There is no special formatting technique for text in a Layout Text Box. Use the text formatting techniques shown in Chapter 2.

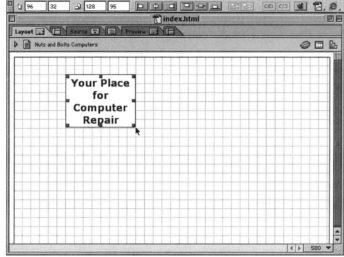

Figure 3-7:
Layout Text Boxes hold text that you place in a grid on your Web page.

GoLive 5 treats Layout Text Boxes as objects and not as text. If you have several Layout Text Boxes on the same page, select two or more of them and use the Objects toolbar to help arrange them. If you select the text within a Layout Text Box, however, notice the both the Inspector and toolbar change to text mode. In text mode, you can use all the text-formatting tools in GoLive 5. (No, you're not schizophrenic — but GoLive 5 may be.)

Placing your image anywhere

Adding a graphic to your page is just as easy as adding a Layout Text Box. If you place a graphic on your page without using a grid, the graphic automatically gravitates to the top and left of your page. If you're using a grid, however, you just drag and drop the graphic exactly where you want it to go. Before you start, make sure that the Site window is open and your graphic file is in the site root folder. (Remember, if you see the file in the Site window; then the file is in the root folder.)

1. **Choose Window⇨Objects to open your Objects palette (if it's not open and selected already).**

   The Objects palette appears, displaying the contents of the Basic tab.

2. **Open the Inspector by choosing Window⇨Inspector or undock it by clicking the Inspector tab at the side of the screen.**

   Sometimes I forget that the Inspector lies in the same window as the View Controller. Remember that, if the View Controller is on-screen, all you need to do to change it to the Inspector is to click the Inspector tab. Just think of them as roommates.

3. **Click to select the Image icon (the fifth icon from the left in the first row on the Objects palette's Basic tab) and drag and drop it on the grid where you want it to go on your Web page.**

   An Image icon now appears on your Web page right where you put it. The Inspector (now in its Image Inspector guise) shows the Point-and-Shoot button and is providing image information.

4. **Pull the point-and shoot-line from the Image Inspector to the Select Window button on the toolbar to bring up the Site window. After you bring up the Site window, pull the point-and shoot-line from the Image Inspector to your graphic image file located in the Files tab of the Site window.**

   The graphic image now replaces the Image icon and stays put where you had it on the grid. (Alternatively, you can drag the graphic directly from the Files tab of the Site window onto the grid.) Figure 3-8 shows how a point-and-shoot line selects the graphic, with the grid on the Layout view in the background.

Placing links in the design

Links are just as much a part of a basic Web-page design as text and graphics are — mainly because links are just text and graphics with a twist: You can make them act as springboards to enable people to jump to other pages, either on your own site or elsewhere on the World Wide Web. Placing a word, phrase, or image that you want to act as a link, therefore, is no different than placing a standard word or phrase of text or a graphic image. The twist comes if you want to make a particular word, phrase, or image "hot" so that it can act as a hyperlink to another page.

To place phrases or words, just choose Window⇨Objects to open the Objects palette and then click the Basic tab (if it's not already selected). Select the Layout Text Box icon (the second icon from the left on the first row of the Objects palette's Basic tab), drag the icon onto your page where you want it to go, and then type the word or phrase that you want to use as a link into the text box. (See the section "Getting your words down pat," earlier in this chapter, for details on how to place text.) To place images, grab the icon for the graphics file that you want on your page from your Site window and drag it onto the page. (The preceding section, "Placing your image anywhere," shows you how to do just that.)

Now you need to transform your run-of-the-mill word, phrase, or image into a link. To do so, follow these steps:

1. **For words or phrases, go to the Layout Text Box on your Web page and select the word or phrase that you want to change into a link; if you want an image to act as a link, select the image.**

   The word, phrase, or image that you select doesn't matter. You can turn almost anything into a link.

2. **Open the Inspector by choosing Window⇨Inspector or undock it by clicking the Inspector tab at the side of the screen.**

3. **Click the Link button (the one showing the two links of a chain joined together) on the toolbar.**

   In the Link tab of the Inspector you see a window with an (Empty Reference!) message in the URL text box, a Point-and-Shoot button, and a Browse button (showing a folder icon). (*Note:* You see the same link information in the Inspector whether you select text or an image.)

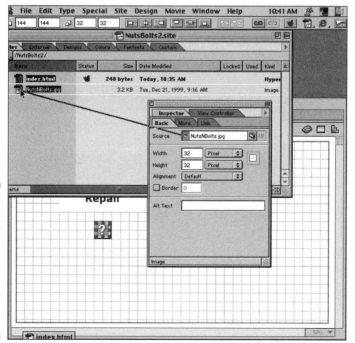

Figure 3-8: Just point and shoot objects onto your page and place them where you want on the grid.

4. **Type the name of the file that you want to serve as the target of the link in the URL text box of the Inspector.**

   Figure 3-9 shows how this setup looks on the grid and on the Link tab in the Inspector. Leave the Target text box blank for now. In Chapter 9, where I discuss frames, you will find out how to use targets.

5. **In the Title text box, type a short descriptive name for the link's target.**

   As a viewer passes the mouse pointer over the link word or image, a little message appears on-screen in your browser displaying that title. You can leave this text box blank if you want, but adding a title gives the user more information and looks sort of cool. (How'd that designer *do* that?)

   Although typing the name of the file is sometimes just as quick as using the point-and-shoot method, the Point-and-Shoot tool doesn't make typos that end up linking your page to a nonexistent URL or file. Dragging the mouse from the Point-and-Shoot button to the file in the Files tab of the Site window is all you need to do. (Refer to the section, "Placing your image anywhere," earlier in this chapter. Point-and-shoot works the same if you're placing an image as it does if you're selecting a link to a page.)

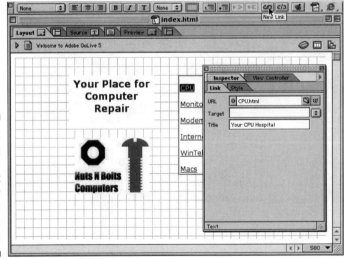

Figure 3-9:
Create a link
from text in
a Layout
Text Box by
using the
Inspector's
Link tab.

Forgetting to click the Link button on the toolbar whenever you want to make a link is all too easy. One way to remind yourself to do so is to look at the URL text box in the Inspector. If you *don't* see (Empty Reference!) in the Inspector's URL text box, that means that you *didn't* click the Link icon. This feature works the same whether you're linking text or images so you just need to remember the same thing for two different operations. (Well, it helps a little.)

Try selecting text or a graphic and use the following key combinations: Ctrl+L; Ctrl+comma; Ctrl+B in Windows or Cmd-L; Cmd-comma; Ctrl-B on a Macintosh. (The word "comma" is an actual comma [,] but it might be confusing had it not been written out.) A directory opens as soon as you press Ctrl+B/Cmd-B and the file you choose will be the linked file. If the current directory is not your root folder, navigate through the directories until it is. Then you will have a shortcut to both links and your root directory.

Adding the finishing touches

To finish the text chores in your Web page, you can color the text. You select the text in the Layout Text Boxes and color text by first clicking on the Text Color well in the toolbar and then selecting the color that you want from the Color palette, as I describe in Chapter 2. To color the text links, just select the Page icon in the upper left-hand corner of the Layout view and then fill in the Color wells in the Inspector, as I also describe in Chapter 2 (in the section about hooking up your site pages). In attempting to color text, make sure that you're selecting the *text* and *not* the boxes.

Now just in case you have any interest in looking at the source code for a page that you create by using the grid (either by choosing Window⇨Source Code to open the Source Code palette or selecting the Source view in the Document window), prepare yourself for a surprise. GoLive 5 uses HTML tables and table cells to create a page that puts everything where the designer (that's you) wants it. (For more information about tables, see Chapter 5.) You see a lot of <TR> and <TD> tags, but don't let them bother you. Those tags are just keeping things where they belong on your page. The tables that I show you how to create in Chapter 5 are for the same purpose but function in a much simpler way. GoLive 5 can put tables on a regular layout or on a grid. It does all the work so that you can design your Web pages with fewer limitations, more creativity, and less pain.

Line 'Em Up and Move 'Em Out

Alignment and balance are two elements that are crucial to a good-looking Web page. If you use the grid, aligning the page components becomes quite easy. To show you how to align objects on the grid, I designed a page that incorporates nothing but graphics. (Skip ahead to Figure 3-13 if you want to see the finished version of this page.) Even the text with the fancy shadowed backgrounds I created by using graphic images. The real problem to solve isn't the placement of elements on the page — that's relatively easy. The hard part (and it's not really all that hard) involves getting everything to line up just right.

Selecting and aligning graphics

The first step for any Web designer is to situate everything on your page in the general arrangement that you want. Grab stuff from your Site window, as I explain in Chapter 2, enter text by using text boxes, and format that text to your heart's content by using the Text toolbar. Figure 3-10 shows what I initially came up with for my page, before I had a chance to fix the alignment.

To get that neat shadowed effect, by the way, you need to use a tool such as Photoshop, ImageStyler, LiveMotion, Fireworks, CorelDRAW, Illustrator, FreeHand, or some other graphics program that offers an option for creating a shadow on JPEG, GIF, or PNG files. Creating the effect isn't hard if you have the right tool. Remember, too, that by putting graphics on your page, both the size of the file and the load time for the page in a Web browser will be greater than if you were just using regular text. (If you're very resourceful, you can create drop shadows by using Cascading Style Sheets, or CSS, as I discuss in Chapter 10, without needing to use graphics at all.)

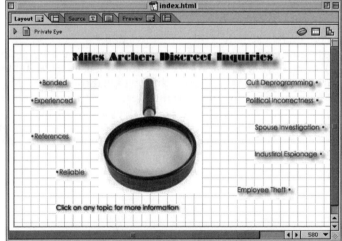

Figure 3-10: Scattered objects need alignment on your Web page.

The first thing that I want to do is line up my three central components (heading, magnifying-glass image, and informational banner at the bottom) down the center of the page. To align such elements, follow these steps:

1. **Shift+click the graphics that you want to select.**

   On my Web page, I shift+click the magnifying glass image, the heading, and the informational banner. By holding the Shift key as you select objects, each object remains selected even as you click another object. After you select it, a frame with little blocks at each corner and on each side appears around the image. (Figure 3-11 shows these three objects selected.)

2. **Choose Window⇨Align from the menu bar.**

   The Align palette appears on your page (see figure 3-11). The Align palette's two roommates are Transform and Tracing Image. So if either one of those palettes are on the page, click the Align tab to bring up the Align palette.

3. **Click the second icon from the left in the Align Objects row of the Align palette.**

   You see the three figures align themselves relative to each other's center. If you want to align the three objects to the center of the page, you select instead the second icon from the left in the Align to Parent row of the Align palette. You can also align the objects to a common horizontal center, to the left or right, or to a top and bottom point relative to each other by selecting one of the other icons. The vertical or horizontal line on the various Align icons indicates the orientation and placement of the alignment.

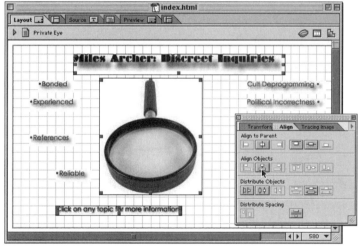

Figure 3-11: The selected objects align relative to each other after you choose an icon in the Align Objects row.

Automate your distribution

Lining up the big guns down the center of your page is one thing, but how do you distribute any smaller elements evenly along the right and left sides of your page? Follow these steps:

1. **Shift+click each object on the left side to align and distribute all the objects.**

   You can tell that each is selected if a rectangle with little blue boxes on the lines surrounds each selected object.

2. **Click the first icon in the Align Objects row of the Align palette.**

   The selected graphic text objects left-align. (But don't deselect the objects just yet.)

3. **With the same objects still selected, click the far right icon in the Distribute Objects row of the Align palette.**

   The Distribute Objects icons evenly distribute selected objects horizontally (the first three buttons in the Distribute Objects row) or vertically (the second three buttons). If you have several objects in a column or row, make sure that you select all the objects to ensure even distribution. Otherwise, GoLive 5 distributes only the selected objects and leaves the others alone.

4. **Follow steps 1 – 3 for the objects on the right side to align and distribute all these objects, except in Step 2, click the *third* icon in the Align Objects row of the Align palette.**

   Figure 3-12 shows both the left and right sets of graphic text images aligned and evenly distributed.

If you want objects on your pages distributed evenly on a diagonal you must place them initially on the page in rough diagonal order. Then you select all the objects on the diagonal and use the Distribute Spacing row in the Align palette to space them evenly horizontally and vertically by using both icons in the row. (You usually must click both icons until the diagonal straightens out and the objects are evenly distributed.)

Figure 3-12:
The far-right icon of the Distribute Objects row of the Align palette distributes selected objects vertically so that even spaces appear between each object.

The page is now ready, but to really see what you created, you first want to view it in Preview view to examine the results. Just open the page that you want to preview and click the Preview tab in the Document window (see Figure 3-13). As you can see in the Preview of the page I just created, the grid is invisible (probably the result of magic), and if you view the page itself in a browser, it looks clean, clear, and professional. Far more options for placing text or images by using the grid are available to you, by the way, than simply placing them all on the left side, all in the center, or all on the right side. But what you now see on this Web page is the design that you want with all the parts sitting in the right places. Compare Figures 3-10 and 3-13 to see the difference that good alignment and distribution make.

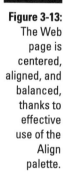

Figure 3-13:
The Web
page is
centered,
aligned, and
balanced,
thanks to
effective
use of the
Align
palette.

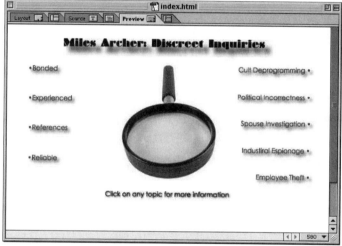

Resize Up the Situation

In the process of getting everything lined up and squared away, you may resize an image. "Resize" occurs when you adjust the size of an image after you have loaded it by changing the image's height and width in the Image Inspector or by dragging a corner or side of an image to make it larger or smaller. The image may not look bad if the proportions are maintained, but if the image looks like an elephant stepped on it, it is easy to restore it to its original dimensions. This will probably call for realignment of the objects, but with *GoLive,* that's easy using the grid. Here's how to fix a goofy-looking image that has been unkindly resized.

1. **Begin in the Layout view of the Document Window.**

2. **Undock the Inspector or select Window ➪ Inspector from the menu bar to open the Inspector.**

3. **Click to select the resized image.**

   Resized images are identified by a Resize Warning icon in the lower right quadrant of the image. The Inspector becomes the Image Inspector.

4. **Click to select the Basic Tab of the Image Inspector.**

5. **Click the Resize Restore button on the Image Inspector.**

   The Resize Restore button (see Figure 3-14) resides in the right portion of the Image Inspector window and resembles the Resize Warning icon. As soon as you click the button, the image is restored to its original size.

Resize icon   Resize Restore button

Figure 3-14: Resized image and resize restore button in Image Inspector.

It is always better to make your images the size you want them in your graphic editing program — not in the Layout view of GoLive. If you have a big image and you resize it to a small one, the big image is still loaded into memory. You just waste bandwidth that way. If you load a small image and resize it, often it looks bad, and it might be distorted. (Adobe Photoshop does a good job of changing image size.)

Use Adobe ImageReady or Macromedia Fireworks to optimize the size of your graphic images for the Web. They do it automatically, saving time and guesswork.

Tracing

What if you could get a preview of all of the images on your page before you actually put them on the page? And what if you could crop your images to just the right size *without* resizing the image? Well, with GoLive 5, you can do that and more using the Tracing Image palette (with a little help from the Transform palette).

The process works by importing an image file (including both Web and non-Web images). You can import Photoshop 8-bit RGB images as well as JPG, GIF, PNG, BMP, TARGA, PCX, PICT, PIXAR, and Amiga IFF. Once you import the images for tracing, the entire image or parts of it can then be cropped and saved as Web-safe files to then be placed on your Web page. Here's how you do it:

1. **Begin in the Layout view of the Document Window.**

2. **Undock the Inspector by clicking the Inspector tab at the side of the screen or select Window ⇨ Inspector from the menu bar to open the Inspector.**

   A generic Inspector appears on the screen.

3. **Choose Window⇨Tracing Image from the menu bar.**

   The Tracing Image palette appears with its roommates, Align and Transform. You may need to use Transform with the Tracing Image Palette.

4. **Click on the Source checkbox of the Tracing Image palette and select the file you want to import by clicking the Browse button (the one with the image of a folder) and selecting your file from the list in the directory window that opens.**

   If you drag the file to the page from the Files tab of the Site window, the page treats it as a regular file and you won't be able to trace it; so you have to use the Browse or point-and-shoot method of transfer. You see a dimmed image on the page if the link is successful.

5. **Drag the Opacity slide tool to the left (less) or right (more) to adjust the opacity of the image on the page.**

   I find that setting the Opacity around the middle works fine. If it's too opaque, you cannot distinguish the image from any other actual images you have on the page. If there is not enough opacity, you can't see it at all.

6. **Click on the Move Image tool button (the little hand icon).**

   Now you can drag the image around the page to position it where you want it to go. Find a good place for the image and release the mouse button.

7. **Click on the Cut Out tool located between the Move Image tool and Cut Out button.**

   A cross-hair icon mouse pointer appears. Drag around the image until you see a cropping window with pull-tabs.

8. **Adjust the cropping window with the mouse by dragging the pull tabs until you have selected the part of the image you want on your page, or until it surrounds the entire image, and click on the Cut Out button.**

   The Save for Web dialog box opens. Even if you are using a Web-safe image, you are given four windows, each with a rendering of the image you just cropped. You may adjust the settings in the dialog box or just click on the image you like the best.

9. **Click the OK button after making your selections.**

   You are first given a directory Save window and a name with an extension (png, gif, or jpg); select the directory you want and rename the file if you want to change the default one generated by GoLive.

10. **Click the Save button once your directory and name selections are made.**

   The image you just cropped and saved appears on your page in a floating box. (Chapter 16 fully explains floating boxes.) If you pass the mouse pointer over the sides of the floating box the hand pointer will change from a vertically pointing hand to a horizontal one. When it is in the horizontal position, you can move the box. Move the box with the image in it until it resides where you want it.

When you find that you need to use more than one palette or Site window view at the same time, GoLive 5 provides a handy function. If you drag the tab of the palette or view away from the window it is in, it separates the tab from the window. You don't have to go back and forth clicking tabs because both are open simultaneously. Figure 3-15 shows the Tracing Image palette pulled from its window. When you want to put them back, just drag the tab back into the home window. (If you really want to have some fun, drag a tab from one window and back into another.)

This process is to get everything ready for your page. As each image is cropped and saved, you accumulate the images that you need. The preview positioning is accomplished by dragging the cropped images in the floating boxes anywhere you want on the page. Once you have everything where you want it, you remove all the items from the page, place a grid to cover the page, and then bring in all of the images you have saved and position them using floating boxes where you had them before. Figure 3-15 shows a traced image and the cropped image (robot's head) in the floating box. Only the cropped image is saved to a Web-safe format.

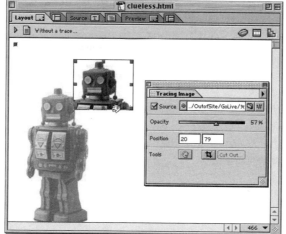

Figure 3-15:
Tracing images can be cropped and placed to assist in the design of a page.

Designing with Templates

Another neat feature for designing Web pages with GoLive 5 involves using the template. For inexperienced designers, a template offers a professionally designed Web site *as a starting point.* Basically, a template in GoLive 5 is a designed page with all of its components. Images and text that serve only design purposes are *placeholders* for actual images and text that you provide. Essentially, templates are designs without content. You provide the content and don't have to worry about the design. Here's how to get one up and running:

1. **Launch GoLive 5 by double-clicking the GoLive 5 icon.**

   A blank page appears in the Document window.

2. **Close the document by choosing File⇨Close or pressing Ctrl+W in Windows or Cmd-W on a Mac.**

   The only thing on the screen will be the menu bar plus any toolbar or palettes you had on the screen when you closed Document window.

3. **Select New Site⇨Copy from Template**

   The New Site from Template dialog box opens, as shown in Figure 3-16. Thumbnail images of the layout — usually the index page and the structure — show you a general idea of the design.

4. **Select the design you want, type in the name you want for your new site in the Name New Site text window and click the OK button.**

Note: When you first select your design, the default name for that design appears in the Name New Site text box. Be sure to type over the default name in the Name New Site text box with the site name you want to use. Otherwise, you'll get the generic template name that may be hard to find if you have seven other sites with the same name.

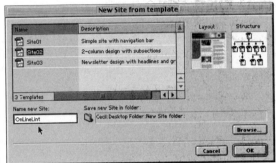

Figure 3-16:
Select a template from the New Site from template dialog box.

Web page design can be one of the most satisfying endeavors you can undertake. The more you study good design technique, the better your designs will be, and while templates are the last GoLive 5 feature covered in this chapter, it may well be one of the first you will want to try out. With the Web, remember that the whole world can see your work, and that means you can look good to a pretty big audience.

Chapter 4

More than One Way to Navigate a Web Site

In This Chapter

▶ Using the Site window to organize files

▶ Creating anchors and setting up links to them

▶ Organizing the site by using the Navigation and Link windows

▶ Making links out of images

▶ Creating image maps and using them to make links

▶ Using the In & Out Links palette

*T*hink globally and act locally. That piece of political populism applies to your Web site. You need to think of your Web site as something that people all across the World Wide Web are viewing and using, from What Cheer, Iowa, to Katmandu, Nepal. That's what thinking globally means. But to get your Web site working correctly, you need to think *locally,* and in GoLive 5, that means that you must gather your pages together in your *Site folder* — otherwise known as your *Site window.* The site folder is the *root folder* for your entire site, and all links are relative to the root folder. If you square away your root folder, you find that, as you place your pages on the Web, all the pages perform just as you expect.

Navigating the Reefs of the World Wide Web

I dedicate this chapter to dealing with the link issues for a Web site and the tools available in GoLive 5 that help you create links. GoLive 5 provides a really great way of organizing all your pages and page elements in its Site windows. It helps you organize everything on your Web site, and it makes doing so easy.

You find the basics of linking text to internal and external pages in Chapter 2. This chapter shows you how to put the pieces of a Web site-to-be in the Site window by using the Navigation and Link windows. In addition, you will see how to place page navigation links called "anchors" on a Web page.

In GoLive 5, you quickly find that you need to use different palettes all the time. Opening them from the menu bar can prove tiresome and time-consuming. By pressing the Control (Ctrl) key on your keyboard and clicking the top bar of the palette, you can "dock" the palette on the right side of your screen with only the tab and palette label in view, as shown in Figure 4-1. To return the palette back to the page (undock) just click the tab.

Figure 4-1:
You can dock palettes to the right side of your screen.

Adding text links

Figure 4-2 shows the starting page of a Web site that's still very much under construction. You can see the handy grid lines that all smart Web designers use to line up elements on a page cleanly and efficiently. (For more information on using grids, see Chapter 3.) You also see a nice heart-shaped graphic in the center of the page and a few blocks of text. Hovering over the starting page is an open Site window containing a number of graphics files ready for you to link to this starting page.

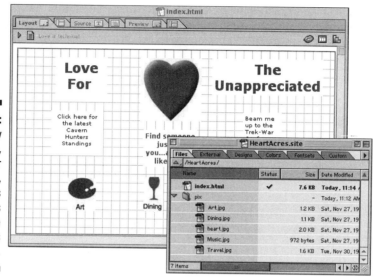

Figure 4-2:
This new
Web site,
still under
construction,
needs links
to other files
to increase
its usefulness
to visitors.

To get things going, you may want to link the text block Click here for the latest Cavern Hunters standings to an HTML page in a folder sitting on your desktop. The following steps show how to establish that link:

1. **Access your site by choosing File⇨Open from the main menu bar or by pressing Ctrl+O (in Windows) or Cmd-O (on the Mac). Select the site that you want from the list in the Open dialog box that appears and click the Open button.**

   The Site window for the site that you choose appears. The name of the site appears at the top of the Site window. In my example, my site's name is HeartAcres.site. In GoLive 5, all sites use the extension SITE. The extension helps to distinguish them from Web pages in the site with similar names.

2. **Find the file name of the page that you want to open in the Name list of the Site window's Files view and double-click that file's icon.**

   Your starting page now appears in Layout view. (The name of my starting page, as you can see in the Site window's Name column in Figure 4-2, is index.html.)

3. **Select on the page the word that you want to act as the hotspot for the link and click the Link button (the one displaying two intertwining links of a chain) on the toolbar.**

   I'm selecting the word here in the phrase Click here for Cavern Hunters Tournament Standings. (I use the term *hotspot* to refer to any text or graphic that acts as a link or initiates an action.) After you click the Link button, the button becomes pale, indicating that your hotspot is ready to accept a link.

4. **Undock the Inspector by clicking the Inspector tab at the side of the screen or by choosing Window⇨Inspector from the menu bar.**

   The Inspector appears with (Empty Reference!) in the URL text box for you to replace with the name of your link file or a URL.

5. **If you know the name of the file to which you want to link, type the file name into the URL text box of the Inspector and press Enter.**

   This action establishes the link — and you're done! If you don't know the name of the file to which you want to link, please continue on with Step 6. Figure 4-3 shows the selected hotspot highlighted and the Inspector standing by for a URL to be selected using the Browse icon button.

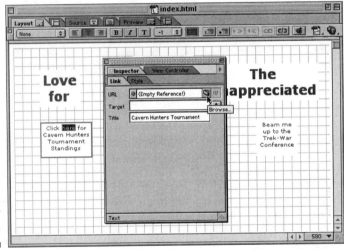

Figure 4-3: The Inspector provides several ways to help find the files for your links.

6. **If you're not sure of the name of the file to which you want to link, click the Browse button at the right side of the Text Inspector.**

   An Open dialog box appears, as shown in Figure 4-4. By using this dialog box, you can navigate through your directories to find the file that you want. The name of the Cavern Hunters Web page file on the Desktop is cavh.html in my example. Figure 4-4 shows a preview of the page's source code (which usually isn't much help with HTML pages) and the page that you want selected.

7. **Navigate to the file to which you want to link, select its name in the list, and then click Open to establish the link.**

   The dialog box disappears after establishing the link. Now, whenever you click the hotspot here on your first Web page, you instantly jump to a page displaying the contents of your linked file.

If you select an HTML file for possible linkage, you see some code in the Preview area of the Open dialog box. This view is the same as you'd see if you select a graphics file for linkage, except that, instead of getting to look at a nice, comprehensible image, you see some incomprehensible code. Sometimes the code can help, but usually there's not enough there to enable you to identify the file you're seeking.

Figure 4-4:
The Open dialog box enables you to navigate to the file to which you want to create a link.

Establishing a link is simple enough in GoLive 5, but the real power of the program lies in its capability to gather in all the internal links. You need to round up and corral all the stray Web pages in the Site window. (Ride 'em, cowboy!)

Corralling all your links

You want to keep any and all internal links for your Web site in your Site folder. Web sites are dynamic, so you need to update and change your links as time passes. With all your files in the same Site folder and visible in the Site window, keeping track of even complex Web sites becomes as easy as pie. If you can't see an internal link in your Site window, you want to move it there. Keep in mind that the files you see in your Site window represent the root folder of your site. Just follow these steps to round up the strays.

1. **Establish a link, as I outline in the steps in the preceding section and then click the Site button on the toolbar (the third button from the right).**

   The Site window appears in all its glory.

2. **Click anywhere in the Site window to select it and then choose Site➪ Explorer ➪Add Files in Windows (or Site➪Finder➪Add Files on the Mac) from the menu bar.**

   The Add dialog box appears, as shown in Figure 4-5.

Figure 4-5:
Use the Add
dialog box
to add files
to your Site
window.
GoLive 5
sends any
files that
you want to
add to your
site to the
bottom
pane.

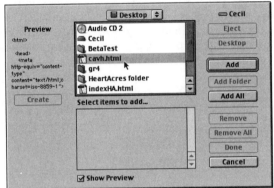

3. **Use the top pane of the dialog box to navigate through your directories to the file that you want by clicking the scroll arrows to scroll up or down the list or by selecting and opening folders or directories by using the pulldown list.**

   You may see a code preview of the file in the Preview area, but don't count on the code gibberish helping you identify the file that you want.

4. **Select the desired file or folder and click the Add or Add Folder (or Add All if you want everything in the window) button to include the file in the Select Items to Add pane at the bottom of the Add dialog box, repeating this process for every file and folder that you want to include in the Add pane.**

   After you add a file or folder to the bottom pane, it disappears from the top pane. Don't worry. GoLive 5 isn't deleting your file or folder from the directory or drive. Removing items from the top pane is just GoLive 5's way of helping you keep track of what you want to copy into the site folder. (If you grab the wrong ones, you click the Remove button to send them back to the top window.)

5. **After all the files and folders that you want appear in the Select Items to Add pane, click the Done button next to the bottom pane.**

   GoLive 5 copies the selected files to your Site window.

After you copy any file from its original folder to your Site folder, GoLive asks whether you want to update your file. Yes! Of course, you want to update your file! After all the work you go through to get it into your Site window, you're darn tootin' you want to update it. (GoLive 5 doesn't assume that your brain's addled, by the way; it's just reminding you that, after you change a file's location, the link information also changes.)

GoLive 5 is a Web-*site* development tool. The more that you think in terms of creating a site and not just a single page, the more sense all these instructions are going to make. GoLive 5's a powerful Web-page tool as well, but good Web pages that appear disorganized aren't a pretty sight (or site!). Just imagine writing a book and working on a single page without any thought to the page's relationship to all the others in the book. What a mess you can end up with if you don't know where you're storing the link's target! By helping you to think about the site as a whole instead of just about individual pages, GoLive 5 helps you avoid that kind of mess.

Anchor Your Page, Matey

To understand *anchors,* you need to know what they do. Some Web pages scroll beyond the limitations of your screen, so you need links to jump to anywhere on the page that lies beyond the screen's limits. Anchors are targets on a page that can serve as links to various page locations.

As a general rule, you don't want your pages to scroll beyond two vertical screens, but sometimes you need more than two screens of information on a single page. This situation especially becomes the case if your page is a long index, menu, or text list. The following text layout, for example, shows a long list that scrolls right off-screen as soon as you put it on a Web page. You can get a hint of how anchors work, however, because the page consists of four levels that align along the top of the page.

Cavern Hunters Tournament Leaders

Click the Desired Level

Level 1 | Level 2 | Level 3 | Level 4

Level 1 Cave Dwell Division

1. Captain Mine Light
2. Princess Strongheart
3. Queen Sunray
4. Lord Dark Force
5. Fairy Sparkle
6. Troll Blunderstrum
7. Giant Arm

Level 2 Dark Room Division

1. Knight Blade
2. Empress Teal
3. Mistseeker

4. Fountain Demon
5. Tunnel-Digger Jennifer
6. Dwarf Arnold
7. Dragon-Slayer Heather

Level 3 Night Light Division

1. Wizard Qulaf
2. Prince Former
3. Emperor Johnny
4. Phoenix Creek
5. Griffin Catcher
6. Hemlock Giver

Level 4 Monster Chase Division

1. Magic Cure
2. Wonder Dell
3. Hero Melvin
4. Arch Beast Kimberly
5. Dwarf-Netter Art

Anchors provide some much-needed help for this page. Whenever you place text in the Layout view (the default view for any new Web page), the page is just about ready for adding anchors. One thing, however, is still missing — a way to get back to the top of the page after jumping to a lower level. That situation's easy to remedy by inserting an anchor link word (Top) that returns you back to the top of the page after you click it.

Placing anchors and anchor link words

To place anchors and anchor link words on your page, follow these steps:

1. **With your page open, access the Objects palette by either undocking it by clicking the Objects tab at the side of the Window or by choosing Window⇨Objects from the menu bar.**

   The ever-helpful Objects palette appears on-screen, displaying the contents of its Basic tab.

2. **Drag the Anchor icon (the second icon from the left in the third row on the Basic tab — the one that looks like an anchor, of course) to the location on the page where you want the page to jump to, as shown in Figure 4-6.**

   The Anchor icons appear on the page wherever you place them. In my example, I want to jump from the top of the page to each succeeding level of my Cavern Hunters Tournament leaders, so I place an anchor at the top of each level (Levels 1 through 4). The heading of each section serves as a good positioning point for the anchors. The word "Top" is placed at the bottom of each level and will become a hotspot when it is linked to an anchor at the top of the page. (All the "Top" links are connected to a single anchor at the top of the page.)

3. **Repeat the process that Step 2 describes for any other anchors that you want to place.**

4. **Close (or dock by Ctrl+clicking the top bar of the palette) the Objects palette after you finish placing your anchors.**

   Nothing more is required of the Objects palette for the time being, and it's a good idea to move it aside to make more room for other palettes you may need.

Drag the Anchor icon to the layout page

Figure 4-6:
Use the
Anchor icon
in the Basic
tab of the
Objects
palette to
place
anchor links
on your
page and
name the
selected
anchor in
the
Inspector.

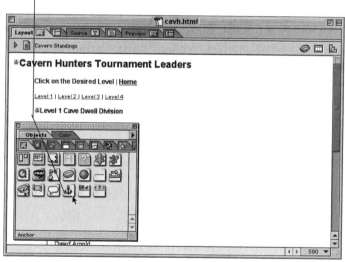

 Sometimes an anchor doesn't take you to the place on the page that you expect. Depending on where the Anchor icon and its information appear on the page, relative to the size of your screen, the screen either shows you what you want after you arrive at the target location of the anchor . . . or it doesn't. You may need to experiment with placing anchors to get them set so that the page goes exactly where you want it to, especially in different browsers that your visitors may use. (And remember to view the page in different configurations in your Preview view so that you can see what the other guy's going to see!)

Naming anchors

After you place an anchor, you still must name it so that GoLive 5 can keep track of it for you. Fortunately, naming anchors is as easy as 1-2-3-4. Just follow these steps:

1. **With your page open, undock the Inspector by clicking on the Inspector tab at the side of the screen or choose Window⇨ Inspector from the menu bar.**

   The Inspector appears.

2. **Select an anchor on the page in the Layout view by clicking it.**

   After you select an anchor, the Inspector displays a text box for you to use in naming the anchor.

3. **In the Name text box of the Inspector, type a name for the anchor that you select.**

   Use a name that's descriptive and relates to the anchor on the page, as shown in Figure 4-7. For the different levels, a simple level number works fine. The anchor at the top got the name "Top." Now all those "Top" labels at the bottom of each level has an easy name to link to.

4. **Repeat Steps 2 and 3 for each anchor on the page, but make sure that you give each anchor a unique name.**

   You can use the same name for anchors on *different pages,* but for any single page, make sure that you give each of your anchors a unique name. Figure 4-7 shows that I'm giving the anchor for Level 2 the startlingly original name of **Level 2.** By the way, you *never* see the anchor's name on the Web page. It's just a target name so that a hotspot has something to hook up with.

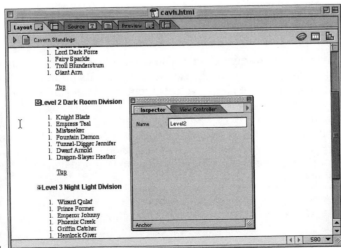

Figure 4-7: Use the Inspector to give each anchor on a page a unique name.

Use intuitively clear names for anchors. Names such as *top, middle,* or *bottom* help you remember the placement of the anchor. Using esoteric names is fine, but remember who must recall what they mean six months from now as you're updating the pages. (Pachyderm? Why did I use *that* anchor name?) Now with "Top" both the anchor name *and* the hotspot name are the same. That's really hard to forget!

Linking to anchors

After you place and name all the anchors on a page, you need to create the actual links so that all these carefully named anchors can actually do something for you. The process of linking anchors is virtually identical to that of making any other kind of link. Just follow these steps:

1. **On your page, where you placed the anchors, type the text that you want to use for your hotspots — the text that you want to use to link to the anchors.**

   In my example, I want to link from the top of the page to the various levels, so I type **Level 1, Level 2, Level 3,** and **Level 4** below the text reading `Click the Desired Level`.

2. **Select the text that you want to use for a hotspot for a particular anchor and click the Link button on the toolbar — the one showing the two chain links.**

   Make sure that you pair up your hotspot text blurbs and anchors correctly. Linking up the wrong pair is easy if you're not careful. After you click the Link button on the toolbar, it goes pale, and the Inspector displays a text window for the anchor (the URL window) along with a Point-and-Shoot button (the button with the corkscrew icon) and a Browse button (the one showing a folder).

3. **Drag the point-and-shoot line from the Point-and-Shoot button to the anchor to which you want the hotspot to link and then release the mouse button, as shown in Figure 4-8.**

   If you can't see the target anchor from the hotspot text, drag the point-and-shoot line down or up, and the Layout page scrolls until the target anchor becomes visible. The point-and-shoot operation automatically puts in the name of the anchor along with the pound (#) sign in the URL window. So you will see #Level3 in the URL window if you select the Level 3 anchor with the point-and-shoot line.

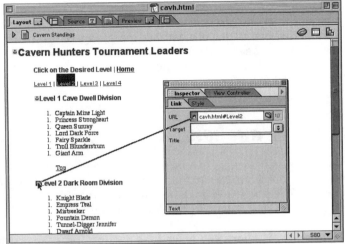

Figure 4-8:
Creating a link from a hotspot to an anchor by using the point-and-shoot line.

After you establish your link by releasing the mouse button, you can see the anchor name in the Text Inspector window whenever you select the hotspot text. A link to an anchor automatically includes a pound sign (#) in the link name, even though you don't actually use that symbol in naming the anchor. During the point-and-shoot operation, the name of the Web page appears along with the anchor name, as you can see in Figure 4-8. Don't worry however. As soon as you release the mouse button, the Web-page name disappears and you get the anchor name with the pound sign only.

This Tool Is Outta Site!

One of the handiest site tools for working with your links is the Site window's *Navigation window.* By using this window, you can add pages to your site that you can actually see, providing you with a better sense of your overall site. Figure 4-9 shows my HeartAcres site from the Navigation window. I don't have much there yet, but as I build it, I can easily keep track of the pages in the site by using this window.

Adding pages for link targets

At this stage of the site development, I need to add another page to handle information about the fascinating world of Trek-War conventions. Instead of choosing File⇨New from the menu bar to start a new page, however, I can simply develop the new page right in the Site window, and GoLive 5 automatically places the page in the Site's root folder. To start and develop a new page in the Site window, follow these steps:

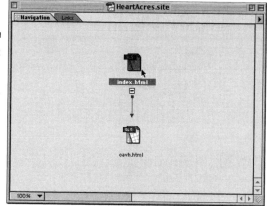

Figure 4-9:
The
Navigation
window
provides a
graphic
picture of
your site
as you
develop it.

1. **Choose File⇨Open from the main menu bar or press Ctrl+O (in Windows) or Cmd-O (on the Mac). Select the name of the site that you want from the list in the Open dialog box that appears and click the Open button.**

   The Site window for the site that you select appears on-screen.

2. **Choose Design⇨Navigation window from the menu bar.**

   The Navigation window appears. You see all the pages in your site with lines indicating navigation links (refer to Figure 4-9). Notice that the tool-bar changes from the Site toolbar to the Navigation window toolbar.

3. **Select in the Navigation window the page icon *from* which you want to link a new page.**

   In my example, *index.html* is the file from which I want to link, as shown in Figure 4-10. The selected page darkens so that you know which page you're selecting.

4. **Click the eighth icon from the left in the toolbar (the one that displays the label `New Child Page` after you rest the mouse pointer over it).**

   A new untitled page appears in the window (see Figure 4-10, lower right side).

5. **Choose the Select Window button on the toolbar to bring the Site window to the forefront and click the Files tab on the Site window.**

   In the Files view, you can now see that GoLive automatically creates a folder by the name NewFiles along with a file, "untitled.html" that goes in the folder. Put differently, the file is placed in the site folder and given the filename untitled.html (see Figure 4-11).

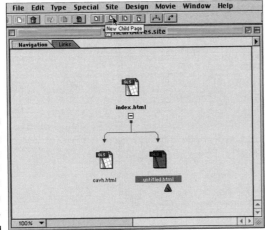

Figure 4-10:
Adding a
new page in
the
Navigation
window.

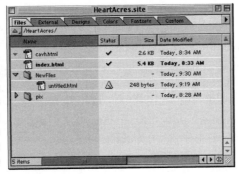

Figure 4-11:
The new
file that you
add in the
Navigation
window
automatically
goes into a
NewFiles
subfolder in
the Site
window.

6. Change the name of the file to one that you want to use by selecting the file name in the Name column of the Site window's Files view and then typing the new name to replace the existing one.

You haven't yet starting working with the page at this time, so a yellow triangle appears in the status column next to the new file.

In addition to adding a new Child page, you also can add a Parent or Sibling page. A Child page enters the hierarchy below the selected page, and a Parent page enters the hierarchy above the selected page. Guess where a Sibling pages appears in the Navigation window? Sibling pages appear at the same level as the selected page. (No surprise there.)

The next thing that you need to do is to create a link from your index page to the new page. Just follow these steps to create your link:

1. **With your Navigation window open, double-click the page from which you want to create a link.**

   The page that you select appears in Layout view. Because I want to open index.html, I double-click it in the Navigation window.

2. **Select the text on the page from which you want to establish a link and press the Ctrl key (in Windows) or the Command key (on the Macintosh) to insert a Point-and-Shoot button.**

   The Point-and-Shoot button is pretty easy to recognize, by the way; it combines a pointer arrow with a distinctive spiral figure. In my example, I want to establish a link between the index page and my Trek-Wars Convention page, so I select the Beam me phrase from the sentence Beam me up to the Trek-War Conference, as shown in Figure 4-12.

3. **Continuing to press the Ctrl key (in Windows) or the Command key (on the Mac), drag the resulting point-and-shoot line to the target page icon in the Navigation window.**

   Your link is now established between the source and target page. Creating links in this manner by using the Point-and-Shoot button helps you see the pages in the context of a Web site and not just as one Web page linking to another.

Keep a steady hand while pulling the point-and-shoot line from the Layout view over to the Navigation window. If the Navigation window is behind the Document window, it will appear after you drag the point-and-shoot line onto any part of the Navigation window. If you find the point-and-shoot method awkward, you can always use the Browse feature of the Inspector. Using the point-and-shoot technique, however, guarantees that the connection you make is in your root folder.

Improving the view

Establishing a link doesn't even raise a sweat. The perspiration may come, however, if you start adding more and more pages to your site with more and more links joining them together. How's a person to keep everything straight?

A closer look at Figure 4-12 shows that GoLive 5 already offers a solution to that problem. The Navigation window provides you with a graphical representation of pages in your site. If you look closely, you see that the Navigation window has a roommate with the name *Links.* From the Links window, you can see the direction and number of links from any of the pages to the other. Although the Navigation window provides you with a good idea of the site's navigational structure, the Links window gives you the nitty-gritty on the actual links. In Figure 4-13, you can see the links between the pages and even to the graphics.

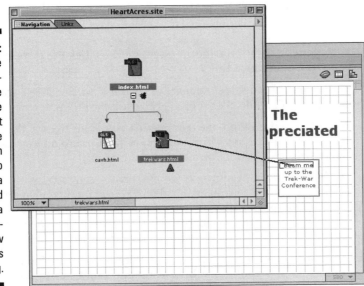

Figure 4-12:
You pull the point-and-shoot line from the Layout view the Navigation window to establish a link and provide a visual picture of how the site is developing.

In selecting a style for displaying items on your page, you get your choice of four options from the Display tab of the View Controller. (To access the View Controller, just select Window⇨View Controller from the menu bar or undock it by clicking the View Controller tab at the side of the window. Also, remember that the View Controller's roommate is the Inspector, so if you have the Inspector on your page, just click the View Controller tab.) You can choose icons, thumbnails, frames, or ovals. In Figure 4-13, I'm selecting to show the items as Thumbnails, but you can see in the figure that an icon still represents one of the pages (trekwar.html). I added that page but I've yet to work on it. Nothing's on it, so it has nothing to show other than an icon. You can also select frames or ovals. Select the one that works best for you. Remember that the goal is to clarify the links in your site. To use the Links window, follow these steps:

1. **If your site isn't already open, choose File⇨Open from the main menu bar or press Ctrl+O (in Windows) or Cmd-O (on the Mac). Select the name of the site that you want to open from the list in the Open dialog box that appears and then click the Open button.**

   The Site window for the site that you select appears, open to its Files view.

2. **Choose Design⇨Links View from the menu bar.**

   The Links window now appears on-screen.

3. **Choose Window⇨View Controller from the menu bar or click the View Controller tab if the Inspector is already on-screen.**

   The View Controller appears on-screen, ready to use.

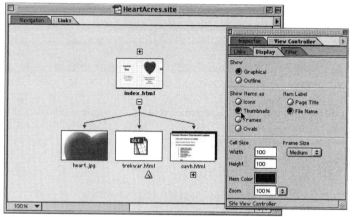

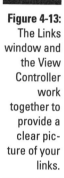

Figure 4-13:
The Links window and the View Controller work together to provide a clear picture of your links.

4. **Click the Display tab of the View Controller to open it.**

   The Display tab of the View Controller displays options for showing the files in graphical or outline format.

5. **Select in the View Controller the options that you want for your display by clicking the appropriate radio buttons, filling in the text boxes, and choosing from the drop-down list.**

   Outline format looks pretty much like the display of the Files view in the Site window, and so I generally select the Graphical option in the Show area. Displaying the images as Thumbnails helps visualize the pages you're building in relationship to the other pages in the site. The selections available in the Cell Size area enable you to make the images larger or smaller depending on how many pages you're viewing. If you have a lot of pages, you want to use the smaller size. You can even color them if you want by selecting a color from the Item Color well.

Graphic Links

In addition to linking to text hotspots, you can also use graphics to create links. For the most part, little difference exists between the processes of linking a text or graphic hotspot in GoLive 5. These *little differences,* however, are most important.

To start, imagine that you've already added some nice graphic images to the starting page of your Web site. Now you want to use these images as links to four separate areas of interest — say art, dining, travel, and music. (Figure 4-13 shows what I may use as images for such areas, but you may have your own take on these things.) You must now transform your four images into link hotspots and then add four new pages to your site to act as the new hotspots' targets. A tall order, you may think, but the following sections show that it's not that tall an order after all. (Check back to Chapter 2 to see how to add graphic images.)

In using graphics as links, you want to avoid being overly clever and creating abstract graphics that the user may not understand. My globe image in Figure 4-14, for example, can mean any or several different things — international politics, global peace, or travel, to name a few. In using image links, therefore — especially if they're abstract ones — you want to add a text label below or above the graphic so that the graphic and text are both telling the user what to click next.

Figure 4-14:
Using images instead of text to link pages.

Hooking up graphic links

After you place your graphic image where you want it on your page, you link it to a page in your Site window by using the Point-and-Shoot button and line in *almost* the same way as you do with text. And, as you also do with text, you need to put your graphics into the Site folder. Follow these steps to create a link to an image:

1. **If your site isn't already open, choose File⇨Open from the main menu bar or press Ctrl+O (in Windows) or Cmd-O (on the Mac). Select the name of the site that you want from the list in the Open dialog box that appears, and then click the Open button.**

   The site appears on-screen in the Files view of the Site window.

2. **Find the file name of the page that you want in the Name column of the Files view and double-click the file's icon.**

   Your page now appears on-screen in Layout view.

3. **Find and select the image that you want to use as a hotspot.**

4. **Undock the Inspector by clicking the Inspector tab at the side of your screen or open it by choosing Window⇨Inspector from the menu bar.**

   Because you're selecting an image, the Inspector appears in its Image mode.

5. **Click the Link tab of the Inspector.**

   You see the Link button and the URL text box appear in the Inspector.

6. **Click the Link button (the one displaying two links of a chain) in the Inspector *or* click the one on the toolbar.**

   Both the Link buttons do the same thing, so which one you use is strictly a matter of your preference.

7. **Click and hold the Point-and-Shoot button on the Link tab of the Image Inspector and drag the resulting point-and-shoot line into the Site Window and to the file to which you want to establish the link, as shown in Figure 4-15.**

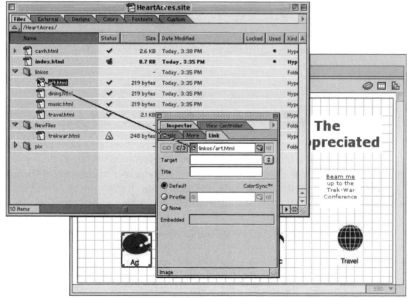

Figure 4-15: Making a link to a file by using a graphic: The Inspector's Link tab provides the correct Point-and-Shoot button to use in hitting the HTML file in the Site window.

Be very careful that you click the *Link tab* in the Image inspector. The Basic tab also contains a Point-and-Shoot button, but you use that button for placing graphics and not for creating links. So watch it!

Deleting unwanted borders

GoLive 5 automatically assumes that you want a border around a graphic if you're designating it as a link. (It gets the idea from the blue complexion that many text links adopt after they become hot.) For the most part, however, you probably *don't* want a blue border around your link images. To get rid of the border, just follow these border-removing steps:

1. **Select the linked image displaying the blue border that you want to delete.**

   Remember that you're just selecting it to get rid of the border — not the graphic!

2. **Undock the Inspector by clicking the Inspector tab at the side of the screen or open it by choosing Window⇨Inspector from the menu bar.**

   Check to make sure that the Basic tab is selected. If not, just click it.

3. **Click the Border check box and type a zero (0) in the text box next to the check box.**

   Of course, if you want a bigger border around your linked image instead of no border, you can type a bigger number here. Who knows? Maybe a bigger border actually makes the page look better than an image without a border.

Creating and Using Image-Map Links

If you divide a single image into different *zones,* or *hotspots,* you call that image an *image map.* Image maps are great tools, because you can have a single image with many different hotspots. Instead of dividing up an integrated image into several little images and attempting to align them, however, you can easily set up a whole image in GoLive 5 so that you can click it in various spots for different links. Just follow these steps:

1. **As always, access your site by choosing File⇨Open from the main menu bar and selecting from the list in the Open dialog box that appears the name of the site to which you want to add an image map.**

   The site appears on-screen in the Files view of the Site window. If you have not done so, drag a graphic from one of your computer's directories to the File view of the Site window to secure it in the site's root folder.

2. **Find in the Name column of the Files view the file name of the page that you want and double-click the file's icon.**

   Your page now appears on-screen in the Document window's Layout view.

3. **Drag the image that you want to use as an image map from the Files tab of the Site window to the Layout view.**

   If you don't use a grid, the image defaults to the upper-left open space on the page. Where you place it doesn't matter for you to use it as an image map.

4. **Undock the Inspector by clicking the Inspector tab or open it by choosing Window⇨Inspector from the menu bar.**

   Because you're selecting an image, the Inspector appears in its Image mode.

5. **In the Inspector, click the More tab.**

   The More tab of the Inspector comes to the front. In the middle of the More tab, you see a Use Map check box.

6. **Select on the page in the Layout view the image that you plan to use as an image map and click the Use Map check box on the More tab of the Inspector.**

   In the Name text box next to the check box, GoLive automatically enters an image map name, basing it on the file name of the graphic you're generating. If you have a graphic by the name of place.jpg, for example, you get an image map with a name something like *placeb541e65b*. Don't worry. You don't need to remember that code. More important, the toolbar changes into the Image Map toolbar to display the image map region tools on the left side of the toolbar.

7. **Click one of the buttons for the Region tools (Rectangle, Circle, or Polygon) on the toolbar.**

   You can use whatever tool you select to drag an area around the part of the image that you want to use to create a hotspot — an area of the image that you can then use as a link, as shown in Figure 4-16. (Notice in Figure 4-16 that a rectangle outlines the cities of Kandy and Ratnapura.)

8. **Select the pointer button (the arrow) from the far-left side of the toolbar and select one of the outlined areas on the graphic.**

   After you select an image map hotspot, you see the little boxes appear on the perimeter of the hotspot, as is the case with the city of Kandy in Figure 4-16. The Inspector becomes the Map Area Inspector.

9. **Type the URL for the target of the link in the URL text box of the Map Area Inspector.**

   In the example shown in Figure 4-16, I type the URL because the target's external and doesn't appear in the Site window. Chapter 11 describes how to place external URLs in the External view of the Site window. If you have external URLs stashed away there, you can use browse or point-and-shoot to make the link instead of typing in the URL.

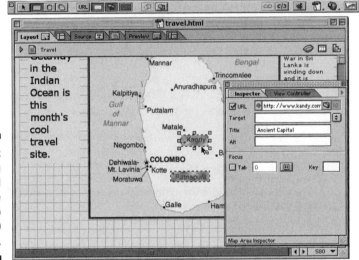

Figure 4-16:
You can turn selected areas of the image map (hotspots) into links.

As you see, you generate links for image-map hotspots just as you do links for text or graphic hotspots. Image mapping is efficient because you can use a single graphic for as many hotspots as you can fit into the graphic. Image maps also offer viewers a very intuitive way to navigate through your site. Map your hometown and put hotspots on all the hot spots! In that way, you can even create an online Chamber of Commerce.

Make sure that you add some text to alert viewers to click the areas that you're using for hotspots. Otherwise, all they see is a graphic image with no discernable clue that the graphic is an image map. Although the hotspots are visible during development in the Layout view, they're invisible in a browser window.

Up Close and Personal with the In & Out Links Palette

The Navigation window used with the Site window gives you a nice graphical representation of your site as a whole, offering the Big Picture perspective on all the pages and links in your site. At times, however, you want to narrow your focus and zoom in for a closer look at a particular page. The In & Out Links palette is the perfect tool for providing such an ant's-eye perspective on a particular page. Think of the In & Out Links palette as a magnifying glass for your Site window, except that, instead of seeing all the pages and links in a site, you see the details of a single page. To use the In & Out Links palette, follow these steps:

1. **Choose Window⊏⊃In & Out Links from the menu bar.**

   The In & Out Links palette appears on-screen.

2. **Access your site by choosing File⊏⊃Open from the menu bar or pressing Ctrl+O (in Windows) or Cmd-O (on the Mac). Then, from the list in the dialog box that appears, select the name of the site that you want to inspect and click the Open button after you find your site.**

   The Site window appears on-screen in Files view, displaying your site.

3. **Select any file in the Name column of the Files view by clicking its name.**

   The In & Out Links palette provides you with a graphical representation of all the links to and from the page that you select. On the left side of the window, you see all the files with links *to* the selected page, and on the right side of the window, you can see the files with links *from* the selected page (see Figure 4-17).

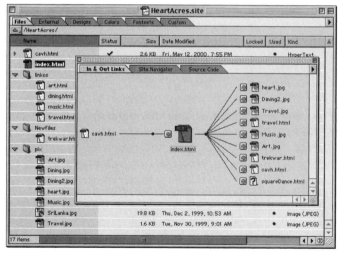

Figure 4-17:
The In & Out Links palette at work.

4. **Click the mouse pointer on any file in the In & Out Links palette that displays a link to or from your selected page.**

   The file that you select now replaces the current file as the central file in the In & Out Links palette and displays all the links to and from the file.

Use the In & Out Links palette to get a quick look at any page's links to other pages, graphics, or other media. The In & Out Links palette also indicates any broken links. In Figure 4-17, for example, the link to "squareDance.html" is broken, indicated by a question mark in the page icon. If you have only a few pages in your site, the In & Out Links palette probably isn't a great help. After your sites start getting large and you need a way to inspect the links on each page quickly, however, you're going to be glad that you have the In & Out Links palette to check out what's connecting to any given page.

Substituting site links by using the In & Out Links palette

Getting the inside dope on all the links to a page is a great help, but the usefulness of the In & Out Links palette doesn't end there. After you finish inspecting the pages of your site, you can use the In & Out Links palette for some major rearranging as well.

Take another look at Figure 4-17. Notice the Point-and-Shoot buttons right next to the center page, as well as those next to all the linked files on the right. Using your steady hand, you can point-and-shoot your way into swapping a new file for one already on your site. Just follow these steps:

1. **Click the Files tab in the Site window (if it's not already open in Files view) or open it by following Step 2 of the preceding steps if it's not open at all.**

   The Files view appears, displaying the various files in your site in the Name column.

2. **Choose Window⇨In & Out Links from the menu bar to open the In & Out Links palette.**

3. **Select the file for the page that you want to rearrange in the In & Out Links Palette by clicking its name or icon in the Files view of the Site window.**

   The file appears in the In & Out Links palette window, showing links to and from the file. Web pages, graphic files, and other media files, such as QuickTime movies or SWF (Shockwave) files, all qualify for selection in the In & Out Links palette. (It's a very democratic palette.)

4. **Locate the replacement file in the Name column of the Site window's Files view.**

   If the replacement file that you want is in a folder, you first need to open the folder so that you can see the file in the Name column of the Files view. You may need to move your In & Out Links palette window slightly to the side to see all the files that the Files view lists in the Site window.

5. **Pull the point-and-shoot line from the file or object in the In & Out Links palette that you want to replace to the one in the Files view with which you want to replace it.**

   The file that you select by using the point-and-shoot line now replaces the file that you chose to replace.

After you complete the point-and-shoot operation, the next time that you open the page in the Navigation window, the new link file shows up in the window's graphical representation of your site. Figure 4-18 shows that I'm swapping the file that I call Dining.jpg for a file with the name Dining2.jpg. If you then view the page index.html in the Layout view, you see that the file Dining2.jpg is now replacing Dining1.jpg.

At first you may think that the In & Out Links palette is a nice little extra but not something you're likely to use a lot. If you're maintaining a big Web site and you want to update your pages regularly without needing to open each page in the Document window, select a current link, click the Unlink button on the toolbar, select the Link button again and put in the new link, you're going to treasure this nifty little tool. All you need to do is to create the updated page, pop it into the Files tab of Site window, and then point and shoot it to replace the old page.

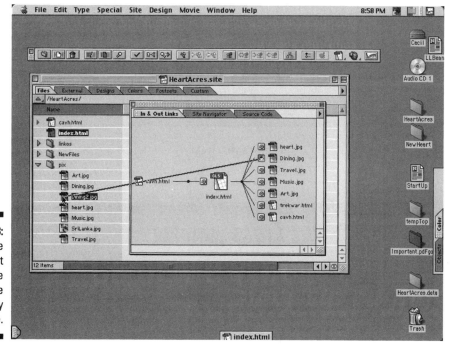

Figure 4-18: You can use the In & Out Links palette to change links to any kind of file.

If you swap image files by using the In & Out Links palette, GoLive 5 maintains the parameters (height and width) for the original file. If you make such a swap, therefore, you need to make sure that the files are of the identical size, or you need to change the parameters. You get a visual clue that an exact fit doesn't exist between the two images that you want to swap if the Resize Warning icon appears (a dotted rectangle with a solid rectangle within the dotted one) More dramatically, the new graphic file looks warped as you view it on your Web page. If the image is selected, the Image Inspector's Resize Warning icon comes alive. If clicked, it will re-mold the selected image to its original size. See Figure 4-19 for the location of the Resize Warning icon on both an image and in the Image Inspector.

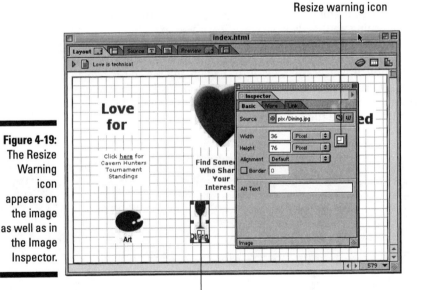

Figure 4-19: The Resize Warning icon appears on the image as well as in the Image Inspector.

Viewing external links in the In & Out Links palette

If the links don't appear in the Navigation window or they reside on an entirely different site, the In & Out Links palette uses a different icon. The In & Out Links palette is a good tool to use if you're changing a page's links or you're trying to figure out what connects to a given page. In looking at wider connections, you can use the Navigation window and then zero in on a page by using the In & Out Links palette to examine and make the necessary adjustments for links to Web pages and media. Figure 4-20 shows how the off-site icons appear. The links from the page travel.html are from image maps, and GoLive 5 shows them as it does any other link to an external site.

Icons for external sites

Figure 4-20:
The In & Out
Links palette
displays dif-
ferent icons
for different
types of
links.

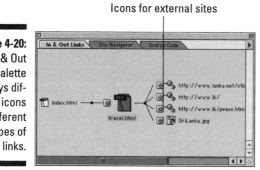

Chapter 5

The Contents of a Table

*U*sing tables is a great way to organize and present text, numbers, and graphics. You can place any object from a Web page into a table; each cell in a table can have its own background color or graphic, different-sized borders, and placement of objects relative to the margins and sides of the cell. Sometimes I like to think of a table as a photo album, too. Each page of the album is like a Web page, and the arrangement of the photos and captions in the album make up the various cells in a table. The table gives you a great deal of flexibility and control for creating a page that looks just as you want it to look. And if you use GoLive 5's new Table palette, making your page a masterpiece is even easier than before.

This chapter covers all the tools GoLive 5 has to make your tables look great. I include examples and explanations on how to format, color, configure and reconfigure tables to meet your needs. Also, you get to see how to save time designing a table by using GoLive 5's new Table palette to format a table automatically.

Setting the Table

You can place tables directly on your page in the Layout view, or you can place tables on a grid. (I introduce GoLive 5 grids in Chapter 3.) Tables act the same as other objects that you place on your Web page in the Layout view. If you lay them on a grid, tables pretty much stay where you place them, but if you place them directly on the page without using the grid, they migrate to the upper-left corner relative to other objects on the page. So, in many ways, tables act the same as any other object that you put on a page in the Layout view.

To start using tables on your Web pages, follow these steps:

1. **Launch GoLive 5 by double-clicking the GoLive 5 icon on your computer's desktop.**

   A new page appears on-screen in the Layout view with its Welcome to GoLive 5 message in the upper-left corner of the Document window.

2. **Choose Window⇨Table from the menu bar.**

   The Table palette appears on-screen. It's blank because you haven't yet placed and selected a table on your page. Notice that the Table palette contains two tabs — Select and Style. Click the Select tab to bring it to the front.

3. **Choose Window⇨Inspector from the menu bar.**

   The Text Inspector appears on-screen.

4. **Choose Window⇨Objects from the menu bar.**

   The Objects palette appears on-screen.

5. **Click the Basic tab if it's not already open as the palette appears.**

   Note that the fourth icon from the left in the top row is the Table icon.

6. **From the Basic tab of the Objects palette, drag the Table icon onto the new page in the Document window.**

   After you drag the icon to the page, a table replaces the icon on the page displaying three rows and three columns with big fat bars for frames. The Table Inspector comes alive, and the Table tab of the Table palette displays the rows and columns of your table.

Now you're all set to do some serious table design. The ever-useful Inspector is on hand again to help out, but now the Table palette stands along side it as its companion to make controlling tables even easier than with the Inspector alone.

The Table palette and Inspector are here: Mind your manners!

The Table Inspector provides a host of adjustments for your table. The three tabs in the Table Inspector offer you plenty of control over on-screen details for working with tables in the Layout view, as shown in Figure 5-1. The Table tab sets the general parameters for your table, so look at it first. It's easy to use, and for such a handy little window, it sure packs a lot of power. You need to keep in mind, however, that the Inspector remains in its Table mode only as long as you're working on a table — while some portion of the table remains selected. (If you deselect the table, the Inspector changes to another mode depending on what you next select.)

The Table palette works together with the Inspector in helping you work with your tables. Its job is to provide sorting and design assistance. If the Select tab is open on the Table palette, whatever cells that you select in the Table palette you also simultaneously select in the table . . . and vice versa. Just click any cell in one or the other and you see that you're actually selecting the same cells in both. If the Style tab of the Table palette is open, you can add designs to a table with a simple click of the mouse. Styles range from serious Budget styles for laying out facts and figures to the colors of the '70s that you can use as a photo album for the Days of Disco.

Figure 5-1:
The Table
Inspector,
with its
Table tab
open, and
the Table
palette, with
its Select
tab open,
show you
the default
settings of a
new table.

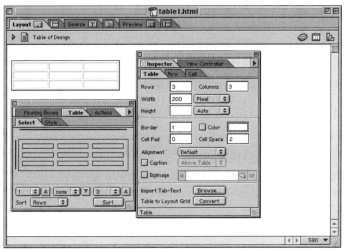

Too many palettes to see everything? Press Ctrl+Tab to toggle *all* your palettes and toolbar on and off the screen. Or press Shift+Control when clicking the top bar of a palette (or its tab) to toggle *all* palettes and toolbar on and off dock.

Set the table properties

To start working on your table, you need to make a number of decisions about how you want it to look. Step through the options on the Table Inspector and Table palette to see what's available. After creating your table by following the steps in the section "Setting the Table," earlier in this chapter, you can set the basic dimensions of your table by following these steps:

1. **On the Table tab of the Table Inspector, enter the number of rows and columns that you want in your table in the Rows and Columns text boxes.**

   The default dimensions provide three rows and columns. Nothing's magical or even particularly useful about the default number of rows and columns, so don't hesitate to make a change. After you set the number of rows and columns for your table, the Table palette changes to reflect the new version of your table, showing the number of rows and columns that you specify in these text boxes.

2. **Set the width and height of the table in terms of one of three units of measure — Pixel, Percent, or Auto — by entering values in the Width and Height text boxes and selecting the appropriate unit of measure from the drop-down list box to the right of each text box.**

   The kind of measurement that you use affects how your table reacts on other computers. The following paragraphs further discuss how to decide which unit of measurement to use and the consequences of using each type. (To continue setting up your table, continue on with the set of steps that appear in the following section.)

Selecting the whole table or parts of it can be tricky. When you move the cursor along the left side of the table, look for the hand icon. When you see the hand, give the mouse a click to select the whole table. The I-beam cursor means you're in a cell so that you can write text in it or place media in the cell. When you see the arrow pointer on the side of a cell that means you can select the cell for formatting.

After you decide on the number of rows and columns that you need for your table, you need to decide what units of measure to use. Often, the other elements on your page determine the unit of measurement your table can use. If you have two graphics that take up exactly 300 pixels horizontally together, for example, you may want to select Pixel so that you can limit your table width to that number of pixels (plus a few more for margins). If you have a lot of different graphics to insert into the table's cells of different sizes, however, you probably want to select Auto so that the table automatically adjusts itself to the widest row or column that the graphics take up. Designers often use the Percent selection so that, no matter what size screen the viewer is using, the table's width takes up only a given percent of the viewing window. Such a setting preserves the page's design proportions.

In other circumstances, you may want the design to preserve a certain size that you measure in pixels. You may choose the Pixel setting, therefore, to maintain sufficient room for a text layout or some other design element. What's really important, however, is that you use the measurement *that works best for your design* and that you don't just assume that the default values are the best ones. As Groucho Marx once remarked, "Who you going to believe? Me or your eyes?" Believe your eyes!

Don't forget to look at your table from the view of different browsers and types of computers. Click the View Controller tab in the Inspector (they're still roommates) and look at your tables from different perspectives. Chapter 2 gives you the techniques for mastering different views with the View Controller.

Looking after your table's appearance

After you set your table's basic dimensions, you're ready to go to work on how your table's going to look. The Appearance area (bottom half) of the Table Inspector provides these options. The basics I describe in the following steps give you the control that you need over how your table's going to look.

Watch where you click the table in the Layout view. If you click a single cell, the Inspector jumps from the Table tab to the Cell tab. You may find yourself filling in values that work for only the selected cell when you actually want those values to apply to the whole table. D'oh! To select the entire table, move the cursor along the left side of the table and look for the hand icon. When you see the hand, give the mouse a click to select the whole table. (Oddly, if you select a row, the Inspector *doesn't* jump to the Row tab. It jumps to the Cell tab.)

Follow these steps to set the appearance of your table:

1. **Making sure that you first select the entire table in the Layout view, enter a value in the Border text box of the Inspector's Table tab.**

   As a rule, less is better. On the great majority of my tables, I set the border to 0 or 1. If it's too thick, a border can sometimes get in the way of the overall message of your design, with the viewer paying more attention to the border than to the text and graphics in the table. Creating a really ugly table that detracts from the message is all too easy if you're not careful. See the tip at the beginning of the chapter for grabbing the whole table and individual cells.

2. **Enter values in the Cell Space and Cell Pad text boxes.**

   The distance between cells (the *cell space*) refers to the distance between the cell's borders. *Cell padding* is the distances between the materials inside the cell and the cell border. If things look too crowded or spaced apart in your cells, just change the cell padding and spacing values until they look right. (In the example shown in Figure 5-2, the padding is set to 2 and the spacing to 1.)

3. **If you want a table color, click the Color well in the Table Inspector's Table tab.**

   The Color palette appears, and you color the table by clicking on the colors in the Color palette. (Magenta? The board's going to *love* that.) Once you're finished coloring, Ctrl+click the top bar of the Color palette to dock it.

4. **Select a table alignment from the Table Inspector's Alignment drop-down list if you don't want to use the default alignment setting.**

   You can use the Inspector to align your table to the left or right of the page. I recommend, however, that you initially leave it in the default mode unless your design definitely calls for it to align to the left or right. (See the Tip that follows these steps for the lowdown on why to keep the default setting for now.)

5. **Click the Caption check box to put a check mark in it and then select from the drop-down list box whether you want the caption to appear on your page above (default) or below the table.**

If you prefer no caption, leave the check box blank. Although the Caption text box is part of the table, it's not a table cell, row, or column and has no borders. Figure 5-2 shows how a table looks after you select the Caption check box and then select Above Table from the list box. (To continue setting up your table, follow the steps in the section "Stuffing the Table," later in this chapter.)

At this point, you have your basic table. Other than the background color, your table consists of just an empty set of cells.

If you leave your table's alignment in the default mode, you can align your table on the page by using the text-alignment buttons of the toolbar. Just place the cursor to the left of the table and click the alignment button that you want on the Text toolbar (Left, Right, or Center). (Of course you can also use the Grid feature that I discuss in Chapter 3 to place your table exactly where you want it on your page.) Figure 5-2 shows a sample table that I created by using the Inspector and the Text toolbar's Center alignment button.

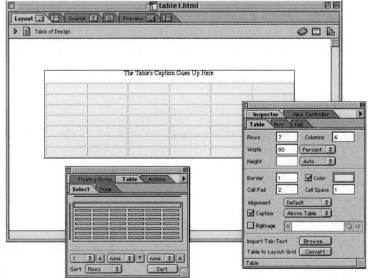

Figure 5-2:
A table on a page in the Layout view, all set for you to add text and images.

Easy styler

The Table palette is a new feature that GoLive 5 is introducing. Before, you had to create your own styles for your tables using the Table Inspector. Now, the Style tab of the Table palette provides some ready-made styles that you can just plunk onto your table. This section describes how to use the Table palette to give your table a quick, new style that looks good without a lot of work. Follow the six steps in the section "Setting the Table," at the beginning of this chapter, to place your table (along with your Table palette) on the page and then follow these steps:

1. **Select your entire table in the Layout view by moving the cursor along the left side of the table and clicking when you see the hand icon.**

   In the Select tab of the Table palette, you should see a blue line across the top and left side of the thumbnail of the table in the Style tab.

2. **Click the Style tab of the Table palette.**

   You see a pattern of colored cells appear in the palette. (The style that you selected the last time that you used the Table palette determines which style you see now. You may, for example, see an orange layout with the name Orange appearing in the Style tab's drop-down list.)

3. **Open the Style tab's drop-down list by clicking on the list located directly under the Style tab's actual tab and to the left of the Apply button.**

   The style that you select now appears in the Style tab of the Table palette. Go through several different ones to find one that you like. Some styles like "Budget" and "Just the Facts" don't tell you a lot about the colors, but others like "Rainbow" or "Green" give you a better idea. (Watch out for "Yellow Press" — it's color scheme is black and red, but "Yellow and White" are . . . well, I'll let it be a surprise.)

4. **Click the Apply button next to the drop-down list.**

   Quick as a wink, your table transforms in color pattern and possibly in size to that of the style you select. (A certain style may affect only the colors in the table, but some styles may also change the cell padding, borders, and cell space.) Figure 5-3 shows the Table palette's Grey style and the resulting appearance of the table on your page. (I'd show you a colorful one, but you may have noticed that the book's figures appear only in black and white.)

To be sure, setting the color scheme and layout of the table can be done by using the Table Inspector to select colors for the table, row, columns or individual cells. However, using the Style tab of the Table palette, you can do everything at once.

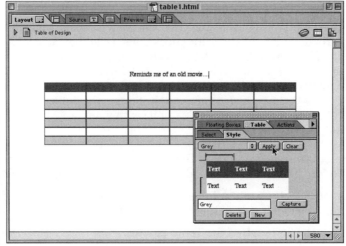

Figure 5-3:
Applying a
style from
the Table
palette's
Style tab to
a table.

Stuffing the Table

After completing the basic table setup (and perhaps some additional styling) as I describe in the preceding sections, you still need to add text and graphics to the table. By placing the cursor in the different cells and in the Caption area of your table, you can easily see where everything goes. Just follow these steps to fill in your table:

1. **Select the table by moving the cursor along the left side of the table and clicking when you see the hand icon and then place the cursor anywhere in the Caption area above (or below) the table on the page in the document window.**

   You now see an I-beam cursor centered in the Caption area and the Text Inspector appears. You can change the alignment to left or right using the Text toolbar's alignment buttons. Type the caption for the table.

2. **Select the new text in the Caption area and change it to the style and color that you want.**

   No difference exists between changing text style and color in a table and changing it on the page directly. Just select the text and apply the style and color by using the Text toolbar. (See Chapter 2 for more on using the Text toolbar.)

3. **Place the cursor in the different cells in the top row and type column headings in each cell (assuming that you want column headings).**

   For example, you may have a price list with the cost, shipping, and tax labels in the column headings and items and prices below.

4. **Choose Window⇨Inspector from the menu bar to open the Inspector or undock it by clicking the Inspector tab at the side of the screen.**

   The Inspector appears.

5. **Re-select the Table.**

   The Inspector becomes the Table Inspector.

6. **Choose Window⇨Table from the menu bar to open the Table palette or undock it by clicking the Table tab at the side of the screen.**

   The Table palette appears.

7. **Click the Select tab of the Table palette (if it's not already open) and then place the pointer to the left of the top row of icons in the tab and click the mouse button to select the entire row.**

   The row appears darkened in the Table palette, indicating that you successfully selected the entire row. (If you experience any eye/hand-coordination problem in placing the pointer correctly to select the entire row, just press and hold the shift key and click all the cells in the row one at a time.)

8. **Click the Row tab of the Table Inspector.**

   Notice the Color well and check box that appear as this tab opens.

9. **Click the Color well on the Table Inspector's Row tab.**

   If the Color palette isn't already open or undocked, it now appears on-screen (see Figure 5-4).

10. **Click any of the colors in the Color palette to change the color of the selected row.**

    You don't need to drag the color from the Color pane (the big column of color on the left of the Color palette that contains the currently selected color) of the Color palette. Just click the colors to watch the row change to those colors. If the row doesn't respond click the Color well on the Table Inspector's Row tab again.

    If you put a style on your page by using the Style tab of the Table palette, it locks the colors for that style on your page and you can't use the Color palette to color your cells. You can easily change these set colors, however: Just select the table, click the Style tab of the Table palette, and click the Clear button on the Style tab. The set colors for that style disappear, and you can now use the Color palette to color your cells.

11. **Open the Horizontal Alignment drop-down list on the Row tab of the Table Inspector and select Right to make the text align to the right side of each cell.**

    You often use the Right alignment selection for text in tables that consist mainly of numbers. That way it's easier to line up the decimal points.

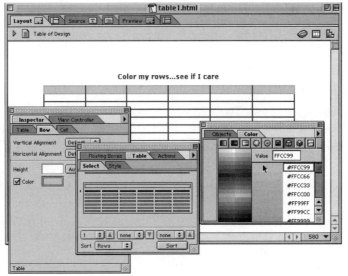

Figure 5-4:
Coloring a
table row by
using the
Table
Inspector,
Table
palette, and
Color
palette.

12. **Open the Site window by choosing Window➪Site from the menu bar
    and drag any media files that you want to place in your table from the
    Site window into the appropriate cells, as shown in Figure 5-5.**

Drag media files from site window to table cell

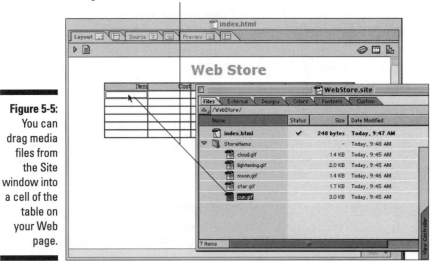

Figure 5-5:
You can
drag media
files from
the Site
window into
a cell of the
table on
your Web
page.

Remember that you can also toggle between the Document window and
the Site window (if it's already open) by clicking the Select Window
button on the toolbar (the third from the right). You place image files in

the cell of a table the very same way that you place them on the grid, as I describe in Chapter 3, or on a blank page. You can also place more than a single media file in a cell, just as you can place more than one on a Web page. (See Chapter 2 for placing images on a page.)

Adjusting Your Table

The table makes automatic adjustments to graphics and text that you place in the table cells. After you place everything that you want in the table, however, you may want to make your own adjustments. You may, for example, want to change a font in the table. You change fonts in table cells the same way that you change fonts outside of a table, as I describe in Chapter 2. After you put your text and images into a table, however, you may need to make adjustments to the table because the materials that you add may distort its appearance.

You may face the temptation to resize the graphics in the cells so that they better fit the size that you want or conform to the size of the other images. Resizing is very easy to do in GoLive 5, but by resizing such graphics in tables, you can actually slow down the load time of your page. Smaller graphics do take less time to load, but graphics that you resize to make smaller still take the same amount of time to load as they do as full-sized graphics. For an important page — one that you want to load as quickly as possible — take the time to actually change the image size of your graphics instead of merely resizing them. Changing the size of images is really very easy to do in programs such as Adobe Photoshop.

The difference between resizing an image and changing an image's size lies in two different processes; one for Web pages and the other for graphic editing. The size change in Web pages distorts the image because it takes the actual graphic file and shrinks or stretches it to fit in a table cell. In graphic editing, unnecessary pixels are removed when a file is made smaller and pixels are added to make it larger. So if you resize an object to make it larger, there aren't enough pixels to make it look good, and if you make it smaller, you don't get rid of the extra pixels but you still carry the weight of the file. (See the end of Chapter 4 for recognizing the Resize Warning icon on both the graphic and Image Inspector.)

Adjusting table sizes

The first thing that you may want to adjust is the dimension of the table itself. Table dimensions are originally set to 75 percent of the page and remain at that size until you change the table's dimensions. To change a table's dimensions, follow these steps:

1. **Choose Window⇨Inspector from the menu bar to open the Inspector or undock it by clicking the Inspector tab at the side of the screen.**

   The Inspector appears on-screen.

2. **Select the table on your page by moving the cursor along the left side of the table and clicking when you see the hand icon.**

   The Inspector becomes the Table Inspector.

3. **In the Table Inspector, change the setting for both the Width and Height drop-down lists to Pixel.**

4. **Change the values in the Width and Height text boxes by entering new values until the proportions of your table look better.**

   Notice in Figure 5-6 that the table is 300 x 400 pixels.

Adjusting cell sizes

After your table is adjusted to the dimensions you want, you can now make adjustments to the individual cells.

1. **Choose Window⇨Inspector from the menu bar to open the Inspector or undock it by clicking the Inspector tab at the side of the screen.**

   The Inspector appears on-screen.

2. **Choose Window⇨Table from the menu bar to open the Table palette or undock it by clicking the Table tab at the side of the screen.**

3. **After the Table palette appears on-screen, click its Select tab if that tab isn't already open.**

4. **Select any cell by clicking the cell in the Table palette.**

   You can select a cell for editing in either the Table palette or on the table itself. Sometimes I find it easier to use the Table palette because I know I won't accidentally select the cell for entering text or media (the I-beam cursor shows) when I want to select the cell for editing (the arrowhead cursor appears).

5. **In the Cell tab of the Table Inspector, change the setting for both the Width and Height of the selected cell drop-down lists to Pixel.**

   Using pixel units to measure a cell provides closer matches between the size of the media in the cell and the cell size than does a percent unit of measure.

6. **Change the values in the Width and Height text boxes by entering new values until the proportions of your table look better.**

   If the table width is set, sometimes when a single cell's width is changed, it affects the width of other cells. For example, in Figure 5-6, you can see that the column label "Shipping Time" is stacked because the cell width was reduced due to a cell in another column being expanded.

The tricky part of changing a single cell is its effect on the rest of the table. Suppose, for example, that you have a table set to 400 pixels wide. If you have four cells in each row, and each is 100 pixels wide, when you change any one of those cells, it ripples through the entire row. So, for example, if you changed one cell to 160 pixels with, the other three cells would automatically change to 80 pixels to maintain the table width of 400.

Adjusting color and alignment

After you make the necessary adjustments so that the size looks better, as I describe in the preceding sections, you may find that the rows of your table also look better if you make each row a different color and align the text in the center of each cell so that it better lines up with the column headings. To do so, follow these steps:

1. **Choose Window⇨Inspector from the menu bar to open the Inspector or undock it by clicking the Inspector tab at the side of the screen.**

   The Inspector appears on-screen.

2. **Choose Window⇨Table from the menu bar to open the Table palette or undock it by clicking the Table tab at the side of the screen.**

3. **After the Table palette appears on-screen, click the Select tab if that tab's not already open.**

4. **Select all the rows in your table by dragging your mouse pointer down the left margin of the table in the Select tab of the Table palette.**

   All the rows in the Table palette are highlighted with a thicker border. Why not select the entire table? If you select the whole table, the Row tab alignment pulldown menus are inactive.

5. **Click the Row tab of the Table Inspector (if that tab's not already open) and use the Vertical and Horizontal drop-down list boxes on the Row tab to change the vertical and horizontal alignment of the text to Center and Middle, respectively.**

   By selecting all the rows at once, you adjust the horizontal and vertical alignment of the rows in a single operation.

6. **Select an individual row by clicking to the left of the row in the Select tab of the Table palette.**

   Note that when you select a row, the arrowhead mouse pointer changes orientation to the right and changes from black to purple. When it makes the orientation change, you are ready to click yourself a row. (Hold down the shift key to select multiple rows in this manner.)

7. **On the Row tab of the Table Inspector, click the Color well.**

   The Color palette appears on-screen (if it's not already there). The selected color appears in the Preview pane in the Color palette and the selected row takes on the color that you select. Repeat Steps 6 and 7 for all the rows in the table that you want to color.

8. **Select the entire table by moving the cursor along the left side of the table and clicking when you see the hand icon. On the Table tab of the Inspector, change the value in the Border text box to zero to remove all the borders from around your table.**

   Now different colors separate the rows of your table instead of borders, as shown in Figure 5-7.

To color columns, you just select the column that you want to color in the Select tab of the Table palette by placing the mouse pointer at the top of that column and clicking it after the pointer turns downward. Then, on the Cell tab of the Table Inspector (click that tab to open it), click the Color well. Doing so opens the Color palette; from there, just click the color that you want for the column. Repeat this procedure for every column that you want to make a different color.

You can probably see the design problem with the page shown in Figure 5-7. Transparent GIF graphics, which display white backgrounds to pick up any drop shadows, cause a big block of white space to appear around the shadow. You can fix that problem by using one of two methods: You can either get rid of the drop shadows or change the background of the column to white. To use GoLive 5 to fix this problem, simply press Shift, click all the cells that you want to change, and then drop in a white background by using the Cell tab of the Table palette. Click the Color well and choose white from the Color palette. This procedure doesn't affect the rest of the cells in the row. Figure 5-8 shows how the table looks after you change the background color of the cells this way. Compare Figures 5-7 and 5-8 to see the difference.

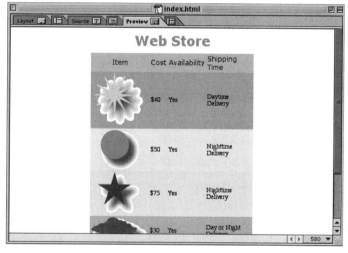

Figure 5-7:
You can use colors to separate rows (or columns) in your table.

Figure 5-8:
Cell backgrounds and graphic backgrounds match in the first column of this table.

Expand Those Rows and Columns!

Sometimes you need a row or a column to consist of more than one cell. When you expand a cell to cover more than a single row or column it's known as a *span.* (You can add a span to either rows or columns.) In the sample table shown in Figure 5-9, for example, you can combine the Lightning and Clouds rows into a single row. That example serves to show you first how to add a row span and then how to add a column span.

Adding a row span

To add a row span, you use the Cell tab of the Inspector. (***Note:*** Although the expression *row span* uses the term *row,* you're expanding only a single cell at a time.) To add a row span, follow these steps:

1. **Choose Window⇨Inspector from the menu bar to open the Inspector or undock it by clicking the Inspector tab at the side of the screen.**

   The Inspector appears on-screen.

2. **Select the table on your page by clicking its left side.**

   The Inspector goes into its Table mode.

3. **Choose Window⇨Table from the menu bar to open the Table palette or undock it by clicking the Table tab at the side of the screen.**

4. **After the Table palette appears on-screen, click the Select tab if that tab's not already open.**

5. **Select the Cell tab in the Table Inspector.**

6. **On the Select tab of the Table palette, click the cell to which you want to add a row span.**

   Row spans create an additional row downward from the selected cell. After you complete a row span, the color and text from the selected cell extends into the span.

7. **In the Row Span text box of the Table Inspector's Cell tab, enter the number of rows that you want to add to the selected cell to create the span.**

   If you enter a **2** in the Row Span text box, the cell then takes up two rows — it doesn't *add* two more rows to the existing row. Figure 5-9 shows how to create such a row span from the original selected cell in the Table palette by using the Cell tab of the Table Inspector. As soon as you click the newly expanded cell, the Table Inspector shows a miniature representation of the expanded cell in your table at the bottom of its Select tab.

Selected row drops the indicated number of rows in the Row Span Wind

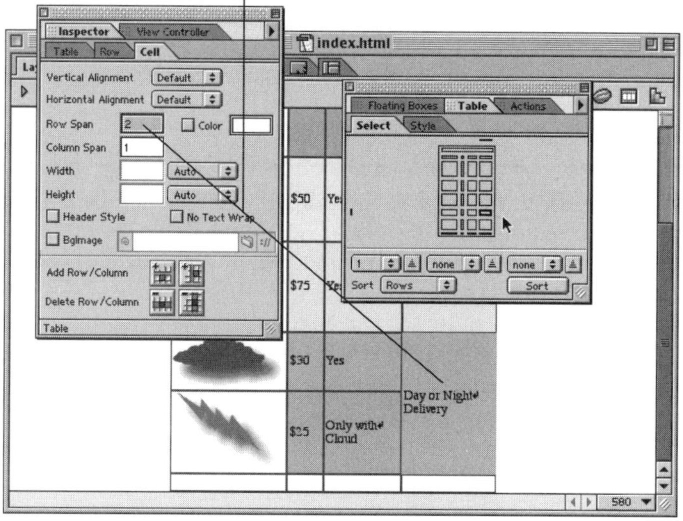

Figure 5-9:
The Row
Span value
that you
enter on the
Cell tab of
the Table
Inspector
expands the
cell into the
next row by
the entered
value
minus one.

All spans must extend into existing rows or columns. You can't create a row span in a cell if that cell is in the bottom row of a table, because the spans extend *downward.* If you attempt to span a cell beyond the borders of a table, the span value simply stops at the highest possible value for that cell. (You can always add more cells by increasing the number of columns and rows in the Table tab of the Table inspector and then span into them.)

Adding a column span

Besides adding another row to a cell, you can span a column as well. Columns all *span to the right.* To add a column span, follow these steps:

1. **Choose Window⇨Inspector from the menu bar to open the Inspector or undock it by clicking the Inspector tab at the side of the screen.**

   The Inspector appears on-screen.

2. **Select the table on your page by clicking its left side.**

   The Inspector becomes the Table Inspector.

3. **Choose Window⇨Table from the menu bar to open the Table palette or undock it by clicking the Table tab at the side of the screen.**

4. **After the Table palette appears, click the Select tab if that tab's not already open.**

5. **Click the Cell tab in the Inspector.**

6. **On the Select tab of the Table palette, click the cell to which you want to add a column span.**

   Column spans merge the selected cell with the cells in the next chosen columns. The color and text from the selected cell extends into the new span.

7. **In the Column Span text box on the Cell tab of the Inspector, enter the number of columns that you want to add to the selected cell.**

   The number that you enter includes the cell itself plus the number of spans you're adding to the right. A value of **3**, for example, creates two spans to the right (two additional cells plus the original cell, making three altogether).

The table in Figure 5-10 now shows a column span in the row with the lightening bolt (in addition to the row span already there). The only other difference between this figure and the previous one is that a value now appears in the Column Span text box on the Cell tab of the Table Inspector and a different cell is selected in the Table palette.

Figure 5-10:
Column
spans
expand to
the right of a
selected
cell, as is
the case of
the middle
cell in the
last row of
this table
containing
any
information.

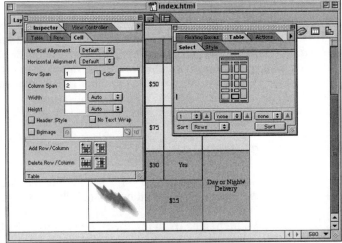

To remove a span, just select the cell and enter a **1** in the Row or Column Span text boxes in the Table Inspector. The sample table for this chapter really doesn't need the column span, so I'm deleting it by placing a 1 in the Column Span text box. After you remove a span that way, you also delete all the text you add to the span including that of the original cell. If you add a span that you don't really want and realize it immediately, use the Edit⇨Undo command from the menu bar or Ctrl+Z (in Windows) or Cmd+Z (on the Mac). You can also use your History palette to more precisely undo materials. Select from a list in the History palette the point you want to undo back to.

(It's like a time machine — just select the part you want to restart at and everything goes back to that point.) By undoing a span, you get back your original cell and its contents.

Deleting and Adding Rows and Columns

In developing a Web site, you often find that you need to pare down or expand a table. New information comes in, you add a new product or service or delete an old one, or some other kind of change requires you to change the table. In GoLive 5, you don't need to rebuild the entire table — just cut and paste your rows and columns as necessary.

Making row and column deletions

If you refer back to Figures 5-9 and 5-10, you may notice an extra row at the bottom of the table that contains nothing in its cells. I put it there as a sacrificial lamb to show you how to remove a row. Just follow these steps:

1. **Choose Window⇨Inspector from the menu bar to open the Inspector or undock it by clicking the Inspector tab at the side of the screen.**

   The Inspector appears on-screen.

2. **Select the table on your page by clicking its left side.**

   The Inspector goes into its Table mode.

3. **Choose Window⇨Table from the menu bar to open the Table palette or undock it by clicking the Table tab at the side of the screen.**

4. **After the Table palette appears, click the Select tab if that tab's not already open.**

5. **Click the Cell tab in the Table Inspector.**

6. **On the Table palette, select any cell in the row or column that you want to delete.**

   You need to select only a single cell in the column or row awaiting deportation into silicon vapor (and *any* cell works); you don't need to select the entire row or column.

7. **Click the appropriate Delete Row/Column icon in the Cell tab of the Table Inspector (the first icon to delete a row and the second to delete a column).**

   The left icon is for rows and the right icon is for columns. Make sure that you click the left one to delete your row. Otherwise, you lose a column instead. Notice, too, that the delete icons are red and the add icons are green. (You can't tell if you're looking at the Inspector in a figure in this book, but on-screen the colors are quite apparent.)

Because the little Delete Row/Column icons are right next to each other, you need to be very careful not to click the wrong one! If you do, immediately use the Undo command to retrieve your lost element: Ctrl+Z (in Windows) or Cmd-Z (on the Mac). *Do not* try to get a row or column back from row/column heaven by immediately clicking the Add Row/Column icon. If you do, you get a row or column back, but you still lose all the text and media in the cells of the deleted row or column. So practice using Ctrl+Z/Cmd-Z (or choosing Edit⇨Undo from the menu bar if you prefer doing things the hard way). As Ms. Sternum used to say back in the third grade, *"Pay Attention!"* (especially if you're deleting rows or columns).

Creating new rows and columns

Deleting rows and columns is pretty straight forward, but adding them is a little trickier — although not much. Follow these steps to add a column or row:

1. **Choose Window⇨Inspector from the menu bar to open the Inspector or undock it by clicking the Inspector tab at the side of the screen.**

   The Inspector appears on-screen.

2. **Select the table on your page by clicking its left side.**

   The Inspector becomes the Table Inspector.

3. **Choose Window⇨Table from the menu bar to open the Table palette or undock it by clicking the Table tab at the side of the screen.**

4. **After the Table palette appears on-screen, click the Select tab if that tab's not already open.**

5. **Select the Cell tab in the Inspector.**

   Notice the two green icons near the bottom of the Inspector.

6. **On the Table palette, select the cell *to the right* of the area where you want the new column to go or *below the row* where you want to add the new row.**

   New columns are inserted to the left of the selected cell and new rows are inserted above the selected cell.

7. **Click the *second* icon in the Add Row/Column in the Cell tab of the Table Inspector to add a column or the *first* icon to add a row.**

GoLive 5 employs a handy method of showing you exactly where you can expect to see your new row or column appear in your table. A green bar appears above or to the right of a green box in the appropriate icon at the bottom of the Table Inspector. The green box represents the selected cell, and the bar shows you where in the table you can expect to see your new row or column appear.

Ta-Da! The completed table

Before going any further in this book, take a look at the completed table that I'm using as an example in Figure 5-11. It doesn't even look like a table but rather like a clearly organized set of information. The purpose of a table is to help you organize information in text and image forms. The borders are optional, and in this example, instead of using borders to delineate rows, I'm using background colors. Color on Web pages costs the same as black and white, so use it generously to communicate and clarify data in a table.

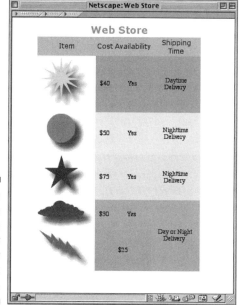

Figure 5-11:
A table on your Web page may not actually look like a table.

Before you start making a serious table for yourself or a client, play around some with GoLive 5's table tools. Experiment with row and column spans, background colors or border sizes, and try adding and deleting rows and columns. You find that these tasks become quite easy after you play with the program for a while, and you build up the intuitive skills that GoLive 5's design encourages by doing so.

Chapter 6

Looking Under the Hood: How HTML Runs Your Web Pages

· ·

In This Chapter

▶ Looking at HTML

▶ Setting Source Code Preferences

▶ Changing the Way Code Looks

▶ Speaking in Tags

▶ Using Attributes in Code

▶ Setting Meta Tags

▶ Giving Body to your Pages

▶ Using Format Tags

▶ Editing source code in the Outline view

· ·

*U*sing GoLive 5 relieves you of needing to write HTML (HyperText Markup Language) code into your Web pages. GoLive writes HTML code automatically as you drag and drop graphics, enter text, and format your page. Knowing something about how HTML works, however, can come in handy. You may, for example, see features on someone else's Web page that you want to incorporate into your own. By looking at the page's source code, you can find out how to create those features. HTML code can reveal anything from a simple background color to more advanced features like a rollover graphic.

HTML is the universal code for the Web, and so code written in Tokyo, Bombay, Nairobi, or New Haven is all from the same source. Sometimes, either by Web page designer error or because of a glitch in the way a Web page is put together, little problems can crop up. Knowing something about the way HTML works will help you identify and correct some of the little problems. For the most, part, though, GoLive 5 takes care of such problems for you.

Looking at HTML

GoLive gives you three tools to enter and edit HTML code — Source view, Source palette, and Outline view. The most direct way to edit code is by using either the Source view or Source palette. The Source view turns your Document window into a view where you see nothing but source code made up of HTML and generally some JavaScript. You cannot see the elements on your pages as you can from the Layout view. The GoLive Source palette enables you to look at a page in the Layout view and at the same time see the code that generates the page at the same time. (Using both the Source and Outline views requires you to close one to see the other.) I focus on the Source palette to explain the basics of HTML and how to create and edit HTML in GoLive 5.

If you're familiar with HTML and want to tweak your pages, the built-in HTML editor in GoLive 5 serves as a simple and helpful code editor and debugger.

More experienced HTML and JavaScript users (as well as those who use ASP, CDML, XML, FileMaker or Cold Fusion) are sure to be happy that GoLive 5 uses *360Code*. Essentially 360Code means that GoLive 5 accepts coded scripts from these other languages and any HTML editor.

Switching from a view to a source code

The easiest way to familiarize yourself with HTML is to begin with a Web page created in GoLive 5 and then to look at the code in the Source view. Figure 6-1 shows a page that contains basic elements — text, a graphic, and a link.

Figure 6-1:
A basic Web page containing text, a graphic, and a link.

Keep in mind that a Web page is really made up of HTML instructions that your browser interprets, so the underlying is really a description of how you place different elements on the page. Think of the code as a set of commands that tell the text, graphics, and links what to do. Follow these steps to look at HTML code for a page:

1. **Choose File➪Open➪filename.html to load a page into the GoLive 5 Document window.**

   If you're already working on a page, you don't need to open another one. Save any page you're working on in the Document window before you go to the Source view. Choose File➪Save from the menu bar or press Ctrl+S in Windows or Cmd-S for Macintosh.

2. **Click the Source view tab of the Document window.**

   All of the text, media, and links disappear and you see a sea of code.

Voila! You just entered the realm of HTML code. Not as exciting as a bungee jump, but you can now see the inner-workings of a Web page. Figure 6-2 shows the code for the My Dog Fred page.

If you want to take a peek at source code of some recently completed pages or site, take advantage of GoLive 5's ability to quickly grab a recent page or site. Select File➪Open Recent Files to see a list of both recently opened pages and sites created in GoLive 5.

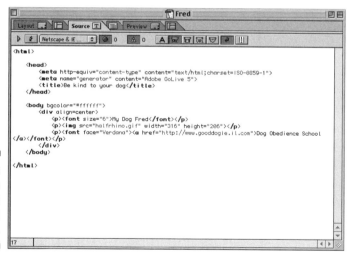

Figure 6-2:
An example of source code for a Web page.

Both Netscape Navigator and Internet Explorer enable you to look at HTML code. To see a page's code in Netscape Navigator, choose View⇨Page Source. In Internet Explorer, choose View⇨Source. Sometimes a page's code is hidden, but most of the time, if you can see the page, you can see the code.

Viewing the page and source code

GoLive 5's new Source palette lets you look at the source code *and* the page in the Layout view at the same time. If you make a change in the Source palette, you see those changes immediately in the Layout view. Figure 6-3 shows the page and its source code together on-screen. To open the Source palette on the screen, simply choose Window⇨Source Code. The Source palette appears on-screen with its Source Code tab open.

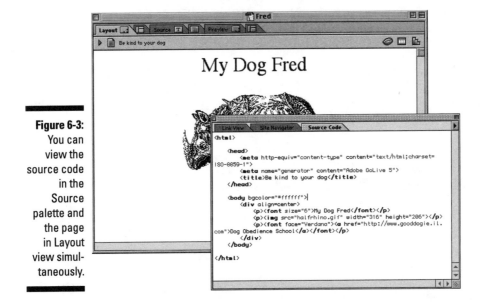

Figure 6-3: You can view the source code in the Source palette and the page in Layout view simultaneously.

Stating Your Preferences

Preference settings affect what you see in the Source view of the Document window. You may not need to change preferences, but seeing how they affect what you see in the Source view is a good idea. Follow these steps to look at or set preferences for the Source view:

1. Choose Edit⇨Preferences.

The Preferences window appears

2. **Click the Source icon in the left pane of the Preferences window.**

   Settings for the Source view appear in the right side of the Preferences window, as shown in Figure 6-4. If a check mark appears in the check box for the options in the right pane of the Preferences window, that option is currently selected and active.

You're ready to set preferences. All changes can be reversed; so don't be shy because you are changing the way *you want* your source code to appear.

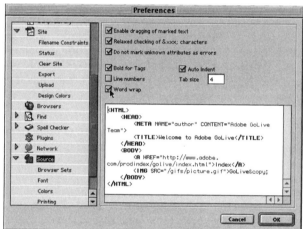

Figure 6-4:
The Preferences window enables you to set your preferences for the Document window's Source view.

GoLive 5 gives you the following eight preference settings from which to choose:

- **Enable Dragging of Marked Text:** This option is a good one to keep unless you want to minimize the possibility of dragging text or code to the wrong place.

- **Relaxed Checking of $XXX; Characters:** You need certain kinds of characters for certain kinds of formatting in HTML. One of the most common formatting characters is the ampersand (for example, * ,* which stands for nonbreaking space). Unless you select the Relaxed Checking check box, however, the character-checker may think that any ampersand it finds is an error.

- **Do Not Mark Unknown Attributes as Errors:** This choice can prove a little tricky. I leave it selected because sometimes GoLive 5 marks more script than necessary. However, if you're coding a whole page in HTML in the Source editor to practice how to code, you may want to leave it unselected.

- **Bold for Tags:** Checking your source code is easier if only the tags appear in bold. Leave this option selected to make debugging easier.

✔ **Auto Indent:** Usually this option is a good one to leave selected because you can better distinguish whether your coding is correct if it's indented — see "Containers and nests" below. Spotting a bug or editing is also simpler with indents.

✔ **Line Numbers:** Line numbers can clutter a page, but if you know that you have a bug on line 572, these numbers make that line easier to find. (You can leave the Line Numbers option unselected here, however, and then toggle it on and off from the Source toolbar.)

✔ **Word Wrap:** Selecting this option enables you to see all the code in a horizontal window: If you don't select this option, code listings can extend beyond the right side of your screen, requiring you to scroll left and right to see it all. The soft wrap doesn't include a carriage return at the end of each line, but you can see and edit code in a single eyespan. Selecting the Word Wrap option in Preferences is the only way to wrap code listings in the Source palette. (The Source view has its own Wrap icon that you can toggle on and off.)

✔ **Tab Size:** The amount of indent for each level is the "tab size" of the indent. Generally, I like 4 or 5 for my tab size. It's enough to clearly indent but not so much as to cause word wrap with too many of the indents.

You can set other options by clicking additional items in the left side of the Preferences window; click the arrow next to the Source icon and open its drop-down list. Select which parameters you want to change and make those changes you want, including those that I describe in the following list:

✔ **Browser sets.** Prepare code that works for both of the major browsers and in different versions of those browsers. Versions before Version 3 are pretty archaic and don't support Dynamic HTML and other nifty features of Web pages. I usually prepare my code for both browsers from Version 3 onward. This decision is important because excluding earlier versions of a browser means that certain features of a Web page don't work if a viewer sees them in an older browser. (Yeah, I know. Browsers are free, and why would someone refuse to upgrade a browser?)

✔ **Font.** Select a font to appear on the editing page, the colors used for characteristics of HTML coding, and printer settings. Consider applying different colors to different HTML properties so that coding and debugging are easier.

✔ **Colors.** Pick colors for Syntax highlighting and different page elements. Experiment with both different colors and numbers of colors. Important elements to be sure to include in color highlighting are Media and Links at a minimum. In that way your media (such as your graphic images) and your links codes are highlighted. Since both links and media are common places for code to go haywire, it helps to make them stand out.

However, I usually select the Detailed selection because I want to see several key elements of the code stand out, including Media and Links, URLs, and Server Side code.

✔ **Printing.** Select from Printer Specific settings and Special Fonts. Generally, I set these to be different from what's on the screen. Unless using a color printer, I'd suggest you leave Syntax Highlighting unchecked and go with Bold Typeface for Tags. Line numbers I find generally in the way, but for long scripts they can be useful. Also, I like a font like Courier because it is monospaced (that helps distinguishing code elements from one another).

Changing the Way Code Looks

If you change views in the GoLive 5 Document window, the context-sensitive toolbar changes. In the Source view, however, a separate toolbar appears as part of the actual window. Figure 6-5 shows the Source Toolbar with its several options.

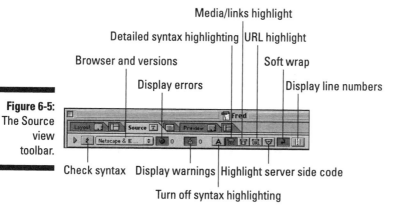

Figure 6-5:
The Source
view
toolbar.

The Source Toolbar is unique because its functions affect the appearance of HTML source code in the Source view, not how the Web page itself looks. You can toggle features on and off by clicking the buttons on the toolbar. The following list describes the functions of each button on the Source view toolbar:

✔ **Check Syntax:** Opens at the top of the Source view window, showing errors and warnings.

✔ **Browser and Versions:** Changes the browser and browser version the syntax-checker examines. The older the version, the more warnings you see telling you that some of the code isn't acceptable.

- **Display Errors:** Warns you if you make a coding mistake that's unacceptable in all browsers or versions (such as including a closing tag without an opening tag). The warning appears with a red ball next to it in the Syntax window. Toggle this button on or off to display errors. (I leave mine on all the time!)

- **Display Warnings:** Appears if one of the selected browsers or a selected version doesn't recognize a tag.

- **Turn Off Syntax Highlighting:** Turns all the HTML script to a single color.

- **Detailed Syntax Highlighting:** Turns on all the color coding for the HTML script.

- **Media and Links Highlight:** Highlights only media (movies, graphics) and links.

- **URL Highlight:** Highlights only URL file names and addresses.

- **Highlight Server Side Code:** Highlights code such as ASP (Active Server Page) or other server side code. *Always* highlight server side code if you're working with it so you don't get it mixed up with the client side code. GoLive 5 generates a lot of code and if server side code is part of that generation, you want it to stand out. Server side code communicates with the code in the various server configurations, such as Common Gateway Interface (CGI). If you use the Dynamic Link software, you will see ASP code generated in your source. Therefore, you may find having a special highlight for the server code useful.

- **Soft Wrap:** Makes lines of HTML code wrap around rather than scroll off the right side of the window.

- **Display Line Numbers:** Appears along the left margin of the window to identify lines. Each line has a separate number; wrapped text is not considered a separate line. (Don't worry, line numbers are not left on your Web pages. If they were, they'd totally distort them.)

Whether you're an old hand at coding HTML in text editors or a novice to HTML coding, you're sure to find the Source view helpful. The Source view is as easy to use as a text editor is, and it formats HTML so that the code's easier to debug and edit.

Speaking in Tags

HTML is a language that uses tags to describe a page; meaning that it uses a set of tags to tell objects on pages where to go. HTML gives a page *formatting* (also known as *markup*) and incorporates links to other sources of information — usually other Web pages. Those links are known as hyperlinks, or hypertext, which explains the name HyperText Markup Language. Nothing really too exotic about it.

A tag is a code that instructs the browser how to convert text, graphics, and links. You identify a tag by its enclosure in arrow brackets (also known as *angle brackets, greater than/less than brackets* or *those pointy things*). The first tag you see on a Web page, for example, is ⟨HTML⟩ (refer to Figure 6-2). That tag tells the browser that what follows is an HTML document.

Some tags have start and end identifiers that mark text for a particular application. Italicized text, for example, opens with the ⟨I⟩ tag and closes with the ⟨/I⟩ tag. All the text between those tags is italicized. The slash mark (/) always denotes the ending tag.

Other tags only have a single state. For example, the tag that calls up an image, ⟨IMG⟩ uses a start tag but no end tag. Figure 6-2 contains a line of code that begins with ⟨IMG....⟩ but the tag has no end tag with the same code. A few tags such as the paragraph tag ⟨P⟩ sometimes have end tags ⟨/P⟩ as you see in Figure 6-2 — GoLive automatically generates them no matter what — but in other Web pages, you find plenty of ⟨P⟩ tags but no ⟨/P⟩ tags.

You can write or edit HTML scripts in text editors such as Notepad in Windows or SimpleText on the Macintosh. If you want to do some simple editing, such as changing a page's background color, you can load one of the basic text editors and make the changes. Using a simple editor is a good idea if you have other programs loaded and memory is tight. However, most of the time, straight HTML editing in the Source view is much more effective because of GoLive's syntax-checking and code formatting capabilities.

Containers and nests

If text and code lie between start and end tags, they're in *containers*. For example, look at the following line of code from Figure 6-2:

```
<h1>My Dog Fred </h1>
```

This line shows a container beginning with ⟨h1⟩ and ending with ⟨/h1⟩. The ⟨h1⟩ (or ⟨H1⟩ if you like to use caps) stands for *Heading 1,* and all text within the ⟨h1⟩ container takes on the format of Heading 1. The text, *My Dog Fred,* lies within the container. (I need to contain Fred!)

In Figure 6-1, the text, graphic and link are all centered on the page. That's because they're in the container that the tags ⟨center⟩ and ⟨/center⟩ describe. Within the ⟨center⟩ container are other tags that also use start and end tags. They're *nested* inside the ⟨center⟩ container.

Mixing nesting code is a common problem in editing and creating HTML code. If a tag opens in a container, it *must* close in the same container. Notice in Figure 6-2 that the container for *My Dog Fred* opens and closes within the

<center> container. If it opened in the <center> container and closed outside of it, you'd see an error and the Web page wouldn't work. The following examples show the right and wrong way to nest tags:

Right:

```
<center> <I> <h3> Look at this! </h3> </I> </center>
```

Wrong:

```
<center> <I> <h3> Look at this! </center> </h3> </I>
```

In the wrong example, notice that <h3> is nested in two containers — <center> and <I>. That means that </h3> should come before *both* </I> and </center>.

When fine-tuning your HTML code, mixing up the nesting sequence is easy. As GoLive automatically creates HTML code, it never makes nesting-code errors. So if you edit your Web page code, be sure that any changes you make nest all the tags correctly. And if your page disappears after some fine-tuning in the Source view, check to make sure your nests are set up right.

Leaving in part of a container while deleting the rest of it is another common nesting and container error that frequently happens during editing. For example, if you decide to get rid of italicized text, you might just go in and remove the opening <I> tag and leave in the closing </I>. If you make the change while working in the Layout view, GoLive 5 removes both tags automatically; but in the Source view, you must remove both yourself. Leaving part of a container can cause your page to be formatted in a way you do not want or intend.

One of the greatest things about HTML is that it's *not* case-sensitive. That means you can write the code in uppercase, lowercase, or a combination of cases. So you can type in <B> or <b> or even <br> or <Br>. Live it up with this loosely coded tag language!

You've Got Attributes!

Some tags have attributes. An attribute in the context of HTML is something like a parameter — a variable value to set and change. For example, the <body> tag has several attributes, and I use the following attribute in the sample Web page script shown in Figure 6-2.

```
<body bgcolor="#ffffff">
```

The attribute is the background color (bgcolor) and the value of the attribute is the color white. Other <body> attributes include the color of the links, visited links, and active links. If you include no attributes for <body>, GoLive uses the default values: a gray background, blue links, purple visited links, and red active links.

Another tag in the sample Web page script that displays an attribute is the <IMG> tag. Here the attributes belong to the image called in by the tag.

```
<img src="halfrhino.gif" width="316" height="206">
```

The three attributes are height, width and src. The image name, "halfrhino.gif" is the value of the attribute src, while the height and width values are culled from the size of the graphic. The src attribute names the *source* of the file being brought into the Web page. The src value can be the name of the graphic file alone if the Web page and graphic are in the same folder, or a full URL such as the following:

```
"http://www.outermongolia.com/recipes/yakbread.html"
```

If you change the attributes of a graphic's dimensions, it distorts unless the changes are proportional to the original values. Similarly, if you change the src value but don't change the height and width values, the new image also distorts. The moral to this story is to be careful changing attributes unless you know what can happen. (Either that or goof around with attributes on pages you don't care about to determine more about how they affect your page — that sounds like more fun.)

Telling What's on Your Pages

The first part of an HTML script is usually the head. It's easy to spot because the <HEAD> </HEAD> tags contain it. The title goes here, along with other code not shown directly on the Web page. Common tags that you find in the head section include <META> tags, <TITLE>, and JavaScript function definitions. You use the <META> tags to tell the world what's in your Web pages. Search engines use <META> tags to locate various topics and page contents. For example, the following <META> tag tells the search engine the contents of my page:

```
<meta name="keywords" content="dogs, training, big">
```

GoLive automatically generates <META> tags for the character set, file format and the generator named "Adobe GoLive 5."

To describe what is on your page beyond the keywords, use the following `<META>` tag :

```
<meta name="description" content="We specialize in training
        large and difficult animals. See us before your
        pet eats you.">
```

Keep in mind that GoLive generates most of the HTML code seen in the script's head and not your own tedious coding. In fact, one of the Object palette tabs is the Head, which includes icons for all the different things that you can drag and drop into the Head area of the Layout view. That little arrow next to the page icon in the upper-left corner of the Layout view toggles the Head area open and closed. You can fill the Head with lots of valuable information, including `<META>` tags that don't appear on the Web page but can affect other aspects of the page.

Declaring Your Page's Look

As soon as your Web browser sees the `<BODY>` tag, it knows that everything in the Body container is to appear on the Web page. The attributes of the opening `<BODY>` tag affect the entire page and you can override them only by using specific containers that tell the browser to do otherwise. For example, the following `<BODY>` tag declares that the page will have a tan background color, firebrick links, and red text.

```
<Body bgcolor="tan" link="firebrick" vlink="firebrick"
        alink="firebrick" text="red" >
```

If you develop a color scheme that you like, rather than defining the majority of your work by using individual font color changes, just put it all in an attribute of the `<BODY>` tag.

Formatting Tags

In the Source palette, you're likely to run across one or more HTML formatting tags. The good thing about the tags is that they provide a consistency across platforms, monitors, and browsers. The bad thing is that they're severely limiting.

Heading tags

HTML provides six heading tags. Each tag begins with an *H* followed by a number. The largest heading is `<H1>` and the smallest is `<H6>`. Think of these tags as containers that affect blocks of text rather than single characters. A typical heading container appears as shown in the following example:

```
<H2> This is the second largest heading. </H2>
```

Style tags

Styles are also rather limited in HTML (nothing fancy here). The following list displays an example of bold, italicized, and underlined styles, and each includes its opening and closing tag.

<B>: **Boldface** </B>

<I>: *Italicized* </I>

<U>: Underlined </U>

You use other styles in HTML less often, but they may come in handy in certain applications. (The last of these I hesitate to provide because of its use to annoy the viewer.) The following list displays these additional styles and their tags:

<STRIKE>: ~~Strikethrough~~ </STRIKE>

^{: Superscript}

_{: Subscript}

<BLINK>: The text blinks... </BLINK>...until the viewer exits the page screaming.

Using the <FONT> tag and its attributes is another and a far more flexible way to style how your code looks. Basically, the <FONT> </FONT> container has three attributes; color, size and font. The color values can either be the six-character hexadecimal values for the color or one of the reserved HTML color words. (Hexadecimal values are a base-16 numbering system from 0 to F that your microprocessor finds friendly.) Font size is a value from 1–7, but these values have nothing to do with point or pica size. The following illustrate a <FONT> container employing all three attributes:

```
<FONT color="green" size="3" font="verdana">
```

You can use any one or combination of attributes in the same tag. If you change the color, size, or font of even a single letter in GoLive 5's Layout view, GoLive 5 generates a <FONT> container that it reveals in the Source view.

Alignment tags and attributes

The alignment tags and attributes work with both text and graphics. You accomplish most of the general alignment in combination with either a heading tag — such as <H3> — or a paragraph tag <P> in which alignment is an attribute. One tag, <CENTER>, works as a container with </CENTER> and has no attributes. The following examples show different alignment options in HTML:

```
<P align="left"> All of this is to the left. </P>
<H3 align="center"> The middle of the road. </H3>
<P align ="right"> Is this too conservative? </P>
<Center> Front and Center </Center>
```

Another interesting type of alignment tag is <BLOCKQUOTE>. Each instance of <BLOCKQUOTE> indents the text at a tab stop on the page. For example, the following HTML creates text that steps across the page at one, two, and three tab stops.

```
<blockquote>This is in one.
<blockquote>This is in two.
<blockquote>This is in three.</blockquote>
</blockquote>
</blockquote>
```

On the Web page, the text steps across the page like this:

This is in one.

    This is in two.

        This is in three.

Each instance of the <BLOCKQUOTE> tag bumps the text over one more tab. Because the sentence, This is in three has three <BLOCKQUOTE> tags before it before any closing instances of the tag, it's set three tabs in.

Basic lists

The *Ordered* and *Unordered* lists constitute the two basic HTML lists. The Ordered list generates a sequential set of numbers and the Unordered list appears something like a bullet list. Each list works with two types of tags. The first tag defines the container as either an Ordered list (<OL>) or an Unordered one (<UL>). Each item in the list is tagged with (<LI>) with an optional (</LI>) at the end of each item. (Usually, coders just leave off the closing <LI> tag because the <LI> at the beginning of the next line accomplishes the same thing.) You must, however, use a closing list tag in the form of either </OL> or </UL>. An Ordered list, for example, looks as follows:

```
<OL>
<LI> One for the money.
<LI> Two for the show.
<LI> Three to get ready.
<LI> And four to ao!
</OL>
```

On the Web page, you see the following:

```
1. One for the money.

2. Two for the show.

3. Three to get ready.

4. And four to go!
```

Coding links

The two basic kinds of link codes apply to graphic files and other Web pages. First, you initiate *hyperlinks* (or just plain *links*) by using the <A> tag followed by the HREF attribute. You need to terminate the hyperlink by using a closing tag, </A>. The HREF is the *H*yperlink *REF*erence that can be any page's URL, from a page in the root folder to a site in Outer Mongolia.

Cutting off the </A> tag is a common error in editing HTML code. If you change the hotspot text or graphic, sometimes you clip the </A> tag as well. That's probably because the closing </A> tag seems divorced from the beginning tag that usually begins <A HREF...> rather than simply <A>. And while discussing a warning around <A> tags, I probably need to add that in editing HTML, you can also clip out the hotspot words or graphics that the <A> container surrounds if you're not careful.

The most common link is simply one to another URL as the following example shows:

```
<A href="http://www.adobe.com"> Click here. </A>
```

If you have several folders in your site and your script calls for links to pages in different folders, you see different references to the file and their folders. The following three examples show the basic types of references to different levels:

✔ **Link to a level down:** The link is to a folder that the folder in which the linking Web page resides *contains,* as in the following example:

```
<a href="Bottom/botFld.html">Link below.</a>
```

✔ **Link to the same folder:** The link is to a file in the same folder, as in the following example:

```
<br><a href="level.html">Link level.</a>
```

✔ **Link to a level up:** The link is to a folder that *contains* the folder in which the linking Web page resides, as in the following example:

```
<br><a href="../topFld.html">Link above</a>
```

The links to an image file follows the same rules of reference as to links to other Web pages. In the example page shown in Figure 6-2, the reference is to a file in the same folder. However, where all graphics are together in a media file residing in a folder within the folder containing the Web page calling (linking) the graphic file, the reference would have to name the folder and then the file name. For example, if all of your graphics are in a folder called (quite originally) *graphics,* for example, first you name the folder and then the particular file. The following line of code, for example, makes this connection:

```
<IMG src="graphics/cow.jpg" >
```

The graphic file cow.jpg is found in the folder graphics that resides at a lower level than the Web page that calls the page.

You can call a graphic file from anywhere on the Web. The problem is that somebody might file a copyright infringement lawsuit if you do. Having a link to someone else's page is one thing (that's okay), but if you just reference a single graphic file that you like and integrate it into your page, you may be infringing on a copyright — even if you never take the graphic off the person's server!

Coding in the Outline View

The other view in the Document window where you enter HTML code is the *Outline view.* This view is very different from the Source view, and the context-sensitive toolbar transforms into the Outline toolbar. In this view, the sample Web page displays a unique look, as shown in Figure 6-6.

The idea behind the Outline view is to provide the designer with a way to enter HTML code while not having to write a single line of code. Not only can you enter tags, but you can enter attributes and their values as well. Using the Outline view is virtually a whole new way of thinking about coding HTML. For tweaking attributes and fine tuning many of the page elements, this view may come in handy. However, it takes some getting used to, and for old hands at coding HTML, it may seem a bit unusual. You really need to consider the Outline view along with the Outline toolbar, so please check out Figure 6-7 before forging ahead.

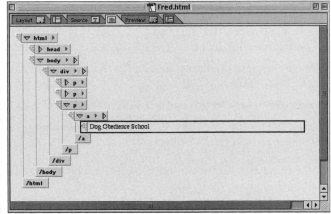

Figure 6-6:
The Outline view clearly shows the hierarchy of the coded page.

New HTML tag

New HTML attribute

New custom tag

Figure 6-7:
The Outline toolbar.

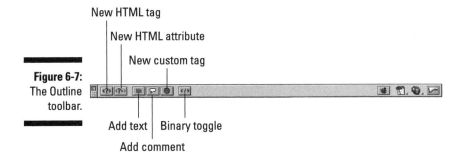

Add text | Binary toggle

Add comment

Adding tags

To get started using the Outline view, you need to use the Outline toolbar and understand how to insert HTML tags. Follow these steps:

1. **From the Document window, click the Outline tab (the fourth from the left).**

   You see a stylized set of tags showing the hierarchy of the coding system. Note the lines connecting the beginning and ending tags of the container.

2. **In the Outline view window, select one of the HTML elements where you want to insert an HTML tag.**

3. **Click the New HTML Tag button on the Outline tool bar.**

   An untitled tag appears at the insertion point.

4. **Take one of the following actions:**

   a. **Type in the name of the tag to replace the untitled tag label.**

      Or

   b. **Deselect the untitled tag and Ctrl+click (Windows) or Command+click (Macintosh) on the name.**

      Be careful here the first time you try this. Up jumps a pop-up menu with a database of HTML tags.

5. **Select one of the tags in the menu and it inserts itself into the script.**

   If you want to close a container, just select the opening tag, and then add a slash in front of it after it appears in the Outline view.

Because GoLive 5 advertises its Outline view as enabling you to create HTML code without needing to write it, you may wonder why you have the option to type the name of the tag. If you know the right code to key in, you can just type it. On the other hand, instead of keying the code, you can just select an HTML tag from the pop-up menu. You must know which tag to use from the pop-up menu, however, and so, although you need not actually type any HTML, you sure as shootin' need to *know* what the tags will do. The value of the Outline view lies in its clarity of structure and its providing appropriate choices when it comes to attributes you may choose to add. If you want to delete an Outline view tag, choose Edit⇨Cut from the menu bar or press Ctrl+X in Windows or Cmd-X on the Mac.

Adding and modifying attributes

You can use one of two methods to modify or add an attribute to an existing tag in the Outline view. Because the methods are so different, I discuss each separately. Go to the Outline view as shown in Step 1 of the previous section and follow these steps to use the first method:

1. **Identify and select in the Outline view of the Document window the tag to which you want to add an attribute (or for which you want to modify an existing attribute).**

2. **Click the arrow to the right of the Tag name in the Outline view to display a pop-up menu and select an attribute from the menu.**

   Depending on the tag, you have a few or a lot of attributes from which you can choose. You can choose more than one attribute by repeating the process for each attribute you want to add. A rectangle appears around the selected attribute and if appropriate, you may write in the rectangle.

3. **If you're adding an attribute, click the arrow to the right of the attribute name to open a menu displaying the attribute's possible values. Then select the value that you want for the attribute.**

   If the attribute is a color, a color box appears. Open the Color palette (choose Window⇨Color to open it if it's not already open, or click the Color tab at the side of the screen if it's docked) and drag a color from the Color palette to the color box to add a color value. You can also type the color name or a hexadecimal color value in the box. If the attribute uses a wide selection of values, as is the case of the height and width of an image, just select the value and type any specific value that you want.

I find this method of modifying and adding attributes much easier and useful than adding tags in the Source view. It's also a good way to discover which attributes associate with various tags.

The second method of adding attributes involves using the Outline toolbar.

1. **Select in the Outline view of the Document window the tag to which you want to add an attribute.**

2. **Click the New HTML Attribute button on the Outline toolbar.**

3. **Type in the name of the attribute you want to add over the *attr* abbreviation that appears where you placed the New HTML Attribute.**

   For example, if you selected the "body" tag and clicked the New HTML Attribute button, you could type in "link", and you would see a little color box appear next to it. Now that you have the attribute in, you can put in the value for the attribute, which in the case of link is a color. (I sort of liked the color "plum.") If you add an unknown or illegal attribute, no values appear. GoLive 5 prevents you from making a mistake. Nice touch.

Adding more content and tags with the Outline view

The remaining buttons on the Outline toolbar provide ways to add text, comments and non-HTML tags. The toolbar also includes a button for showing one or both ends of a container — the binary toggle. See the toolbar in Figure 6-7 for button references for the following buttons:

✔ **Add Text:** Select the area above where you want to add text and click the Add Text icon in the toolbar. Write in all the text you want in the inserted window that appears when you press the Add Text button. Be sure that you add the text in the <BODY> container and not the Head area.

- ✔ **Add Comment:** Select the area above where you want to add a comment and click the Add Comment icon. You can add comments anywhere you want in the script. The comments are just to help you remember what you're doing in the script and don't appear on your Web page.

- ✔ **New Custom Tag:** The tags that you add by using this button aren't HTML tags but rather tags from ASP, XML or some other non-HTML scripting language.

- ✔ **Binary Toggle:** Click the binary toggle icon to show and hide the closing tag. Why do this you may ask? It saves screen space and you can see more of the script.

HTML is a growing and dynamic language, and you can expect to see changes, enhancements, and even conflicts in how the two major browsers use it. I mean this short chapter to serve as only a brief introduction to the language. Even hard-core hackers, however, have enough sense to let GoLive 5 do most of the HTML coding for them, and they use the Source palette, the Source view, and Outline view primarily for fine-tuning a script or adding something more exotic such as JavaScript functions. In this case, a little bit of knowledge isn't a dangerous thing. By experimenting with keying in a little HTML here and there you gain more control over your Web page's appearance and a better understanding of what makes it tick — not to mention cooler looking pages.

Part II
Looking Good — Designs That Delight

"I just resent your suggestion that we place my photo on the 'Jokes' page of our Web site."

In this part . . .

*J*ust when you thought, "This is as good as it gets," in Web site development, you are now about to enter the second realm of mind-blowing enhancements you thought only a genius could do. But no! You find that you can match colors with Picasso, create more forms than a tax attorney, and even partition your Web page into separate parts so that you can display different elements at the same time. (Those in the know refer to such partitions as *frames.*) But that's not all! This part has CSS — those magic Cascading Style Sheets that you could never fathom and now are as easy as a point and click.

If you're totally frustrated by the way HTML deals with formatting text, you'll love CSS. You define the font, its color, the indent, the margin, the background color, and every other CSS feature simply by selecting what you want from one of GoLive's handy windows. You get control over unruly formatting quickly. Oh, and by the way, in this part you discover that after you create a to-die-for style sheet, you can import it to other sites and reuse it.

Chapter 7

Color Me Web!

GoLive 5 makes adding color to your Web page easy by giving you color wells and a Color palette with nine different coloring options. Further examination of the humble Color palette also reveals features that make GoLive 5 more than just a nifty way to add color to a Web page. More revelations are in store! (Film at 11.)

No discussion of color on the Web is complete without including the graphic images that you import into a Web page. Not only do you want your graphics and Web colors to complement one another, but you also need to keep in mind that the method you use to prepare a graphic image for the Web helps determine how the image actually looks on a Web page and how much bandwidth it takes up traveling across the Internet. (*Bandwidth* is the speed that data travels over phone line and other data lines.) This chapter covers methods for adding color to your Web page and includes some discussion about getting your graphics ready for the Web.

Getting a Mix of Color

To access the Color palette, either click the Text Color well in the center of the Text toolbar or a color well in one of the Inspectors or choose Window⇨Color. The Color palette displays nine buttons to use for selecting or mixing colors. (If you can't see the buttons on your Color palette, click the arrow in the upper-right corner of the palette to reveal a drop-down list. At the bottom of the list, select the Show Buttons option, placing a check mark in the box.) All the color buttons work the same way in adding a color from the palette's Preview pane (the largest frame on the left side of the Color palette). Each button, however, uses a different method to actually mix the color. The following list examines each button, from left to right:

- **Gray Slider:** A slider enables you to pick a percentage of black in a color.

- **RGB Sliders:** Color mixes as a decimal percentage of Red, Green, and Blue.

- **CMYK Sliders:** *CMYK* or *Process* provides four sliders that enable you to mix percentages of cyan, magenta, yellow, and black. Because CMYK is for color on paper and not computer screens, it may not meet your expectations. If you're comfortable using CMYK, however, go ahead and do so. *The Designer's Guide to Color Combinations: 500+ Historic and Modern Color Formulas in CMYK,* by Leslie Cabarga, provides a great set of color combinations, all with their CMYK percentages. (The pull-down menu indicated by an arrow in the upper right corner of the Color palette contains a *Percent Values* selection when you want to use percentages instead of decimal values.)

- **HSB Wheel:** Hue, Saturation, and Brightness are the three variables selected in the HSB wheel. Click the color ball to get the color you want and then move the slider to make it lighter or darker. (The pull-down menu indicated by an arrow in the upper right corner of the Color palette contains a *Percent Values* selection if you want to use percentages instead of decimal values.)

- **HSV Picker:** Sets hue, saturation, and value to create a color. The outer ring enables you to set hue by dragging a little box around the ring. Drag the horizontal axis on the inner rectangle to set saturation and the vertical axis to set value.

- **Palettes:** To the right of the default set of color swatches is a pull-down menu. In the menu you may choose from 256 Colors, 16 Colors, 16 Grays, Desktop colors, and Custom colors. The number of colors helps determine the size of the file — the more colors, the larger the file. Custom colors are important for applications where you want a limited set of colors for your color scheme.

- **Web Color List:** These colors are the Web-safe colors that ensure that the color you see on your Web page looks the same to everyone regardless of the computer or monitor a viewer uses. (Well, if the monitor is incorrectly adjusted, the viewer's not going to see the colors correctly.)

- **Web Name List:** If you like to choose your color by name, this button is the one for you. Although color names such as orange, gray, blue, and purple are clear enough in meaning, how such colors as Peru, Moccasin, and Dodger Blue may appear, however, is anyone's guess. (Folks in Los Angeles and Brooklyn may know what Dodger Blue looks like — da bums!) If you choose fuchsia or magenta, you get the same color.

✔ **Site Color List:** This button works only if have your Site window open. The Site colors option is a valuable tool in GoLive 5, and it helps keep your site within a compatible color palette. For more information on installing colors in the Color tab of the Site window, see the section, "Storing a Color Set in the Site Window," later in this chapter. (The fourth tab on the Site window selects the color view.)

Tickled #FFC0CB: Color on the Web

Your Web browser interprets color through hexadecimal codes. (*Hexadecimal codes* are actually a base-16 numbering system that your computer relates to.) If I were tickled pink, I'd be tickled #FFC0CB as far as my Web browser is concerned. Without getting too technical, only certain colors show up consistently in different monitors and computers hooked into the Web. Understanding a bit about these colors and values helps you understand how to use GoLive 5's Color palette and how to make conversions from different ways of mixing colors.

A good way to start learning about color and color combinations is to enter the key words "complimentary colors" in an online search engine such as Excite, Yahoo!, or Lycos. You will find several different Web sites dedicated to color theory.

Practicing safe Web-page coloring!

The 216 Web-safe colors derive from the common values that all computers and monitors can read. What looks a certain way on your Web site on your computer looks the same on everyone else's — and that's important.

In Chapter 1, I discuss the Web Color List button on the Color palette. Now you get to see what makes those colors so safe.

Using the Web Color List button on the Color palette is the best way to ensure that your colors are truly Web safe. In fact, if anyone other than you and your cat looks at your site during development, keeping a Web-safe palette is important.

One of the goofier mysteries of HTML lies in its Web-color names. The button to the left of the Web Color List button is known as the *Web Name List*. Some of the colors on the list are Web safe and will turn out fine on any computer or monitor; however, others on the list aren't Web safe at all. Colors with such names as AliceBlue, GhostWhite, and Papayawhip (my favorite) are *not* Web safe, I'm afraid, and how on earth anyone selected them as part of a set of Web colors is beyond me. Lucky us, however — we can use these names instead of using hexadecimal code. (Which is easier to remember is a tossup.)

You can mix colors in many different ways, and folks with an artistic and graphic-design background often display a decidedly non-Web way of thinking about color. GoLive 5, however, enables people who're smart about color and color mixing to more easily obtain the exact colors that they want for their Web-page development. That's why GoLive 5 offers so many buttons on the Color palette. The following section examines the three main numbering systems that you use for entering color on the Web. So no matter whether you're new to graphics or you're an experienced graphic designer or artist, this section has something for you.

Magic Web values

If you want an exact color match, you can use the values for the *RGB* (*R*ed, *G*reen, and *B*lue) palettes. Three different sets of values define Web colors. First, in the native language of HTML, you have sets of six hexadecimal values. You express these values in terms of 16 alphanumeric values from 0 to F. In an HTML color value, for example, you may see the number CC9933. That number tells your computer to create a color containing the following values:

Color	Hex	Decimal
Red	CC	204
Green	99	153
Blue	33	51

Most Web and graphic tools perform all the numeric conversion for you, and the only real knowledge that you need is to duplicate the value. So if you see the color value CC9933 and you use that same value in another graphic, you know that you get the same color.

Even if you never understand hexadecimal numbers, you can copy them to your Web page. What's more, if your RGB colors use the following set of numbers, they're Web safe:

00	33	66	99	CC	FF

Safe hexadecimal values

Any RGB combination of those values is safe on any Web browser. The value 666699 or the value FFCCFF, for example, is safe, but FFC0CB (pink) isn't, although HTML accepts it as a legitimate color. The following HTML example works like a champ, but it's not Web safe:

```
<body bgcolor="LemonChiffon">
```

So although LemonChiffon may look good enough to eat on your computer, the way that color comes across the Web to the computer of some poor lady in Sheep Dip, New Zealand, may end up dazing and confusing her.

The second button on the left of the Color palette provides RGB colors in percentages — a mixing procedure familiar to graphic artists. Fortunately, mixing Web-safe colors by percentage is even easier than working with hexadecimal values because the percentages are all units of 20 (all except 0, that is). Just remember to count by 20 as you set the percentages of RGB, as the following example shows, and your colors are sure to remain Web safe:

| 0 | 20 | 40 | 60 | 80 | 100 |

Safe decimal values

Another way to select RGB values is to use decimal values (not percentages) instead of hexadecimal value. To access Percentage values, you need to click the arrow in the upper-right corner of the Color palette. A drop-down list appears where you can toggle Percentage values on and off. If you prefer to use decimal numbers rather than percentages, the following are Web-safe ones:

| 00 | 51 | 102 | 153 | 204 | 255 |

GoLive 5 includes decimal values for Windows users because you may be working with graphics that you want to match to a color scheme that you develop in GoLive 5. The graphic editing system (such as Adobe Illustrator or Photoshop) may provide colors that they represent in decimal values. (Remember that fact and keep this book handy whenever you wander over and start cranking up your drawing program.)

A simple trick to use to make sure that your mix of colors is Web safe is to select or mix any color that you want on your favorite Color palette button. After you get it just the way you want it, click the Web Color List button (that's the Web-safe one) and see whether the one you're mixing up matches a Web-safe color. If not, pick the color closest to it. Or you can just go to the RGB button (the second from the left on the Color palette) and see whether all percentages are either 0 or a factor of 20.

Coloring Text by Using the Color Well

Notice the Text Color well button in the center of the Text toolbar — the ninth button from the left. (It's the one that looks like a little box or window.) Other color wells appear in the Inspector palette, enabling you to color different objects in GoLive 5. (Chapter 5 describes how to use color wells in tables and cells.) You can use the color wells with all the different buttons of the

Color palette, except Site Colors. The Text Color well button on the Text tool-bar works just the same as all the other color wells. By using the Text Color well, you can watch your text change colors as you click away on your Color palette.

To color text by using the Text Color well button on the Text toolbar, follow these steps:

1. **Open a page by choosing File⇨New from the menu bar or by pressing Ctrl+N (in Windows) or Cmd-O (on the Mac).**

   A new blank page appears in the Layout view of the Document window.

2. **Type a line of text on the new page in the Layout view.**

3. **Select the text that you type in Step 2 and then select Heading 1 from the Paragraph Format drop-down list at the far-left side of the Text toolbar.**

   You want your text nice and big so that you can see it change colors.

4. **Click the Text Color well** *once.*

   If not already on the screen, the Color palette appears.

5. **Select any of the Color palette's buttons.**

   The coloring scheme of your choice appears on the screen.

6. **Select any of the colors in the Color palette.**

   Not only do the colors in the Text Color well button change, but the selected text changes colors, too.

Coloring text by using the color wells is a little quicker than dragging colors from the Color palette to the selected text. Try different combinations of text colors with background colors and link colors. Take the time to get it just right because poorly chosen colors can ruin even the most sophisticated of Web pages.

Matching Your Web Page to Your Graphics

One of the greatest features of GoLive 5 is its color-copying tool. You can match the color of any object that you add to your Web page (including text, background color, or a graphic image) to the color of an existing object. To do so, just follow these steps.

1. **Choose File⇨Open or press Ctrl+O (in Windows) or Cmd-O (on the Mac) and then select the page containing the colors that you want to copy from the Open dialog box that appears.**

   The page appears in the Layout view of the Document window.

2. **Choose Window⇨Color from the menu bar or undock the Color palette by clicking the Color tab at the side of your screen.**

   The Color palette appears on the screen.

3. **Click either the Web Color List button (seventh from left) or the Palettes Color button (sixth from left) on the Color palette.**

   I prefer to use the Web Color List button because after I match a color, I can make it Web-safe by choosing the color on that button that's closest to the one I'm matching.

4. **Place the mouse pointer on the swatch area of the button.**

   On the Web Color List button, the swatch (it looks like a patch quilt of all different colors) is on the left side of the window. In the Palettes button, the swatch takes up most of the window.

5. **Press the mouse button (the left mouse button on Windows PCs) until you see the pointer become an eyedropper.**

6. **Holding the mouse button down while in Layout view, drag the pointer over the area on your page for the color you want to match.**

   The color in the Preview pane changes as you move the eyedropper pointer over the areas on your page. The color in the Preview pane picks up the color you drag the eyedropper over. (Just for fun, move it anywhere on your computer screen and watch it pick up the colors there and display them in the Preview pane.)

7. **After you use the eyedropper pointer to match the color that you want to use, release the mouse button.**

   The color over which you're holding the eyedropper pointer as you release the mouse pointer stays in the Preview pane, and now you can drag and drop the color from the Preview pane to color anything you want on your page. (You can't change the color on a graphic image, however.) Figure 7-1 shows how to select a color from a graphic image on the page (the robot) by moving the eyedropper pointer over it so that the same color appears in the Preview pane of the Color palette. By collecting colors from the robot, I can create a page using the robot's color scheme for my text and links.

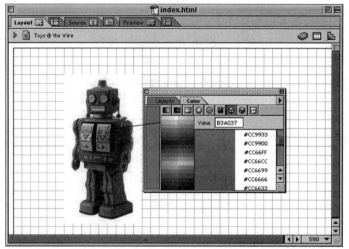

Figure 7-1:
Copying color from a graphic image — in this case, a robot — to the Preview pane of the Color palette by using the eyedropper mouse pointer.

In cases where you have a large dominant graphic figure, you can often collect an entire color scheme for a page or even a site by using the color-copying feature of GoLive 5. You need not use all the colors, and sometimes copying colors from a central graphic may not work. However, integrating colors in your text and graphics is one way to make use of color on your page in a pleasing manner.

Customizing your color scheme

If you go to all the work of creating a color scheme from a graphic, you probably want to save the color scheme so that you can use it on your site or on other pages. GoLive 5 provides an easy way for you to do that. The Custom palette in your Color palette is a well-hidden but valuable tool that you can use for such a purpose. To save your color scheme in the Custom button of the Color palette, follow these steps:

1. **Choose Window➪Color from the menu bar or undock the Color palette by clicking the Color tab at the side of your screen.**

   The Color palette appears on your screen.

2. **Click the Palettes color button (sixth from the left).**

   A set of color swatches appears.

3. **Click the arrow in the upper right-hand corner of the screen to open a drop-down list, and then select Custom from that list.**

   A black color grid with 36 black cells for color swatches appears in the Color palette. You can drag any color from the Preview pane to any of the 36 cells to store a color selection.

4. **Color your Web page by using colors that you capture from a graphic image as I describe in Steps 3–6 in the preceding section.**

   You can store each color you copy from your graphic in your custom palette. Once the selected color from the graphic appears in the Preview pane, drag the color from the Preview pane onto one of the black custom cells. (Of course, if you select black from the graphic, there is no need to drag it on top of an existing black one.)

Once you have your custom palette completed, you can use it to color the remaining text on your page. You may even want to drag the colors to the Color tab of the Site window and use them as site colors.

Transferring color schemes from outside sources

Some excellent design books dealing with color sets provide the values for different sets. If the values for the color schemes are in RGB (*R*ed, *G*reen, *B*lue) or CMYK (*C*yan, *M*agenta, *Y*ellow, blac*K*), you can easily transfer them to your Custom color palette. As I mention in the section "Getting a Mix of Color," earlier in this chapter, Leslie Cabarga's book *The Designer's Guide to Color Combinations* describes percentage colors for a wide range of color sets. To transfer one of these sets to your Custom color palette, follow these steps (as they lead you down the #FFFF00 Brick Road):

1. **Choose Window➪Color from the menu bar or undock the Color palette by clicking the Color tab at the side of your screen.**

   The Color palette appears on the screen.

2. **Click the Palettes button on the Color palette.**

   The top palette is a color grid with swatches of 256 colors.

3. **Click the arrow in the upper right-hand corner of the screen to open a drop-down list and then select Custom from the list.**

   A black color grid appears in the Color palette with 36 cells where any color can be added by dragging the color from the Preview pane of the Color palette.

4. **Select CMYK Sliders by clicking the third button from the left on the Color palette.**

   The CMYK Sliders appear, displaying four sliders, one each for cyan, magenta, yellow, and black. To the far right of each slider is a text box where values appear as the sliders are moved.

5. Click the arrow in the upper right-hand corner of the screen to open a drop-down list and then select Percent Values from the list.

You can add values in either decimal or percent in the text window next to each slider.

6. Enter the following values in the text boxes next to each of the CMYK sliders:

I found it much easier to type in the color values than using the sliders to get exactly the right value for each of the four colors. However, if dragging the sliders is easier for you, then by all means use the sliders.

	C	M	Y	K
Color 1	0	100	45	0
Color 2	40	0	0	100
Color 3	0	3	15	0

After you enter a value for each color, it appears in the Preview pane of the Color palette. Click the Palettes button (the sixth from the left) in the Color palette and you see the same color in the Preview pane of the Custom palette. Drag these colors into the black cells until all three colors are there.

This color set comes with a good Web designer's seal of approval, so you can rest assured that the colors will look real smart when you use them to color your page. Use one for a background, one for headline fonts and one for body fonts. Or you could use one for the page background and one for a table background, making color a central and interesting part of your page.

GoLive 5 preserves the Custom palette that you create on the Palettes button of the Color palette. The next time that you open GoLive 5 and select the Custom Color palette from the menu in the Palette button, you see all the color sets that you've entered. If you're working on a big project, keeping a Custom palette saves you a lot of time. If you want, you can put these customized color sets right into the Color view of your Site window, as I explain in the following section.

The effort to get a compatible color combination may seem to be excessive, but actually it's kind of fun. Good designs generally have good color combinations and if you go through all the work to create an attractive and informative Web page, you should work with the color as well. With all the tools available in GoLive 5, it's not too difficult.

I hate to say it, but the likelihood is pretty low that the custom color sets that you create are Web-safe. You can try to use the closest Web-safe colors or just take your chances that your colors don't distort and look creepy on different monitors. It's a Hobbesian choice for Web-site designers but one that you need to make.

Storing a Color Set in the Site Window

Color is key on the Web. Color is one of the main elements that ties together all the different pages in a site, as well as all the elements on the individual pages that make up the site. A Web site displaying a consistent set of colors feels cohesive to the viewer. You need to work up a color scheme with care, but after you do establish a color set or your site, you want one that's easy to use.

That's certainly the case with any color scheme that you create in GoLive 5. Using the Color tab of the Site window, you have a place where you can store the set of colors you plan to use on your site. Once your site colors are determined and safely tucked away in the Color tab (or view) of the Site window, your color work is virtually complete. Besides, all the colors stored in the Colors tab of the Site window can be accessed through the Site Color List of the Color palette.

Follow these steps to formulate a color scheme on the Color tab of the Site window:

1. **Choose File⇨Open or press Ctrl+O (in Windows) or Cmd-O (on the Mac) and then select a site from the Open dialog box that appears.**

    The Site window appears on the screen. Depending on what view or tab you had selected before closing the site, different site views will appear. If you don't have an existing Site, you can create one by choosing File⇨New Site⇨Blank. (With a new site, the Files view of the Site window appears first.)

2. **Click the Color tab of the Site window.**

    The Color view appears. GoLive 5 may have automatically placed colors there, and you will see them with untitled names.

3. **Choose Window⇨Color to open the Color palette or undock the Color palette by clicking the Color tab at the side of the screen.**

    After you open your Color palette, click any button with which you want to work. A safe bet is to select the seventh button — Web Color List.

4. Create or select a color in the Color palette.

Enter color values in one of the slider palettes or choose from a swatch selection by clicking on the swatches. Whichever method you use, the color appears in the Preview pane of the Color palette.

5. Place the mouse pointer in the Preview pane of the Color palette, press and hold the mouse button, drag the color into the Name column of the Color view in the Site Window, and then release the mouse button.

A new color box now appears in the Name column of the Color tab, as shown in Figure 7-2. This color carries the label `untitled color`. You can give it any name you want. Even the colors from the Web Name List button now — alas — appear untitled in the Name column. (They do, however, retain their original names in the HTML Name column.)

Figure 7-2:
Site colors can be dragged from the preview pane of the Color palette to the Color view of the Site window and named to reflect their use or source in the site.

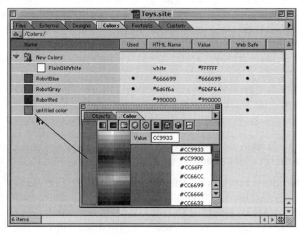

After you have your colors in the Site window, give them names that are easy to remember. Most colors display no names in the Site window until you give them names yourself — GoLive 5 identifies them only by their hexadecimal values.

If you use a name reflecting the nature of the Web site, that identifier helps you to remember the purpose of the original color set. In the sample Site window in Figure 7-2, I copied colors from the robot image back in Figure 7-1 for use as a theme for the entire site. Hence, I name each color as a "RobotColor."

Using Site Colors to Paint Your Pages

After you select and store your site colors, you use them to color your Web page. If you limit the color scheme for your Web page to the selected color set for that site, your pages and site look professional. To select site colors, follow these steps:

1. **On the File tab of the Site window, open a Web page for that site by double-clicking the page's icon.**

   As you create a site, it automatically creates an index.html page file, and you can open that file or any other file in your site by clicking its icon on the Files tab.

2. **Choose Window⇨Inspector or undock the Inspector by clicking the Inspector tab at the side of the screen.**

   The Inspector appears on the screen.

3. **Choose Window⇨Color to open the Color palette or undock the Color palette by clicking the Color tab at the side of the screen.**

   The Color palette appears on the screen.

4. **Click the Site Color List button on the Color palette.**

   You now see all the colors that you dragged to the Colors tab of the Site window as described in the previous section. The names appear in a list and are either the ones you gave them or `untitled color`.

5. **Select an object on your Web page to color by clicking on it.**

   You can select individual passages of text to color, or you can go for a more global approach by using the Page button in the upper-left corner of the Layout view of the Document window. Clicking the Page button sets the Inspector to its Page mode. Click the Page tab in the Page Inspector to find color wells for setting default colors for text, links, and background colors. For more information about the Page tab of the Page Inspector, see the section "Setting the Tone with Background Color," later in this chapter.

6. **Click the color well for the object that you want to color to activate it.**

   Text uses the Text Color well button on the toolbar. You find the color wells for other objects in the Inspector.

7. **Choose a color by clicking on it in the Site Colors List on the Color palette.**

   With a custom set of colors, you don't have to hunt for the color or jockey the sliders into place. The color in the color well changes, and so do the objects that you select or target (as, for example, you do links) to color.

You can also drag the colors directly from the Colors tab of the Site window to the selected objects on the Web page. Dragging is awkward, however, because you must flip back and forth between the Layout view of the Document window and the Colors tab of the Site window. By using the Color palette, you don't need to bother with switching back and forth because the palette shares the screen with the Layout view of the Document window. My word to the wise: Life is complex enough. Make things easy on yourself and use the Site Colors List of the Color palette. (Unless you're showing off for friends; then doing things the hard way is okay!)

If you take the colors from graphic images in your Web page to use as site colors, the combination provides both page and site integration. Figure 7-3 shows a page that gathers all its site colors from a key graphic image on the page. After you select all the colors from the image, you can use them as the text and link colors to create a seamless color integration of graphic, page, and site elements.

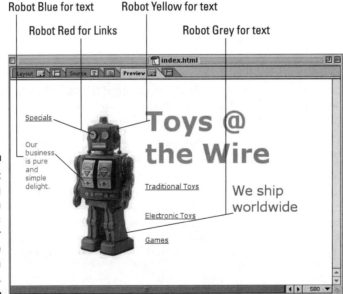

Figure 7-3:
Copying colors from a graphic image for use as site colors on a Web page.

Setting the Tone with Background Color

You want viewers to see but not notice a Web page's background color. The color sets the tone for the page, but you need for the content of the page to contrast with the page's background color. A dark background calls for light-colored text and images so that these elements remain visible, while a light-colored background needs darker text and images to create contrast.

Design and style issues aside, coloring the background of your page in GoLive 5 is easy; just follow these steps:

1. **With GoLive launched, select File➪New from the menu bar.**

   A new page opens in the Document window.

2. **Choose Window➪Color from the menu bar to open the Color palette or undock the Color palette by clicking the Color tab at the edge of the screen.**

   The Color palette appears on the screen.

3. **Choose Window➪Inspector or undock the Inspector by clicking the Inspector tab at the side of the screen.**

   The Inspector appears on the screen.

4. **Select the Web Color List button (seventh from the left) from the Color palette and click the color you wish to use**

   Because the background color affects a large area of the page you want to make sure that you use one of the Web-safe colors.

5. **Click the Page button in the upper-left corner of the Document window.**

   When the Page button is clicked, the Inspector becomes the Page Inspector.

6. **Click the color well in the Background row of the Page tab of the Page Inspector and then click on the color that you want for the background color in the Color palette.**

   The background changes to the new color that you selected in the Color palette. With the color well, you can keep clicking different colors until you get just what you want.

Go to a bookstore or artist supply store and invest in a good book on colors. The more that you know about good color combinations, the better off you are in designing pages. You may also want to look online for software that helps you out in choosing color sets. (Check out www.hotdoor.com on the Web for an Adobe Photoshop plug-in known as Harmony. It helps you select appealing color sets.)

Keeping Up Your Background Image

Besides adding a background color, you can also add a background image to your page. Any Web graphic that you choose can serve as a background image. The browser tiles the image so that it repeats itself in the background of the Web page.

You need to select a background image before you can apply one to your page. Finding or creating the right background image is important. Because a background image acts like tiles on the floor; the wrong background image repeating countless times can look more than awkward. Remember that your Web page must load the graphic file, so try to pick one that is "light" — one with a small file size. You also want to use only a JPG or GIF file for your background image. After you find the file that you want to use as your image, follow these steps to add it to the background of your page:

1. **With GoLive launched, select File⇨New from the menu bar.**

   A new page opens in the Document window.

2. **Choose Window⇨Inspector to open the Inspector or undock it by clicking the Inspector tab at the edge of your screen.**

   The Inspector appears on the screen.

3. **Click the Page button in the upper-left corner of the Layout view of the Document window.**

   The Inspector turns into the Page Inspector.

4. **Click the Page tab of the Page Inspector.**

   The Page tab appears. Near the bottom of the Page tab, you see the Image window.

5. **Click the Image check box in the Background row right beneath the Color well to put a check mark in it.**

   The Link text box in the Inspector activates and you see (Empty Reference!) in the text box.

6. **Enter the path to and the name of the file that you want to use as a background image in the Link text box (or click the Browse button — the one with the folder icon — to find the file on your computer).**

   You can also click the Point-and-Shoot button in the Inspector to select the file from the Files tab of the Site window. Just click on the point-and-shoot button and drag the point-and-shoot line to the graphic file in the Files tab of the Site window. As soon as you select the file for the background, the image appears in the Layout view, tiled as the background for your page.

A graphic background can add depth and interest to a page. Alternatively, it can camouflage all of your efforts. (If you've surfed the Web, you probably have seen sites where the Web Master decided he needed a really cool graphic but neglected to consider the fact that it would hide the content.)

Chapter 8

How to Flaunt a Form: Buttons, Boxes, and Lists

*F*orms provide the Web surfer with a means to enter information into your Web site. The information can be relayed with text elements, selections from pull-down menus, and different types of buttons. The more interactive a Web site is, the more the visitor is involved in the site. Because forms are the primary way that users enter feedback, they're central to Web site planning.

The Line Forms at the Right

Web pages often incorporate forms for viewers to fill out, and GoLive 5 makes creating and using such forms a snap. A lot of different forms are available for use on the Web, and some things that may not look like forms actually are forms. Some forms consist of little (or big) windows in which the viewer writes. Other forms offer buttons for the viewer to click, press, and pound — well, at least to click. Still others consist of menus and drop-down lists that you can put where you want on the page.

Creating your forms is the easy part. Making those forms actually accomplish some specific task requires a bit more help from GoLive 5. A number of buttons on the Objects tab of the Objects palette can prove a big help to you in getting your forms going. Some simple JavaScript programs help extend the useful and creative aspects of forms as well. Again, GoLive 5 even helps with the JavaScript. For example, JavaScript helps move data input into a form back to the site owner via e-mail. GoLive 5 writes the JavaScript to resize the window when a button is selected so that the user can control the window size.

One major use of forms on your Web site is to establish a link with a server. Usually, you form these links by using CGI (Common Gateway Interface) or some other type of communication link that uses special programming such as ASP (Active Server Pages). Unless you know how to program in CGI or one of the other server languages, you need to hire a programmer who does. By using GoLive 5, however, you can create forms that make the site ready to communicate with the server.

Web designers routinely use forms for sending information through what's known as a *Common Gateway Interface* (or *CGI*) on a server. CGI acts on the information and sends a response back to the Web page, which is the client viewer. However, CGI is a set of protocols that's beyond the scope of this book. Programmers use a language called *Perl* to write programs between a Web page and the CGI on the server. Some actions and reactions, however, you consider as *client-side* actions. (They require only the information in the user's computer and not that in the server.) Such actions occur without the use of CGI code. This chapter shows you how to set up your site for CGI connections but not how to use CGI code. Fear not, however, as you do discover in this chapter how to work with some of the client-side operations. To find out more about CGI take a look at *Perl and CGI for the World Wide Web: Visual Quickstart Guide* by Elizabeth Castro (published by Addison-Wesley, Inc.).

See Chapter 13 for a detailed discussion of using GoLive 5's Dynamic Link for ASP. Also in Chapter 13, see the discussion of using WebDAV with other people in developing a Web site. One of the others with whom you may find yourself working is a programmer who can create the code on the server you need and provide the parameters for your forms. If you want to get serious about ASP, take a look at *Active Server Pages For Dummies,* by Bill Hatfield (published by IDG Books Worldwide, Inc.).

If your job is to design Web pages by using GoLive 5, concentrate on how the page is going to look to the user and how to communicate to the user. Don't worry about how you're going to use the CGI and JavaScript or script them to use the radio buttons' and check boxes' data. That's not your job. Get a clear idea of what the page must do and how it must work to make it look good. What's important at this point is for designers to maintain good communications with the programmers who later add the CGI, ASP, or JavaScript to the site.

An Entire Palette of Forms

You use the Form tab of the GoLive 5 Objects palette to place any number of different form elements on your page. The form element goes inside a form *container* represented by a single form icon. Each of the form elements has its own icon. Placing a form element is as simple as opening up the Objects palette (by choosing Window⇨Objects) and then dragging the icon of the form element that you want from the Form tab to your Web page. You have lots of icons from which to choose on the Form tab — a tab-filling 17, which is more than you find on any of the other Objects palette tabs — each with its own unique function. The following list gives you the details on each icon on the Form tab and what it represents on the form itself: (The order of these icons is beginning with the first on the left and proceeding to the right in order of placement on the Forms tab of the Objects palette.)

- ✔ **Form icon:** Placing the Form icon on your page creates a *form container,* a kind of box where you place all the other *form objects* in this list. The Form icon contains both the beginning and ending HTML tags of the form container, which ensures that the HTML code written into the form objects on this list actually gets carried out. (In Chapter 6, I describe how containers use both start and end tags.)

- ✔ **Submit Button icon:** Placing this icon within the form container on your page creates a Submit button, useful for triggering the sending the information in the form to somewhere else. Usually this information goes to a GCI program on a server.

- ✔ **Reset Button icon:** Placing this icon within the form container on your page creates a Reset button. A viewer can use a Reset button to clear all the data he or she entered in the form. (Think of it as a Zap! button. *Zap* — the info's all gone!)

- ✔ **Button icon:** With this icon in your form container, you may end up with a simple button on your form. I say *may* because this particular button only works when the viewer is using Internet Explorer 5 or Netscape Navigator 6; earlier versions of these browsers don't support it.

- ✔ **Input Image icon:** The Input Image is just like a button icon except that you select which image you want to put on the button. When you place the Input Image icon on the Web page, a graphic placeholder appears and you can then, by using the Form Image Inspector, place the graphic just as you would a graphic onto a standard image placeholder (described in Chapter 2).

- ✔ **Label icon:** A Label element in a form is associated with a text field. Basically, the Label element is a button that, when pressed, selects the text field. When you design a Web page by using the Label element, you use the Form Label Inspector to make a connection between the Label element and the text field. A point-and-shoot button on the Form Label Inspector makes it easy to connect the Label element with a text field because you just drag the point-and-shoot line to the text field you want the Label element connected to. You want to use a label element judiciously because not all browsers or versions of browsers support this object. Clicking a Label on a form selects, or brings in focus, whichever field the Label describes. (If a field is *in focus,* that field is selected.) This type of object can prove useful if you have several different text fields on a form; the user needs only to click the label of a specific field to prepare that field to receive text.

✔ **Text Field icon:** Placing this icon within the form container on your page creates a Text Field, great for when you need to add small areas of text to a form, such as fields for a respondent's name, address, and phone number. Drag and drop the Label icon that I describe in the preceding paragraph inside the form container and next to a text field on a form, and you have a labeled text field.

✔ **Password icon:** Placing the Password icon within the form container on your page creates a text field for entering a password. For commercial sites, Password objects can act as gatekeepers to specific sections of your site.

✔ **Text Area icon:** If you want the viewer to enter a good deal of text, such as an entire paragraph, place the Text Area icon within the form container on your page to add to your form an area where she can write down her thoughts, ideas, complaints, and feelings.

✔ **Check Box icon:** Use the Check Box icon's checking feature to provide a user with more than one choice to select. You can determine the status of a check box (as checked or not) by using a JavaScript function that compiles a record of which check boxes contain a check and which don't.

✔ **Radio Button icon:** If you want the viewer to enter only one choice, place the Radio Button icon within the form container on your page to place this object on a form. On a single form containing radio buttons, clicking one button to turn it on automatically turns the others off. (As in "Click one: Male, Female.")

✔ **Popup Menu icon:** A Popup menu provides the viewer with several choices on a menu that appears right in the middle of the page, seemingly out of nowhere. You use these menus to set several links into a very small place or to provide the user with a selection of different page actions. For example, you might use the menu to link users to pages for men's, women's, or children's clothing.

✔ **List Box icon:** Similar in function to the Popup menu in providing the user with several choices, the List Box object, on the other hand, keeps all its choices right there on-screen at all times. Place the List Box icon within the form container on your page if you want the viewer to see all the options at once without having to open the menu.

✔ **File Browser icon:** You use the button and text window that this icon creates to view the contents of a CGI file on a server. You create the path of the file browser to the file browser CGI program with the Form File

Inspector. When you press the button, the contents of the CGI file appear in the text window.

- ✓ **Hidden icon:** The Hidden text window element created by the Hidden icon is great for storing data that visitors can use interactively in the Web-page design. Because the form is hidden, you can put as much information in it as you want without taking up real estate on the viewable portion of the page. Hidden elements are useful if you're storing data that someone can open on-screen only if they need it. Using Hidden elements helps keep a screen clear and clean so that the viewer can focus on what he needs. I like to think of Hidden elements as underground storage tanks.

- ✓ **Key Generator icon:** The Key Generator object applies only to the Netscape browser. It generates three key sizes from which to choose. You then use the selected size to generate an encrypted challenge. Any key does the job.

- ✓ **Fieldset icon:** Place the Fieldset icon within the form container on your page to visually group any of your form elements in a certain area on your form. It works only in Microsoft Internet Explorer, but be careful in using it on the grid. (The grouping mechanism in the Fieldset object likes to generate its own grid.) Using the Fieldset object to visually group form elements aids viewers in responding to data in the forms or that the users input into the forms. When viewed in Internet Explorer, the grouped fields appear in their own window on the page.

Whew! The preceding list describes a *lot* of forms, and although some are marginal because they're browser-specific, you can make your pages do plenty by using the forms that GoLive 5 generates. Remember that any examples that I show you dealing with CGI can only cover the process of setting up the particular form on your Web page; a CGI programmer must make actual the connection on the server side of things so that the form can operate. Most of the examples that I give you are client-side forms, however, so you can work with them on your own trusty computer.

The User Gets a Word In

Two types of text elements, *Text Field elements* and *Text Area elements*, enable you to create a page where the viewer can type words, numbers, or anything else he wants. In the world of CGI and ASP, such text goes to a server for processing. If you set up an e-business by placing order forms on your Web pages, for example, you may use a Text Field element to enable the viewer to type into a field on the form the kind of products that he wants. The word that the user types into the Text Field element then goes to the server for comparison against your company's inventory. The server then returns a response page to the viewer informing him whether that particular item is available.

Name, please: The Text Field element

Setting up a Text Field element consists of two basic parts. First, you must put the element on the page where you want it, and then you must provide values for its attributes. In computerese, an *attribute* is a characteristic or property of a form or element. A text element, for example, has attributes of name and size. The *value* is a property of the attribute. If you use a text element to input two-letter abbreviations of state names, for example, the value for the attribute *name* may be "State" and the value for the attribute *size* is "2." Follow these steps to set up the Text Field element on a Web page:

1. **With GoLive 5 launched, choose File⇨New from the menu bar to open a new page.**

   A new page appears in the Document window.

2. **Choose Window⇨Objects from the menu bar to open the Objects palette on-screen or undock it by clicking the Objects tab at the side of the screen.**

   The Objects palette appears on the screen.

3. **Click the Form tab on the Objects palette.**

   The Form tab is the third from the left on the Objects palette.

4. **Drag the Form icon (first on the left) from the Objects palette onto the open page.**

   A rectangle appears on the page. This rectangle is the form container.

5. **Drag the Text Field icon (seventh from the left) from the Object palette onto the page and drop it inside the form container.**

   The Text Field element is now where you want it on your Web page. In the Layout view you will see the outline of the form rectangle around the Text Field element, but on your Web page you will not. (See Figure 8-1.)

Figure 8-1:
A Text Field element inside a form container with a text label.

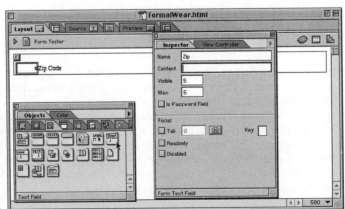

Adding values

After the Text Field element is in place, you need to adjust it to the size that you want and to fill in values for the attributes. Follow these next steps:

1. **Make sure that you have a page open in the Layout view of GoLive 5's Document window.**

2. **Dock the Objects palette by Ctrl+Clicking the top bar of the palette.**

   Docking the palettes that you don't currently need visible on-screen is a good idea so that you don't clutter up the screen too much while you're working.

3. **Choose Window⇨Inspector from the menu bar or undock the Inspector by clicking the Inspector tab at the side of the screen.**

   The Inspector appears on the screen.

4. **Select the Text Field object on your page.**

   The Inspector becomes the Form Text Field Inspector.

5. **In the Name text box of the Form Text Field Inspector, enter the name of the form.**

   Usually, giving the form a name that approximates what the viewer types in it is a good idea. A ZIP code form that you name **Zip,** for example, helps you to remember the purpose of the form. The name is referenced as a unique element name in the form; so be sure that each Text Field element has a unique name within the *same* form. Note also the name will become the fieldname of a database that could be generated. (See Figure 8-1.)

6. **In the Value (in Windows)/Content (in the Mac OS) text box of the Form Text Field Inspector, either do nothing (leave it blank) or type what you want to appear in the text box.**

   Generally, you leave this value blank because you want the viewer to enter the value. If you do enter a value name in this text box — for example, **Enter ZIP code here** — the user can overwrite it with what he enters in the text box. I recommend, however, that you just add a label next to the text box telling the viewer what to do instead of putting a word or phrase inside the text box to tell her.

7. **Specify the width of the visible text field in the Visible text box of the Form Text Field Inspector.**

   The width of the text field on the Web page gives the user an idea of what to write. You abbreviate states, for example, by using two-letter codes such as CA, TX, and NY. If the text field for a state is only two letters wide, the viewer has a better idea of what to actually type in the text field. (He knows that he can't spell out the entire name of the state or even use an abbreviation longer than two letters.) For any text field that you designate for a user's name, you want a wider space — one sufficient to contain a person's entire name, whether she uses Kay, Kate, or Kathryn.

8. **In the Max text box of the Form Text Field Inspector, enter the maximum number of characters that the text field can accept.**

As with the Visible text box, you want the Max text box to reflect how many characters that you intend for the user to enter into the text field on the form. The value in the Max text box, however, terminates any text longer than the amount that you set here. With fields that you designate for names and similar words of unknown lengths, you can leave this text box blank. For fields that you designate for phone numbers, Zip codes, and other values of known lengths, specifying the maximum number of characters that users can enter into the field is a good idea. (They can take it to the Max . . . but no further.)

9. **If you're designating the text field as a Password field, click to select the Is Password Field check box on the Form Text Field Inspector.**

If you designate a text field as a Password field, bullets (or asterisks) appear in the text box instead of the text that a user is entering. This feature helps the viewer feel secure that no one can see his password.

Setting up your attributes individualizes and clarifies your Text Field elements. By doing do, not only do you present the viewer with a clearer set of options, but you also set the stage for using the information that the user will enter. The names of the text fields are used by both JavaScript and the server database to identify fields to use or store the information provided by the people who use your Web page.

Text fields in a single-form container

Suppose that you want to create on your Web page a simple form that asks for a person's name, address, phone number, and e-mail address. You want the form to send this information to the server through a CGI connection. If all the Text Fields are in one form, a single click of the Submit button sends the information the user puts into the forms to the right place.

To make arranging the text fields easier, you can use either a table or the GoLive 5 Grid feature. (For more information about tables, see Chapter 5; for more information about the GoLive Grid feature, see Chapter 3.) As is the case with every other object on a Web page, unless you use a grid or a table, you can never tell just where the objects are going to appear on the page. Figures 8-2 (showing a form in the Layout view) and 8-3 (showing the same form in the Preview view) show several text fields in a single container that I position by using a grid that I put right inside the form container.

To work with forms and the grid, first drag the Form icon onto the page in the Layout view and then drag the Grid icon into the rectangle that the Form icon creates. Otherwise, all the forms that you place inside the rectangle that the Form icon creates on your page pull to the left and top of the page.

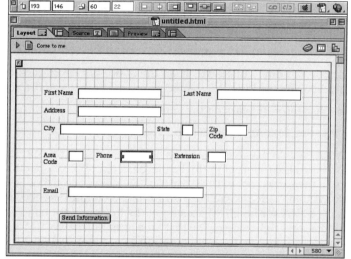

Figure 8-2:
Elements and labels on a grid (in Layout view).

Notice that, in Figure 8-2, the grid lies fully inside the Form rectangle — the Form container that the box containing an F in the upper-left-hand corner of the screen denotes. (The "F" is just an icon label to help you differentiate the form rectangle from the many text field element rectangles that reside within the form container.) As you can see in Figure 8-3, the form-container tag and rectangle don't appear on the Web page (and neither does the grid).

In laying out a page of forms, don't forget to use your alignment tools. Notice in the toolbar in Figure 8-2 that the alignment tools are available for placing form objects. Figure 8-3 shows the page objects centering vertically and hori-zontally on the page — thanks to the alignment tools. (See Chapter 3 for details on aligning objects on the grid.)

Text Area elements

Text Area elements are similar to Text Field elements. They have different attributes and uses, however. You employ text fields to gather specific data, while text areas are for more general or in-depth descriptions or comments. An e-business, for example, may employ text areas instead of text fields to gather customer comments about its service or special shipping instructions.

You place Text Area elements on a page the same way that you place a Text Field element, as I describe in the section, "Name, please: The Text Field element," earlier in this chapter. The exception is that now you use the Form tab of the Objects palette to place a Text Area icon on your page inside the Form container.

After you place your Text Area icon where you want it, you use the Inspector (with different attributes) to fine-tune your text area. Follow these steps:

1. **With a page open in Layout view, dock the Objects palette.**

2. **Choose Window⇨Inspector from the menu bar or undock the Inspector by clicking the Inspector tab at the edge of the screen.**

   The Inspector appears on the screen.

3. **Select the Text Area element on your page.**

   The Inspector becomes the Form Text Area Inspector. Notice that the attributes are different in the Properties area of the Inspector than they are in the same area of the Form Text Field Inspector that I describe in the section, "Adding values," earlier in this chapter. Notice also that *resize points* (or handles) appear on the bottom right-hand corner, bottom, and right side of the text area after you select it. You can push and pull on the handles with your mouse pointer to adjust the text area to any size that you want.

4. **In the Name text box of the Form Text Area Inspector, enter the name of the form.**

   Provide a name that reminds you of the text area's purpose. You may, for example, call it **CusCom** or **SugBox** if you're designing it for customer comments or as a suggestion box, respectively. Keeping the names within eight characters reduces the chances of conflict with database programs that are limited to eight characters. (The name your type in is never seen on the page. It is used by JavaScript and server-side programs to identify a specific form element.)

5. **In their respective text boxes, enter the number of rows and columns that you want for the text area element in the Properties area of the Form Text Area Inspector.**

   If you push and pull on the resize points to resize the text area, the row and column values appear here with the changed values filled in for you, so you needn't fill in these text boxes on the Inspector. The default size for a text area is 4 rows and 40 columns — and any other values appearing here indicate that you already resized the text area. The rows and columns are measured in pixel units.

6. **Use the Wrap drop-down list of the Form Text Area Inspector to select the type of wrap that you want for the text that someone enters into the text area.**

Select Default, Off, Virtual, or Physical. To use the visitor's browser's settings, select Default. Selecting Off ignores the columns that you enter, preventing wrapping. Virtual and Physical wraps force wraps at the column limits. (*Wraps* means it makes the text wrap around in the text window instead of disappearing straight out of the window.)

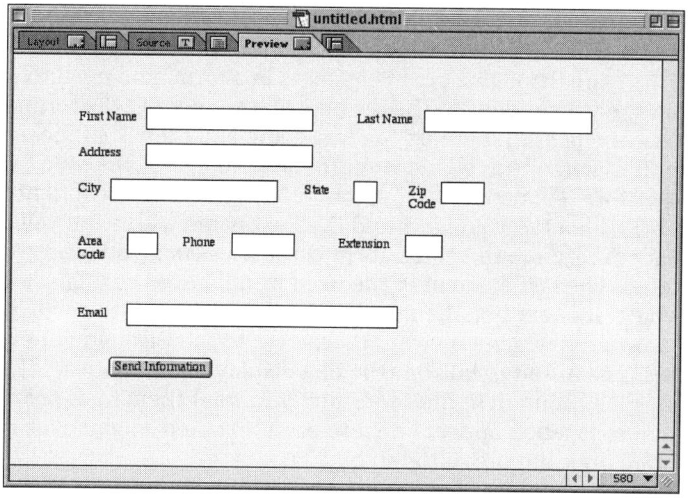

Figure 8-3:
Text fields
and labels in
the Preview
view.

Now you can post both Text elements and Text Area elements on your page. The differences between the two types of elements are subtle but crucial. Using one element or the other depends on what type of information you want the user to enter when she uses your page. Arranging and labeling Text Areas with the other elements in the form container and on the page as a whole determines how and if you get the information from the user that you want.

Tag containers don't enclose text fields, but they do enclose text areas. The `<Textarea>` and `</Textarea>` tags act as a container surrounding all text that someone enters into a Text Area element. By contrast, GoLive 5 considers all text in a Text Field object as a property of the value attribute of the unary `<Input...>` tag.

Focus in elements!

The context-sensitive Inspectors for Text Area and Text Field elements also include a Focus text box. The primary purpose of *focus attributes* is to handle the transfer of information that a user enters into a form element from that form element to a server, although the Focus text box does provide some programming aids as well. Programmers use inactive (disabled) elements of forms to keep information in place and buttons inactive until a CGI or some other script element activates them. (In Figure 8-1, you can see the Focus section in the Form Text Field Inspector.) The concept of "focus" with text elements is akin to "click" in button elements. Essentially, focus refers to the selection of the element — usually it's in use by the user typing in information. You need to address each of the following focus attributes:

- **Tabs:** The Tab text box and button on the Inspector enable you to decide the order of tab stops on your form. If a viewer uses the Tab key to navigate through a set of elements in a form, you need to make sure that the viewer goes to the next correct element in the form. For example, if the user first enters her last name and then is supposed to enter her first name, you would want to make sure that she didn't tab to some other form element than first name. Therefore, you would have the Last name with a tab value of 1 and the First name with a tab value of 2 and so forth through the entire form in the sequence you want the form completed. The last element in the form would have the highest tab value. Type in the text box the tab number that you want to correspond with the order in which you want the viewer to tab through your page. If you press the Auto-tab button (the one displaying the pound [#] sign), you can click each tab in the order that you want them to appear. A little number in a box appears next to each text field as you click it while you're pressing the Auto-tab button.

- **Read Only:** You may want to use a text field or area to leave a message on your Web page or to generate one from a CGI or JavaScript scripts. In that case, you don't want the user scribbling in the text field. On the Web page, the viewer doesn't see the text area or field — only the message it contains. Check the "Readonly" check box in the Form Text Field or Form Text Area Inspector with the element selected. (GoLive 5 collapses the two words into "Readonly.")

- **Disable:** A field that you disable is invisible to the Web-page viewer. So why ever bother to put one on your page if you're going to disable it? (You may well ask!) Sometimes Web page designers want to disable a field until a visitor meets certain conditions and then have the CGI or JavaScript script remove that field from the disabled list so that (like magic) it appears on-screen before your very eyes. Check the "Disable" check box in the Form Text Field or Form Text Area Inspector with the intended element selected.

- **Content (in Text Area elements only):** Typing a message in the Content text box of the Inspector places a message in the text area on your page as soon as the browser loads that Web page. You can use the data of the Contents text box as a message to the viewer, as information that you use in a script, or as a place for JavaScript or CGI scripts to insert information on the page from the server or other from some other type of user-input. For example, using either JavaScript or CGI scripts, you might want to have different messages appear to remind the user to fill in any empty form elements. The message appears in the text area when a Submit button has been pressed and the script launched by the button finds an empty form element. In turn, a message is sent to the text area reminding the user to fill in all form elements.

Click Here: Check Boxes and Radio Buttons

Check boxes and radio buttons provide a way for the viewer to quickly respond to fixed-choice questions. Making responding to a question easy for a visitor increases your chance of getting the information you're requesting; that's why so many Web sites supply a set of either check boxes or radio buttons — to solicit information from the viewer. Educators and trainers use check boxes and radio buttons in online quizzes and tests. The information from these objects goes into a CGI or JavaScript script that either returns the results to the user or sends it to a server for further processing. The following sections describe how to add radio buttons and check boxes to your Web-page forms.

Adding radio buttons to your page

To get radio buttons to work the way that you want, you must first place them on your Web page and then define them appropriately so that GoLive 5 knows exactly what to do with them. (Actually labeling your radio buttons — that is, adding text next to each button on your Web page to define the button for a user — is a separate step, and I cover it in the section "Labeling your radio buttons and check boxes," later in this chapter.)

To place a radio button on your page by using GoLive 5, follow these steps:

1. **With GoLive 5 launched, choose File⇨New from the menu bar to open a new page.**

   A new page appears in the Document window.

2. **Choose Window⇨Objects from the menu bar to open the Objects palette or undock the Objects palette by clicking the Objects tab at the edge of the screen.**

3. **Click the Form tab (third from left) on the Objects palette to select it.**

   The form and element icons all appear in the Objects palette.

4. **Drag the Form icon (first on the left) onto your page in the Document window.**

   The form container appears on your page as a long rectangle. It fills the width of the page and then expands downwards as you add elements to the form container.

5. **Drag the desired number of Radio Button icons (eleventh from the left) from the Form tab of the Object Palette and drop them in the form container on your page.**

   As soon as you drop the icons, they appear as radio buttons.

6. **Select a radio button on your page by clicking it.**

   The selected button now displays a square around it, indicating that you selected it. (Select only one button at a time because you must set each button's attribute individually. If you try to grab more than one at the same time, GoLive 5 won't allow it.)

7. **Choose Window➪Inspector from the menu bar to open the Inspector or undock the Inspector by clicking the Inspector tab at the side of the screen.**

   The Inspector becomes the Form Radio Button Inspector. You can now use the Inspector to work on the selected radio button. (Remember that you must select each button in turn to work on it.)

8. **Enter a one-word description of the category of responses that you expect to get in the Group text box of the Form Radio Button Inspector.**

   The Group text box holds the key to using radio buttons on your form page. A *group* is a set of radio buttons of which the user can select only one. (Users can make only one choice among a set of radio buttons in a single group.) A multiple-choice test, for example, may contain ten questions. Each question offers a *group* of radio buttons next to the possible answers, and only one answer among them is correct. You can, therefore, select only one button. For example, you might name one group "gender" for a question about gender, and another one "income" for a question on about income categories. If the user first selects one radio button in a group and then selects a second button, that second action deselects the first button. No matter how many choices a group may offer, a user can choose only one. (Is that your *final* answer?)

9. **Enter a one-word description of the value for each button that you're associating with the Group in the Value text box of the Form Radio Button Inspector.**

   Several buttons can belong to the same group, but each button in the group must have a unique value. A group that you name **Gender** in Step 8, for example, can have two buttons under the over group name Gender. One of the Gender buttons you want to assign a Value name of

Male and the other a Value name of **Female.** (You select each button individually and type the appropriate names in the Group and Value text boxes of the Inspector.)

That's all there is to creating radio buttons. Be sure only to use them when you want only a single response. (If you want more than a single response to a question, see the next sections on check boxes.) On your Web page, after the user clicks a radio button, only one button in each group stays selected. If the user selects more than one, he deselects the other (turns it to the "off" position). A CGI or JavaScript program returns the value of a selected radio button for use in tabulation. For example, you may want to tabulate the number of men and women who visit your site or some other characteristic of the folks who visit your site.

Placing check boxes on your page

Web page designers use a check box whenever they assume that the user may make more than a single choice for a category. A particular Web page design may, for example, include questions about recreation and offer check boxes for the visitor to select for different types of activities. Setting up check boxes on your Web page forms is similar to setting up radio buttons, with just a few key differences.

To place a check box on your Web page by using GoLive 5, follow these steps:

1. **With GoLive 5 launched, choose File⇨New from the menu bar to open a new page.**

   A new page appears in the Document window.

2. **Choose Window⇨Objects from the menu bar to open the Objects palette or undock the Objects palette by clicking the Objects tab at the edge of the screen.**

3. **Click the Form tab (third from left) on the Objects palette to select it.**

   The form and element icons all appear in the Objects palette.

4. **Drag the Form icon (first on the left) onto your Web page in the Document window.**

   The form container appears on your page as a long rectangle.

5. **Drag the number of Check Box icons (tenth from the left) that you want on your page from the Form tab of the Objects Palette and drop them in the form container.**

   Little square check boxes appear where you drag and drop them in the form container.

6. **Choose Window⇨Inspector from the menu bar to open the Inspector or undock the Inspector by clicking the Inspector tab at the side of the screen.**

   The Inspector becomes the Form Check Box Inspector. You can now use the Inspector to work on the selected check boxes. (Remember that you must select each check box in turn to work on it.)

7. **Click a check box on your page to select it to work on.**

   The Inspector becomes the Form Check Box Inspector.

8. **Enter a one-word description of the category of responses that you expect to get in the Name text box of the Form Check Box Inspector.**

   Unlike with radio buttons, when the user selects only one value from a Group, users can select several check boxes with the same name. Naming several check boxes with the same name, **Recreation,** doesn't mean that the user can select only one check box. Rather, the user can select each check box with the same name and different value. For example, if you want input about gender, you want only a single choice. However, if you want to know about the different types of recreation a person is involved in, you want to make several choices available. The essential difference between Radio Button elements and Check Box elements is that with radio buttons, users can select only one with the same name (group) while with check boxes, they can select several that have the same name.

9. **Enter a one-word description of the value that you're associating with the name of the selected check box in the Value text box for each check box.**

   A set of check boxes with the same name can have as many different values as you want (the only limit being the actual number of check boxes), and the user can select as many of the check boxes as he wants. Among the Check Boxes that you name Recreation, in the Name text box of the Inspector, for example, you may assign such different values as **Hiking, Swimming,** and **Sky diving** in the Value text box. The user may participate in all those types of recreation and, therefore, want to check all the boxes.

Creating check boxes and radio buttons in GoLive 5 is easy. The names and values you provide for these elements are used in linking to server databases or with JavaScript to present calculated data on the screen. Just remember that when you want the user to enter a single choice for a question, use a radio button, and when several responses are possible, use the check box.

Labeling your radio buttons and check boxes

Labeling radio buttons and check boxes is important because, unlike what you can do with some other buttons, you can't placed a label in the radio button or check box itself. The easiest way to label radio buttons and check boxes is simply to type a name next to the button. You can use the grid to make everything look neater and make your designing tasks simpler, especially if you want more than a single column of radio buttons or check boxes on your page. If you're using the GoLive 5 grid, you can drag the Text Box icons next to the radio buttons and check boxes on your form for use in creating labels, as I describe in Chapter 3.

Making the Buttons Behave

Using a form button element is one way to put an object on your page to be used to initiate an action or link to a page. This section examines how to put the button on your page and use it. The Button icon (fourth from the left on the Forms tab of the Object palette) generates a button element on your page when you drag and drop it there. It's only one of the button elements, and, ironically, it is a bit troublesome at the time of this writing. (See Warning below.) Therefore, instead of using the unadorned Button element, I want to use the Submit and Reset buttons as "normal" buttons. In other words, you will see how to make a normal button out of a specialized button element in this section and put it to use on your Web pages. However, before doing that, I want to show you ever so briefly what you *can do* with the Button elements.

Version 6 of Netscape Navigator and Version 5 of Internet Explorer recognize the GoLive 5 Button element. Earlier versions of either browser show only the label with no button on the page. (For some reason, by the way, Netscape Communicator jumped directly from Version 4 to Version 6 with no Version 5.)

When you use the Button element by dragging its icon (fourth icon from the left on the Form tab of the Objects palette), you have a unique advantage: It's the only button that offers you some flexibility of appearance in working a button into your design without requiring you to import a special graphic as an image. By clicking the text area of the button image on your Web page, you can type in any name you want and format the text just as you would any text, as described in Chapter 2. You can even use Cascading Style Sheets to create special background colors for the text on the button. (For more information about Cascading Style Sheets, also known as CSS, see Chapter 10.)

Because this button is somewhat problematic now for cross-browser use, I'll forgo a detailed description of the process for getting it on your page and using. However, if you follow the steps for using the other buttons below, other than the name being derived from the value attribute, the process is almost identical. Use it with the knowledge that many viewers will never see it as a button. Also, as the technical stuff below points out, other form elements can be thrown out of order when this button is employed.

Forms are *arrays,* and you associate a number with each element in a form, beginning (automatically) with *0* and incrementing the number with each form object that you add to the form — that is, all the objects that you place in the form container on your page. So if you have ten elements in your form, they are automatically recognized from 0–9. (This has nothing to do with either the user or designer; it's built into HTML.)

In using code, programmers sometimes refer to an element in a form by its number rather than its name. If one browser doesn't recognize a tag such as `<button...>` (which is used by the button element) as a form but another browser does, the element numbers get all thrown out of whack. If, for example, you have three check boxes, a text area, a `<button.... >` tag, and a text field on a page, in that order, Netscape Navigator counts the text field as element 4. (Remember that it counts the first check box as 0.) Internet Explorer, however, counts the text field as 5 because it counts the `<button.... >` tag as 4. If you're using JavaScript or a CGI script on your page, such differences can result in catastrophic messes.

So the problem isn't only that in one browser you see a button and in the other browser you see only text where you place the button. Rather, if you enter the same data into the forms but the programmer uses numbers instead of name references with the forms and the form elements, the set of information that the scripts on different browsers collects is entirely different in the two browsers.

What if you really want just a plain vanilla button and you don't want to mess with HTML code to create it? The Button icon, fourth from the left on the Form tab in the Object palette really isn't an option if you want to keep the folks using earlier versions of Netscape Navigator happy, but you do have a way to get around this mess. Follow these steps:

1. **With GoLive 5 launched, choose select File⇨New from the menu bar to open a new page.**

   A new page appears in the Document window.

2. **Choose Window⇨Objects from the menu bar to open the Objects palette or undock the Objects palette by clicking the Objects tab at the edge of the screen.**

   The Objects palette appears on your screen.

3. **Click the Form tab (third from left) on the Objects palette to select it.**

   The form and element icons all appear in the Objects palette.

4. **Drag the Form icon (first on the left) onto your Web page in the Document window.**

   The form container appears on your page as a long rectangle.

5. **Drag the Submit Button icon (third icon from the left) into the form container on your page.**

   Earlier versions of both Internet Explorer and Netscape Navigator recognize the Submit button, so it's a good place to start for creating a new button. When you release the icon on the page, you see a button with a **Submit** label on it. Select that button.

6. **Choose Window⇨Inspector from the menu bar to open the Inspector or undock it by clicking the Inspector tab at the edge of the screen.**

   The Inspector becomes the Form Button Inspector

7. **In the Name text window of the Form Button Inspector (where it reads `submitButtonName`) replace the name with the name that you want for the button.**

   This name is the one that programmers use to reference the button. Make this name a single word, but make sure, too, that it's one that identifies what the button does. You may, for example, use a button to launch a calculation script. If you name that button **Calculate,** you can more easily determine what script to link to that button.

8. **In the Button portion (near the top) of the Form Button Inspector, select Normal for the button type.**

   The name on the button changes from Submit to Button. At last! A plain, simple button.

9. **Click the check box next to the Label text box of the Form Button Inspector and enter the message that you want to appear on the button.**

   You want this label to tell the user what to do. The label `Click Here` in the context of the other objects on the page is usually clear enough. If you have a lot of buttons on a page, however, entering a more specific label such as **Click here to calculate taxes** in this text box better clarifies the button's job.

The procedure to make a normal button from a Submit button is fairly simple, and it would be even simpler if you didn't have to change the Submit button into a generic button element. However, you now know how to make your own button; and don't think that because you have to cobble it out of a Submit button that there's anything unusual about your button.

After you create one Normal button by reconfiguring a Submit button, copy as many as you need and paste them to your page. Just select the completed Normal button; choose Edit⇨Copy and then choose Edit⇨Paste and keep on pasting until you have all you want. Then just change the names and labels.

Working with Lists and Menus

You find two main kinds of menus or lists — list boxes and Popup menus — on the Form tab of the Objects palette. You can use either one to give the viewer a choice of options. The designer can designate as the selections on a menu or list anything that he can either link to or create dynamically on the page. (You actually have two sources for the Popup menu — one from the Form Tab and the other from the Smart tab of the Objects palette.) I describe the list box first, in the following section, because it's the least complex of the two.

Using the list box

In a list box, a number of options for a user are always visible on-screen; the view never limits a visitor to just one option, as is the case with a Popup menu. All the viewer needs to do is select one or more choices, and any scripts in the page use these choices. Follow these steps to set up a list box on your Web-page form:

1. **Begin with a page open in the Layout view of GoLive 5's Document window.**

2. **Choose Window⇨Objects from the menu bar to open the Objects palette or undock the Objects palette by clicking the Objects tab at the edge of the screen.**

   The Objects palette appears on your screen.

3. **Click the Form tab (third from left) on the Objects palette to select it.**

   The form and element icons all appear in the Objects palette.

4. **Drag the Form icon (first on the left) onto your Web page in the Document window.**

   The form container appears on your page as a long rectangle.

5. **Drag the List Box icon (thirteenth icon from the left) into the form container on your page.**

   You will see the List Box with First, Second, and Third labels in its window. The List Box object is automatically selected as you first place it in the form container on your page. Leave it selected.

6. **Choose Window⇨Inspector from the menu bar to open the Inspector or undock the Inspector by clicking the Inspector tab at the side of the screen.**

   The Inspector becomes the Form List Box Inspector.

7. **In the Name text box of the Form List Box Inspector, provide a name for the list box to identify its purpose.**

   Use a name that you or a programmer can quickly understand. If you're listing a selection of fruits, for example, enter as the name of the list box **Fruit.**

8. **In the Rows text box of the Form List Box Inspector, specify the number of rows that you want visible on-screen.**

   If you want the user to see all the items without scrolling, enter a number of rows that's equal to the number of selections you intend to show in the list box. If you want to take up only a certain number of rows on the page, regardless of how many items are on the list, enter that number; the viewer must scroll down through the list box's contents to bring the rest of the items into view.

9. **Click the Multiple Selection check box of the Form List Box Inspector if you want to enable the viewer to select more than a single item from the list at one time.**

   Using a list box is a good way to entice an e-customer to make more than a single choice, so don't ignore the Multiple Selection check box. Of course, if the list box shows dress sizes, don't confuse the user by enabling her to choose more than a single size for each item. (Hmmm, I think that I'm going to take a size 8 petite — yeah, right!)

10. **In the Label column in the Focus area of the Form List Box Inspector, start filling in the entries for your list by selecting a row and typing the name of your entry in the text box below the column, repeating this action for every entry that you want to add to your list.**

    These labels that you type appear as selections in the list box. You want to use labels that clearly describe the choices. Click the check box in the rightmost column next to each item if you want an item automatically selected on startup. If you have a list of fruit, examples of what you may enter as labels include **apricots, apples, oranges,** and **pears.** See Figure 8-4 for a list-box selection in the Form List Box Inspector consisting of different vehicles. (E-commerce in *honest* used cars.) If you want more rows, just click on the New button at the bottom of the Form List Box Inspector.

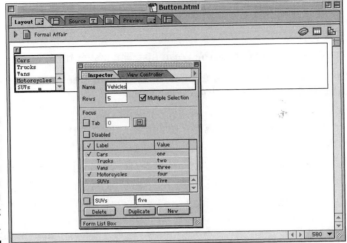

11. **In the Value column of the Focus section, type the value in the text box at the bottom of the column that you want to associate with the label.**

    Depending on the nature of the item and how the script or program is to use the information, you can enter just about any text or number that you want as the value. In Figure 8-4, the value simply refers to the placement of the item in the list. Often, you give the label name to the value, too. What you enter as a value here, however, really depends on what information you want the selection to send to the script.

12. **Use the Delete and Duplicate buttons at the bottom of the Form List Box Inspector to delete or duplicate any of the selected label and values pairs.**

    You may, for example, want to duplicate a label and then either make small edits to each name (say, changing *Cars* to **Cars1, Cars2,** and **Cars3**) or give different values to the same label. Labels and values are deleted as pairs. To change a label or value just type in another name in the text windows at the bottom.

With all the selectable form elements available to you, you can show the initial element in the selected mode by using the Selected check box in both the Form Radio Button and Form Check Box Inspectors to automatically select an item on startup. Radio buttons and check boxes are filled in or checked, and menus display items already highlighted. By making items appear already selected on their Web pages, e-retailers encourage a specific choice that they want to see a visitor make. A line next to a check box, for example, may read, `Check if you want to receive news of new products and services`. The ever-helpful Web page, however, already displays the check box with a check mark inside.

Popups and URL Popups

You can place Popup menus on your page the same way that you place a list box, except that you use the Popup Menu icon (the twelfth from the left) and the Form Popup Menu Inspector. The major difference between Popup menus and list boxes is that Popups generally show only a single message, and the user clicks the vertical arrows at the side of the box side to reveal the rest of the selections.

GoLive 5 does provide an interesting twist on a Popup menu, however — one that's already rigged with script to jump to a choice of other Web pages. Instead of taking the Popup icon from the Forms tab of the Objects palette, you use the URL Popup from the Smart tab of the Objects palette. A URL Popup Inspector enables you to enter, browse, or point and shoot URLs to your heart's content. Follow these steps to set it up and link away:

1. **With GoLive 5 launched, choose File⇨New from the menu bar to open a new page.**

   A new page appears in the Document window.

2. **Choose Window⇨Objects from the menu bar to open the Objects palette or undock the Objects palette by clicking the Objects tab at the edge of the screen.**

   The Objects palette appears on your screen.

3. **Click the Form tab (third from left) on the Objects palette to select it.**

   The form and element icons all appear in the Objects palette.

4. **Drag the Form icon (first on the left) onto your Web page in the Document window.**

   The form container appears on your page as a long rectangle.

5. **Select the Smart tab (second from left) of the Objects palette.**

   The eight Smart icons appear (with a greenish tint.)

6. **Drag the URL Popup icon into the form container on the page.**

   A popup menu bar with the word Choose... appears in the form container. The only difference between this element and ones pulled from the Form tab of the Objects window is the green tab in the upper-left-hand corner.

7. **Choose Window⇨Inspector from the menu bar to open the Inspector or undock it by clicking the Inspector tab at the side of the screen.**

   The Inspector appears, becoming the URL Popup Inspector, as shown in Figure 8-5. You see Label and URL columns in a list box in the Inspector. One label, Choose, appears already filled in for you in the Label column, as does a second label for `Adobe Systems, Inc.`, displaying Adobe's accompanying URL in the URL column. (Figure 8-5 shows several more labels and URLs that I added here.)

8. **Select the sample entry, Adobe Systems, Inc., on the row below** `Choose` **in the sample list box in the URL Popup Inspector.**

   The label and URL of the sample entry appear in the corresponding text boxes below the list, near the bottom of the Inspector. (In Figure 8-5, Netscape is selected.)

9. **Replace the sample label and URL with the label and URL for the Web site that you want to add to your menu.**

   Type the label in the Label text box and either type the URL in the URL text box, select the Browse button (the one displaying a folder to the right of the URL text box) to locate a URL, or use the Point-and-Shoot button (the one displaying the spiral symbol, to the left of the URL text box) to select a URL as described in Chapter 2. (The label simply describes the target URL.) You may, for example, type **Microsoft** as a label and select Microsoft's home page at `www.microsoft.com` for the URL. (Okay, okay — then use Apple, Inc., if you want.)

10. **After you replace the sample label and URL, add another line to the list by clicking the New button.**

    Use the New button to add lines for all the URLs and labels that you need for the Popup menu typing new labels and URLs in the appropriate text boxes for each line.

11. **Click the Delete or Duplicate buttons on selected lines as necessary.**

    If you don't want any of the URL addresses and their labels, just select each one and click the Delete button. You can't delete `Choose...` without going into the source code and changing the word "Choose" to one you want. However, after changing `Choose...` to something else, you *can* change it from the URL Popup Inspector. (Go figure.)

Figure 8-5:
The URL
Popup
Inspector,
displaying
labels and
URLs for
your Popup
menu.

The URL Popup Inspector gives you a great way to include a lot of links in a little space. If your page design gets crowded because you want a lot of information to appear on the page, using the URL Popup Inspector to create Popup menus solves your space problem by placing all your links into just a single, small space. After the menu is open, you have as many links as you want right where you want them. And although the example shown in Figure 8-5 uses only external URLs, you can use this object for links to pages right in own your site as well.

If you want to use the Popup element from the Forms tab of the Objects palette, you find that the instructions for setting up the List Box (see the section, "Using the list box," earlier in this chapter) most closely approximate how to do so.

Chapter 9

The Right Frame of Mind

. . . .

. . . .

*F*rames add a whole new dimension to HTML and Web sites. By using frames, you can organize the look of your Web page in a browser window so that you can display more than a single page simultaneously. Basically, one Web page acts like a latticed window frame with all the glass removed. The empty window frame, divided up by the latticework into separate compartments, is called the *frame set.* The frame set establishes how many frames exist in a set and the dimensions of the frames. No matter what size Web page you bring into a frame, only the portion that fits into the frame is visible.

Defining Frame Elements

GoLive makes it easy to set up and edit frames, but it uses a particular terminology when dealing with frames. The following list spells out what GoLive means when it's talking about frames:

> ✔ **Frame set:** A Web page used to organize and define the frames and load the initial pages for each frame. While the borders defined by the frame set do appear on the screen, no other visual content in the frame set file appears on the screen. (Think of the frame set as the director in a movie — he stays behind the camera. The Web pages are the actors that show up in the different frame windows.)

✔ **Frame:** A single window where a Web page is viewed. Any Web page with a URL can appear in a frame. A link to a Web page anywhere in the world or simply in your site folder can bring that Web page into any or all of the frames in a Web page using frames.

✔ **Frame Border/Separator:** A line separating frames within a frame set. Editing tools enable you to control the width and color of frame borders. (Frame borders are removed by having a value of zero.)

Why Frames?

Because you can bring any page into a browser window by clicking a button, you may be asking why you need frames. Plenty of reasons exist, and you're sure to want to use frames in some application or another. Consider the following features of frames:

✔ **Navigation Aids:** Many designers use one frame in a set to navigate other Web pages in and out of the framed page.

✔ **Multiple Functions:** A Web page with frames can use one frame for calculating values, another frame for displaying products, and still another frame for showing inventory. Different pages within the frame set accomplish different jobs.

✔ **Comparisons:** By viewing two or more Web pages simultaneously, you can compare different elements in a Web site. For example, an art historian may display Web pages with different or similar art styles in a frame set. Because you can include different Web pages in a frame set, the juxtaposition of the pages' content creates dynamic comparisons controlled by the viewer.

✔ **Passing Data:** Web pages within the same frame set read information from another page and write information to other pages. In this way, data can pass dynamically in Web pages without involving Common Gateway Interface (CGI) or Active Server Pages (ASP). By using frames, designers have the opportunity to have multiple databases responding to user input. Designers using CGI and ASP can use pages in a frame set to pass data between the server and the client as well. (See Chapter 8 for more on using CGI and ASP.)

Other uses no doubt abound, and creative Web page designers find new uses for frames all the time. Fortunately, creating and using frames in GoLive is simple.

Setting Up Your Frame Set

The first step in getting your frames up and running is to define your frame set. GoLive has a separate tab for frames on the Objects palette, and like everything else in GoLive, it's just a matter of dragging and dropping. Before you define a frame set, you need to set up a new site. Follow these steps:

1. **Choose File⇨New Site⇨Blank from the menu bar.**

   The New Blank Site dialog box appears.

2. **Type a name for the site in the New Site text field; then enter a folder destination in the In Folder text field. Click OK.**

3. **When the Site window appears, click the File tab.**

   The File view of the Site window appears. You will see one new file named index.html.

4. **Choose Window⇨Objects from the menu bar.**

   The Objects palette appears.

5. **Click the Site tab of the Objects palette and then drag three new Page icons (the first icon on the left) from the Site tab onto the File tab of the Site window.**

   For purposes of understanding how the pages work, I just named them eeney, meeney, and mo. To rename a file in the Files tab of the Site window, either click the right button of the mouse and select Rename from the popup window (Windows only) or click the name in the Files tab and pull the mouse away and type in a new name. Also, you can select the file icon and press the F2 key.

6. **Double-click each of the three pages to open them and write something unique on each page to distinguish them from one another.**

   Because the pages appear in different frames on the page, it helps to see that each page is unique. It also helps to give each a different background color to help differentiate it.

7. **Open Index.html from the Site Window by double-clicking the appropriate file icon.**

   You can rename Index.html to any name you want. For practicing with frames, you might want to name it Frameset.html or FrameUp.html or something similar to let you know that the file is a frame set.

8. **Click the Frames Editor tab in the Document window.**

   It's the tab right between Layout and Source in the Document window. A drop-down label appears when the mouse pointer crosses it.

9. **Click the Frames tab on the Objects palette — it's the fifth tab from the left.**

   In the Frames tab, you see a number of different frame arrangements. Select one you like. (Note that the maximum of frames in each set as displayed is three, but you *can* add more frames to a frame set if you want.)

10. **Drag the Frame Set icon you selected into the Document window.**

    As soon as you release the mouse button, you see the frames with question mark file icons. In the Site Window, you see the page with a green bug next to it. You haven't done anything wrong. It's just the way GoLive tells you your Frame set needs files. Figure 9-1 shows how the page appears in the Document window after the frame set is dropped in.

Figure 9-1:
This is how the first page looks after you drag the Frame Set icon into the Document window within the Frames Editor view.

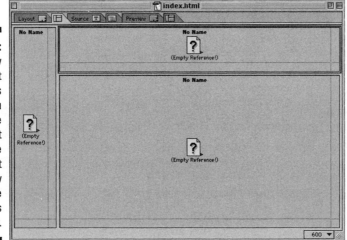

If you drag a Frame Set icon into the Layout view instead of the Frames Editor view, you see a lot of code on top of the page. That's a signal that you just put the Frame Set into the wrong place. Choose Edit⇨Undo or press Ctrl+Z for Windows or Cmd-Z for Macintosh. Click the Frames Editor tab and drag the icon again.

Loading the Frame Set

Your frame set is as naked as a jaybird. You need to assign pages that will appear in the frame set's frames. Each page in a frame set can be loaded and viewed in a browser separately. The pages that go into frame set are not slaves to the frame set, and if you know their URLs, you can load the pages independently anywhere in the world. To load the Frame Set, follow these steps:

1. **Begin with both the File tab of the Site window and the Frame Editor view of the Document window opened by clicking the File tab and the Frame Editor tabs in their respective windows.**

   If docked, undock the Site window by clicking on the Site tab at the bottom of the page.

2. **Undock the Inspector by clicking the Inspect tab at the side of the screen or by choosing Window⇨Inspector.**

   Because the Frame Editor is selected, the Frame Set Inspector appears

3. **Click one of the question mark icons in the Document window.**

   The Inspector becomes Frame Inspector. Notice that a point-and-shoot button is available on the Inspector.

4. **Pull the Point-and-Shoot line from the Frame Inspector to the file in the Site window that you want to appear in the particular frame of the frame set, as shown in Figure 9-2.**

   After the file is connected to the frame, the file's icon replaces the question mark icon in the frame window. Repeat this step until all the frames have a file associated with it.

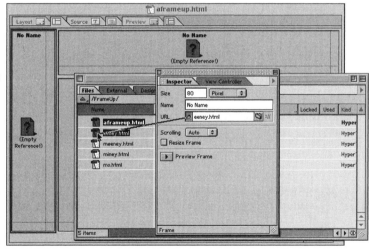

Figure 9-2: A selected Empty Reference icon is replaced with a file in point-and-shoot selection.

Naming the Frames

Each frame in a frame set needs a name. The name of the frame is totally independent of any HTML file that may appear in the frame. Frames need to be clearly named so that when you want a Web page to appear in a frame, it knows where to go. (All right, there's no need to name a frame with THAT name!) The procedure is simple, yet crucial. Here's how to name a frame:

1. **From the Frames Editor view of the Document window, undock the Inspector by clicking the Inspect tab (at the side of the screen) or choosing Window⇨Inspector.**

2. **Click a file icon in one of the frames.**

   The Inspector becomes the Frame Inspector.

3. **In the Name window of the Frame Inspector, replace No Name by typing a name that describes the frame.**

   The name of each frame should remind you of what you plan to put into the frame or at least serve as a point of reference relative to the frame set. For example, you might want to use one of the frames as a menu bar and name the frame "menu." Alternatively, you can name the frames relative to their positions, "side," "top," and "bottom." Use one-word names.

4. **Select and name the rest of the frames.**

   Figure 9-3 shows the Frame Inspector with the name for a frame.

5. **Click the Preview tab (last tab from left in Windows) or Frame Preview tab (last tab from left on Macintosh) in the Document window to look at the pages arranged in the frame set.**

   Preview your frame set periodically to keep a perspective on how the page looks.

Fine-tuning a frame

The Frame Inspector has a few other elements you may want to use:

- **Scrolling:** The Scrolling menu provides three options:

  Auto: A scroll bar shows only if the page scrolls off the top or side. Otherwise, no scroll bar appears.

  No: A scroll bar never appears regardless of whether the page scrolls off the side. Use this option when you don't want scroll bars to interfere with design. (It's also a lesson to those who try to look at Web pages on PalmPilots!) Use this option only when even the smallest monitor can view all pertinent elements of a page.

  Yes: Scroll bars appears whether needed or not. This option makes sense when you want a consistent design at all times on all monitor sizes.

- **Resize Frame:** If checked, the frame can be resized (changed in size), but if it is not checked, the frame cannot be resized. Because a frame design generally does not include changing frame sizes, this attribute is left unchecked. If some frames can be resized and others not, then there is a greater possibility of warping the appearance of the page.

✔ **Preview Frame:** Here's one of those great little buttons in the Frame Inspector that makes Web page development easier. While you're pushing and pulling on the frame, you might want to remind yourself what the initial Web page in the frame looks like. Click Preview Frame in the Frame Inspector, and voila! You get to see the page without having to leave the Frame Editor view of the Document window. (Only available on Macintosh.)

Figure 9-3:
Inspector in the Frame mode with frame named.

Tweaking the frame size and placement

The best visual method of getting the frames just right involves dragging the dividers between the frames left and right or up and down. You can drag columns only left and right, and you can drag rows only up and down. The most effective way of getting the frame just right requires that you preview the initial page while you're resizing it. Here's how to preview your page:

1. **From the Frames Editor view of the Document window, undock the Inspector by clicking the Inspect tab or choosing Window⇨Inspector from the menu bar.**

   The Frames Editor Inspector appears on the page.

2. **Click a file icon in one of the frames.**

   The frame is now selected. Note the changes in the Frame Inspector when you click different frames.

3. **Either double-click the file icon in the frame (Windows or Macintosh) or, in the Frame Inspector, select Preview Frame (Macintosh only).**

   The Web page for the frame opens in the Layout mode of a new Document window. (When you select the Preview Frame, the page has the same configuration as the frame.)

4. **Place the pointer on one of the dividers and move it until the page looks like you want it to within the frame.**

   It's a good idea to preview your completed frame set on different combinations of platforms and browsers in the Preview view of the Document window prior to publishing the page on the Web. Frames have less tolerance for graphics and text being scrolled out of sight, and you probably need to resize your frames more than once to get it just right.

After you get your pages hooked up with all of your frames, you may realize that a frame may look better somewhere else. For example, a column on the far left may look better on the far right, or one at the top of the page may look better on the bottom. Here's an easy way to move your frames in the Document window: From the Frames Editor view, click below the file icon in the frame and drag the frame to a new location. Remember that columns can move only right and left, and rows can move only up and down.

Adjusting the Frame Set

You can start with the selection of adjustments that GoLive provides on the Frames tab of the Objects palette, but you may want to fine-tune the size of the frames in the frame set. The frame set orders the frames in terms of rows and columns using either pixels or percentages. Two rows or columns have to equal 100 percent of the frame set. Using percentages makes it easier to envision how much a row or column takes up.

In some applications, a graphic may consume a certain number of pixels, and the frame dimensions may have to be based on the pixel unit instead of percentages. In these cases, the other frames in the row or column need to be carefully balanced so as not to block the graphic.

The Frame Set Inspector is a great tool for handling such balancing chores. To transform an Inspector into the Frame Set Inspector, simply click on the border between two frames in a frame set. An open Inspector immediately becomes the Frame Set Inspector.

The Frame Set Inspector options can be a little confusing, so check out the following list for the lowdown on what the options actually mean:

✔ **Size:** The size window is a mystery. It is dimmed because, unlike tables, frame sets have no absolute sizes. Tables can take up 80 percent of a window or 241 pixels, but frame sets can't. Ignore it.

✔ **Orientation:** Here's another of those options that are not altogether clear. By selecting other than the default orientation, the frame dividers are arranged in a way that looks nothing like the frame set you dragged over from the Objects palette. Leave it alone, too.

✔ **BorderSize:** Finally! Here's an option you can use. Generally I prefer to minimize the border size to 1, or more often, 0. Like table borders, wide borders in frame sets tend to create a rat-maze effect. Pay close attention to the border attribute and consider a seamless frame set where the borders are invisible.

When editing, it's a lot easier to edit with a big fat border than a skinny one. You have to click on the divider to select the Frame Set Inspector, and with skinny dividers, it's easy to miss and hit one of the frames instead. So while you're editing, leave the border size wide. After you're done editing, you can reduce the border to a smaller size that's compatible with the design.

✔ **BorderColor:** You can use border color effectively. By using minimal size borders and subtle color differences between the background color of the pages and the border, you can distinguish between the frames without a jarring separation. Click the BorderColor well in the Frame Set Inspector (which brings up the Color palette), select a border and click the color you want in the Color palette.

✔ **BorderFrame:** The border frame is made up of narrow lines framing the border. If the border frame is turned off (No), then only the border color shows in the width determined in the BorderSize window. Try different combinations to see what you get. Essentially, you can make the border itself larger or smaller but the frame around the border is a Yes/No option.

Frame sets don't have the cell padding — the distance between the object in the cell and the walls of the cell — that you find in tables. One way to mimic frame padding is to use the border size as the pad. Switch BorderFrame to No and use the same border color as the background color of the Web pages in the frame set. Increase and decrease the size of the border until you have the padding in the frames you want.

✔ **Preview Set/Stop Preview:** These two buttons may not seem like much, but in developing a Web page with frames, you'll love them. While in the Frame Editor view, you frequently need to look at the frame set with the pages in the frames. Rather than leaving the Frame Editor view and clicking Preview view in the Frame Inspector (see Figure 9-4) and then returning to the Frame Editor view for more work on the frame set, you can just turn the preview on and off with these buttons. It's easy and has no calories either. (This feature is only in the Macintosh version.)

Figure 9-4:
The Frame
Set
Inspector in
Macintosh.
The
Windows
version is
the same
except it has
no Preview
Set or Stop
Preview.

Navigating with Frames

Frames done well are a joy to design and develop. However, one area tangles up just about everyone at one time or another: navigating in frames. A link on a normal non-frame page means that when the user selects a link, the linked page replaces the current page. With frames, there are specific targets (frames) you want the linked pages to appear in but not others. For example, if you design one of your frames to be a navigation bar, you don't want it to be replaced by another page.

GoLive automatically includes the names of the frames in the link options in the Text Inspector's or Image Inspector's Link tab when a link is established. (That's why it's so important to name your frames as soon as you can.) A pull-down menu provides two sets of link targets. The bottom set lets you open up a new window to display the page you're linking to, while the top set lets you open the page you're linking to in one of the other (named) frames in the current window. First, consider the menu options for opening a new window to display the page you're linking to:

- **_blank:** Opens a new window and leaves the current window open also. A new page outside of the frame set opens. Usually the page covers up a good portion of the frame set page, which isn't a good thing. However, sometimes the designer wants to open a page and leave at least part of the linking page visible as well. Users can compare the information on the linked page with the linking page. With external links, opening a new window guarantees that the linking frame set will not be lost. (The viewer may have to shift the pages around to get a clear view.)

- **_self:** Technically, _self doesn't open a new window at all, but rather opens the page in the frame with the link. (GoLive must think that consistency is the hobgoblin of little minds.) Essentially, with the _self target, the linked one replaces the linking page.

Don't use _self with a frame housing your menu or navigation page. If you do, as soon as you link to another page, your menu goes "Adios" and in comes the linked page into the frame. (I hate it when that happens.)

✔ **_parent:** The linked page is loaded into the parent frame set. The current frame set is replaced by a new page or frame set. Your whole frame set disappears and a page or new frame set takes its place.

✔ **_top:** The entire frame set is discarded and the new page is brought up in a new window. This appears to work exactly like _parent except in cases where nested frame sets are employed. In a nested frame set, _parent replaces only one of the frame sets and leaves the others. (A *nested frame set* occurs when a page with its own frame set is opened inside a frame. See the last section of this chapter for a discussion of these frame set arrangements.) _top discards all frame sets and brings up a new window. For the most part, _parent and _top work the same if you don't use nested frame sets.

Linking to frames within a frame set

With frame sets in GoLive, you don't need to open a new window to display a page you're linking to; the top set of menu options in the Text or Image Inspector lets you open the new page in any of the named frames of the current frame set. When you name a frame, that name is immediately entered into the menu set, where it's always available for use. (The number of names listed obviously depends on the number of frames you have created and named in the frame set).

Figure 9-5 shows how the sample page menu options are displayed in a pull-down menu in a Text Inspector after a link is established. In this example, the frame set has three frames named Side, Top, and Body; the target for the link from the sample page is set for Body, which means that when a viewer clicks the hot link in the sample page, the page you have set up as the target for the link appears in the frame named Body.

Up to this point in my treatment of GoLive, I've made few references to the term *target* because the default target has been the option of choice. However, with frame sets, the default is almost *never* the right choice. It would be better to select _self as the target than leave it at default (which is _self) just to stay on your toes. In pages without frame sets, the default just replaces the current page with the linked page. That works fine. But if you want to keep your page in place in a frame, you better choose a different target frame than the one the link is from or bring up a new window (_blank) for a target.

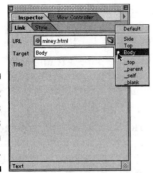

Figure 9-5:
Selections
for links
in an
Inspector.

The procedure for establishing a link in one frame and showing the linked page in another frame uses the target menu extensively. Use the following steps:

1. **Begin in the Frames Editor view of the Document Window.**

2. **Undock the Inspector by clicking on the Inspect tab at the side of the screen or choosing Window⇨Inspector.**

   The Frame Inspector appears. (If the Frame Set Inspector appears, it simply means you have one of the borders selected. Click in a frame to change it to the Frame Inspector.)

3. **Select a file icon in one of the frames on which you want to create a link.**

   A border appears around the inside of the selected frame.

4. **Either double-click the file icon (Windows or Macintosh) or select Preview Frame in the Frame Inspector (only Macintosh).**

   The selected page opens.

5. **Select the text or graphic for the hotspot for the link.**

   Keep the text or graphic selected for the rest of the operation. The Inspector becomes either the Text Inspector or the Image Inspector.

6. **Click the Link icon in the Toolbar or Text (or Image) Inspector.**

   The Link icon's symbol is two chain links.

7. **In the Text (or Image) Inspector, fill in the URL window by using the point-and-shoot button, the Browse... button or by typing in the URL address.**

   Your link is established. The links can either be internally to a file in the Site window or elsewhere on your computer, or to an external source anywhere in the world.

8. **In the Text (or Image) Inspector, pull down the menu next to the Target window.**

   Select the frame in which you want the linked page to appear from the top set of menu options. It replaces whatever page is currently in the selected frame. Usually a menu page in a narrow vertical frame is the source of the link and an adjacent larger frame is where the linked page appears. You can choose any of the selections, from the top or bottom portions of the pull-down menu.

A frame menu

Many page designers want to keep all linked pages within the confines of a frame set. The links are all on a single page that remains in a frame and new pages are displayed in one or more frames. That page is called a "menu" because it has a list of all the links. Follow these steps to make your own menu.

1. **Choose File⇨New Site⇨Blank from the menu bar.**

   The New Blank Site dialog box appears.

2. **Type a weather-related name for the site in the New Site text field; then enter a folder destination in the In Folder text field. Click OK.**

3. **When the Site window appears, click the File tab.**

   The File view of the Site window appears.

4. **Choose Window⇨Objects or undock the Objects palette by clicking the Objects tab on the side of the screen.**

   The Objects palette appears on the page.

5. **Choose Window⇨Inspector or undock the Inspector palette by clicking the Inspector tab on the side of the screen.**

   A generic Inspector appears.

6. **Click the Site tab of the Objects palette and then drag 9 Page icons (first icon on the left) from the Site tab to the Files tab of the Site Window.**

7. **Rename Index.html to Rainset.html and then name each of the other files with the following titles:**

   To rename files in the Site window, just click on the names to select them (right-click in Windows) and type in a new name.

   > Menu.html
   >
   > Weather.html
   >
   > Sunday.html
   >
   > Monday.html
   >
   > Tuesday.html

Wednesday.html

Thursday.html

Friday.html

Saturday.html

8. **Open Rainset.html from the Site Window by double-clicking on its file icon.**

    A blank page appears in the Layout view of the Document window.

9. **Click the Frame Editor tab of the Document window.**

    A blank page appears announcing, "No Frames."

10. **From the Frame tab of the Objects palette drag a two-column frame icon to the Document window.**

    The Inspector becomes the Frame Set Inspector.

11. **In the Frame Set Inspector, enter 2 for the BorderSize and click the check box next to Border Color, and then click the color well.**

    The Color palette appears.

12. **Select a bright yellow swatch from the Web Color List, third button from the right in the Color palette.**

    The color well turns bright yellow and so does the border.

13. **Set BorderFrame to No in the Frame Set Inspector.**

    You don't need no stinkin' border frame. Border frames sometimes get in the way. The bright yellow stands in for the border frame.

14. **Select the left frame of your frame set by clicking in the left frame area.**

    The Inspector becomes the Frame Inspector.

15. **Type** Menu **in the Name window of the Frame Inspector and select No from the pull-down menu.**

16. **Select the right frame by clicking in the right frame area and, in the Frame Inspector, type** Weather **in the Name window; then select Auto from the pull-down menu.**

17. **Drag the file Menu.html from the Site window into the Menu frame and the file Weather.html into the Weather frame.**

    Alternatively, you can click the point-and-shoot button to bring the files to the frames.

18. **Double-click the Menu.html file in the Menu frame to open it in the Layout view of the Document window.**

    A new Document window opens with the Menu.html page in the Layout view. The original Document window with the frame set remains on the screen. Any file in a frame set appears in the Layout view when opened from an icon in a frame. Any open Document windows stay where they are on the screen until you close them.

19. **At the top of Menu.html page, type** Select a Day **and then below type the seven days of the week, beginning with Sunday, as shown in Figure 9-6.**

    Each day of the week will become a link to a page that has that day's predicted weather.

20. **In the Layout view showing Menu.html in the Document window, drag a pale blue color from the Color palette to the Page button in the upper left-hand corner of the Layout view.**

    The menu page will now have a pale blue background.

21. **Select Sunday in Menu.html.**

    The Inspector becomes the Text Inspector.

22. **Click the Link icon on the toolbar and drag the point-and-shoot line from the Link tab of the Text Inspector to connect to the corresponding Sunday file in the Site Window.**

    As you make the link, select Weather in the Target pull-down menu of the Text Inspector. Be sure to correctly specify the target. Otherwise, the daily weather reports appear in the Menu frame, effectively knocking out the menu. (A tornado got the menu!)

23. **Repeat Steps 18 and 19 for each day of the week in Menu.html**

24. **Select the frame set Document window by clicking it and then double-click the Weather.html icon in the Weather frame to open it in the Layout view of the Document window.**

    Type a text announcement on the page telling the viewer to click the menu at the left to select the day the viewer wants to see the weather. You can either type directly on the page or, if you use the grid, type the announcement into a Text box you placed on the grid.

25. **On each of the daily files (for example, Tuesday.html, Wednesday.html), put in the predicted weather for the week.**

    Open the pages from the File tab of the Site window by double-clicking the page icon. Figure 9-7 shows a page using the menu and frame set described. (Tuesday has been selected — hope you're not having a picnic in the later afternoon!)

Frame sets themselves have no background colors. However, notice in Figure 9-4 that you can assign border colors to frame sets. Background colors, however, come from the pages loaded into the frames. Instead of using borders, you can use background colors from pages effectively to distinguish the frames in a Web page, as shown in Figure 9-8.

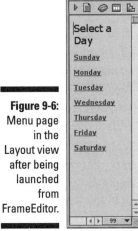

Figure 9-6:
Menu page
in the
Layout view
after being
launched
from
FrameEditor.

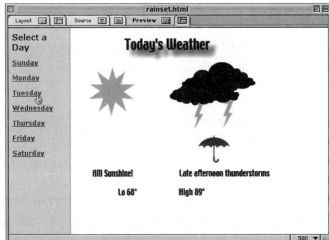

Figure 9-7:
Frame set
using a
menu frame.

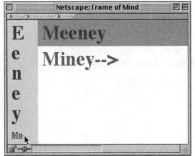

Figure 9-8:
Colors
effectively
define
frames.

Adding Frames

Adding a single frame to a frame set is deceptively easy. In looking at the different arrangements of frame sets in the Frame tab of the Objects palette, you may not see the set you want. Suppose, for example, that you want a frame set with exactly four equal frames — two rows and two columns? No such animal can be seen in the frame set icons in the Frame tab. Fear not, it's easy to fix. Here's how:

1. **Open a new page in GoLive by choosing File⇨New or by pressing Ctrl+N (Windows) or Cmd-N (Macintosh).**

   A new, untitled page appears in the Layout view. Switch to the Frame Editor view in the Document Window by clicking the Frame Editor tab (the second tab from the left).

2. **Choose Window⇨Objects or undock the Objects palette by clicking the Objects tab on the side of the screen.**

   The Objects palettes appears on the page.

3. **Click the Frames tab of the Objects palette and drag the sixth (from the left) frame set icon onto the page in the Frame Editor view.**

   Three frames appear on the page, as shown in Figure 9-9.

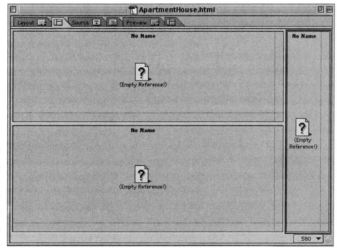

Figure 9-9:
A three-frame frame set on a page.

4. **Drag the single frame (the first one on the left) icon from the Frames tab of the Objects palette into the far left frame of the Frame Editor.**

   Four frames now appear, but they are not even. (See Figure 9-10.)

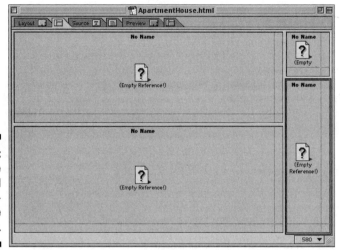

Figure 9-10:
A single
frame added
to an exist-
ing frame
set.

5. **Choose Window⇨Inspector or undock the Inspector palette by clicking the Inspector tab on the side of the screen.**

   The Inspector is on the screen.

6. **Click in one of the frames so that the Inspector becomes the Frame
   Inspector.**

7. **In the Size pull-down menu of the Frame Inspector, select Percent and
   type in 50 in the Size window in the Frame Inspector.**

   Repeat this process with all four frames until you see four equal frames,
   as shown in Figure 9-11.

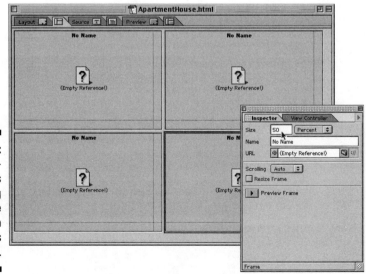

Figure 9-11:
Four equal-
size frames
set up using
the
Inspector in
the Frames
mode.

By adding additional frames and changing the frame sizes, you can come up with virtually any frame set you want. When a frame set of more than a single frame is added to a frame set on a page, it's treated as a nested frame set. You can arrange and rearrange nested frame sets by pressing Ctrl and then clicking and dragging a frame set to a different place on the page. (Remember, to move a single frame, just drag it onto the page.) So if your original frame set displeases you, just move the frames around until the frame set suits your tastes and purposes. And believe me, it's a lot easier than moving furniture.

Chapter 10

Cascading Style Sheets

• •

• •

*B*efore Cascading Style Sheets (CSS), Web page designers pulled out their hair trying to get text to behave like it does on paper. In the whole history of page design, never was there a time that limited styles and layout like the original HTML. However, with the introduction of CSS, a whole new set of possibilities opened up to designers — possibilities that GoLive makes easy to apply. Generally considered part of Dynamic HTML, Cascading Style Sheets were introduced in the fourth version of both Netscape Navigator and Microsoft Internet Explorer.

In the bad old days, Web designers had to rely on tables to do all of the formatting on Web pages. CSS eliminated this dependence on tables, thus letting designers pick and choose if (or when) they wanted to use tables for formatting. (The CSS features of GoLive, for example, don't prevent you from using tables or the Grid — actually a variant on the table form.) Using CSS, you can define entire styles quickly and easily so that if you need a purple, 15-point font in Verdana with a yellow background, all you need to do is define it and then apply it to the text. Moreover, you can indent paragraphs (just like grown-up page designers), set margins, and pretty much make text behave the way you want.

This chapter examines not only CSS, but also the great tools GoLive 5 uses to make generating CSS very simple. With the help of familiar tools like the Inspector and toolbar, you get a chance to create text on your Web page that you thought only the pros could do.

Getting Control with CSS

Style sheets, like JavaScript, are defined in the head of an HTML page. A style container <STYLE> </STYLE> demarcates the area where you place CSS code, but with GoLive, you define your style sheets in a cool CSS Selector Inspector. (Love that name — Selector Inspector.) Understanding a little about the way CSS works under the hood helps you in any tweaking you may want to do. (If you need a refresher course on HTML terminology, including words like heads, tags, and containers, check out Chapter 6.)

Before doing CSS the easy way, it helps to know what CSS looks like in the Source view or Source Code palette, just for a little context. Remember that a *container* is a set of HTML tags with a beginning and end. Anything between the tags is in the container and affected by it. The STYLE container allows you to create as much CSS as you want with different definitions. All of the style definitions are put in the page's Head area. Choose Window➪Source Code to open the Source Code palette, or in the Document window, click the Source tab to look at the code.

Redefining tag

In the <STYLE> container, you can do one of two things: redefine a tag or create a class. When you redefine a tag, your definition replaces the original definition given in HTML. For example, you can use the <A> tag, the tag reserved for links, to redefine how your links are going to look:

```
<HTML>
<HEAD>
<STYLE TYPE ="text/css">
    a {
    color: olive;
    font-family: Arial;
    text-decoration: none
     }

</STYLE>
</HEAD>
```

The redefinition of the <A> tag makes all link fonts olive in color, Arial font, and with no underline. So whenever you make a link on a page with that style definition using GoLive, you no longer get the blue underline in the current font face. For example, if you select a default colored Times font and use the Text Inspector to link it to another page, your link automatically turns the color olive, the font to Arial, and there is no sign of the underline usually associated with linked text.

After you redefine a tag, all you need to do to apply the tag's style is put text into the tag's container. Suppose, for example, that you redefined <H3> to be a purple colored font with a green background. The line,

```
<H3> I look like a grape on the grass. </H3>
```

creates the purple text on a green background. (The style code would look like — H3 { color : purple; background color: green } — in the Head area STYLE container.)

When a background color is applied with CSS, it applies only to the text in the container and not the whole page. If the <BODY> tag is redefined in CSS, the background color applies to the entire page.

Creating classes

CSS provides a way for you to better control what your text looks like. In changing a tag, you are limited to the structures HTML provides. However, CSS offers more. So besides redefining existing tags, you can create your own defining words called *classes*. Classes are used to define the font, colors, and structure of the text you put on your Web page. In defining classes, words beginning with a period (.) signal that the word will be a class — a "dot.definition." Classes are something like new style tags, but there is no need to replace an existing tag's definition. My favorite CSS class defines the text with a yellow background. In a paragraph, it makes the text stand out just like highlighted text in a book. I use it in the following demonstration of making a class.

```
<HTML>
<HEAD>
<STYLE TYPE ="text/css">
    .highlight {background-color : yellow}
</STYLE>
</HEAD>
```

Applying classes is a little trickier in HTML. The dot-defined classes need to be embedded in other tags, like <P>, or put into a <SPAN> or <DIV> container. (This is a new role for <P> that until now just created a new paragraph.) When you apply classes, the period or dot is dropped. As a general rule, use <P> or one of the <H> tags when you want to apply the class to the whole paragraph. Use <SPAN> when you want to apply it to a little part of the paragraph. For example, you would use <SPAN> when you wanted to apply CSS to a sentence in a paragraph but not the whole paragraph. The <DIV> tag is used to apply the CSS to more than a single paragraph. The following script uses both <P> and <SPAN> containers.

```
<HTML>
<HEAD>
<STYLE TYPE ="text/css">
    .backlight {background-color : black; color : white}
    .bigugly {color : purple; size : 24 pt; background-color
            : lime }
</STYLE>
</HEAD>
<Body bgcolor="white">
<P class=bigugly> This is big and ugly.</P>
Only part of this line is <SPAN CLASS=backlight> important.
        </SPAN> The rest is not.
</BODY>
</HTML>
```

Had I used a <P> or <H> instead of <SPAN>, a paragraph jump would break the line. Obviously, doing all this work in HTML may take a while, but with GoLive, it's pretty easy. However, you are provided with many options, and to get rolling on Cascading Style Sheets there's a lot to discover.

Now that you have a little background in CSS and how it works under the hood, this next section should be a relief. GoLive 5 makes it easy to create style sheets without having to enter source code. (Rats! And I wanted to enter code until I'm blue in the face.)

Making Your First Style Sheet the Easy Way

Getting a simple style sheet made in GoLive helps to see how easy it is. So follow these steps for a simple change of tags.

1. **Open a page by choosing File➪New from the menu bar or by pressing Ctrl+N (in Windows) or Cmd-O (on the Mac).**

   An untitled page appears in the Layout view of the Document window. (If it's untitled, why does it have a title, "Untitled.html"?)

2. **Choose Window➪Inspector or undock the Inspector by clicking the Inspector tab at the side of the screen.**

   The Text Inspector appears.

3. **Type "This is not a test. It's the real thing!" on the page.**

   Leave the default settings for the text, changing nothing. (I'll be looking....)

4. **In the right-hand corner of the page, click the CSS Button on the upper-right side of the Document window — it looks like a staircase.**

   The Style Sheet window opens. Notice the toolbar has changed to the CSS Toolbar. The toolbar is easy to overlook in this operation, but it's crucial to getting started with CSS in GoLive. (If the toolbar doesn't change to the CSS Toolbar, click the Style Sheet window to wake it up.)

5. **Click the Tag icon (< >) on the toolbar.**

   The Inspector changes into the CSS Selector Inspector and a new Tag icon appears in the Style Sheet window, labeled "element."

6. **Click the Basics tab of the CSS Selector Inspector (a pencil icon) and, in the Name field, replace "element" by typing H4.**

   You can put any tag you want. H4 gets ignored a lot; so I chose it.

7. **Select the Font tab (second tab from left) in the CSS Selector Inspector.**

   The tab is marked "F" for "Font." Not surprisingly the CSS Selector Inspector provides you with several font options. Read on!

8. **Pull down the menu next to the Color window of the Font tab and select maroon.**

   You will see 16 named colors. Maroon is a nice color for this demonstration. (Okay, pick Fuchsia if you must!)

9. **Pull down the menu next to the Size window of the Font tab and select xx-large.**

   You are presented with 20 different font-measuring units. Use any that you want. I chose xx-large because I want you to see that the H4 size will not be what is was before you used CSS to change it. That's it. You've completed transforming a tag. If you click the Basic tab (the pencil icon one) of the CSS Selector Inspector now, you see the code generated for the new tag. The CSS Window closes automatically when you go on to some other task — just click the page.

10. **Select the text you typed onto your original page and select Header 4 from the Paragraph Format pull-down menu on the left side of the toolbar.**

    A large maroon message appears on the page.

You've only scratched the proverbial surface of CSS, but you can see how powerful it is.

The CSS Selector Inspector and CSS Toolbar appear and disappear between visits to the page. Whenever you select text to try out your new CSS, the Inspector turns into the Text Inspector. To get the CSS Selector Inspector back, you need to click the CSS button — the little staircase in the upper-right-hand corner of the document window. (The CSS Selector Inspector can be an elusive little bugger.)

Discovering the CSS Window, Toolbar, and Style Tab

Getting the CSS button to perform a few simple tricks for you is relatively easy, but if you really want to unleash the true power of CSS, you may want to familiarize yourself with all the options available for CSS in GoLive. To do that, you need to take a closer look at the CSS Selector Inspector as well as the Style Sheet window and CSS Toolbar.

The Style Sheet Window and the CSS Toolbar are fairly simple, but you do need to keep an eye on them and know how to use them if you want them to work effectively with CSS. At this point, you need only concern yourself with classes and tags on the Style Sheet window, and the corresponding icons on the toolbar. IDs, the other option in the Style Sheet window and on the toolbar, are similar to both tags and classes in setup and applications, but they require a little coding. (See the section, "ID, Please" to find out how to use them.)

To get CSS going in GoLive, click the CSS button to open the Style Sheet Window and then add new classes and tag definitions by selecting the Tag (< >) or Class (()) icons on the CSS Toolbar. Classes and tags are named in the Name window of the CSS Selector Inspector. Figure 10-1 combines two screen shots to show how a new class is created as soon as you select the Class icon on the CSS Toolbar. The new class shows up on the Style Sheet Window, the CSS Selector Inspector and in the Style tab of the Text Inspector. (The Inspector cannot be in the Text mode and CSS selector mode at the same time, but to see the connections in CSS the two screen shots have been arranged in the same space so that they appear simultaneously.)

As soon as the designer in the CSS Inspector Selector has defined the tag or class, those changes are echoed in the other Style Tab of the Text Inspector and the Basics tab of the Style Sheet Window. It's important to remember that your selection on the CSS Toolbar sets the sequence in motion. Once defined, by selecting text and using the Style tab of the Text Inspector, you can use the new class or tag to apply the style.

After you're comfortable with the idea that the CSS development sequence begins with the CSS Toolbar, much of the rest is pretty straightforward. So the next step is to look at all the options available on the CSS Inspector Selector.

Inspector in Text mode

Inspector in CSS Selector mode

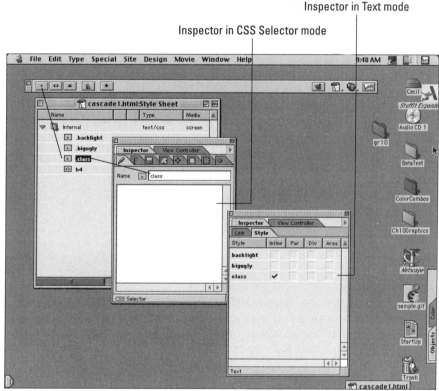

Figure 10-1:
The CSS
tools work
together to
create
Cascading
Style
Sheets.

Modify Your Fonts

The Font tab, the second tab from the left on the CSS Inspector Selector, automatically generates CSS code for the many combinations of options GoLive
makes available for fonts. The following list focuses on each option:

- **Color:** The sixteen choices of color in the pop-up menu echo those of
  the W3C (World Wide Web Consortium), but you need not limit yourself
  to those. Click on the Color well in the Fonts tab to open the Color
  palette and choose any color you want from the Color palette.

- **Size:** Font size is a bit tricky because you have so many options. Unlike
  standard HTML where a few sizes fit all, Cascading Style Sheets provide
  font measurements in picas and points as well as other units of measurement. Use any of the units you want or a combination in your sheets.

- ✔ **Line height:** This dimension is something like leading in traditional line distance measurement. Leading refers to the amount of space between lines. Only new lines receive the values in line height, though. Wrap around lines are automatically determined by the font size, but when a new line is created by a carriage return, CSS applies the line height. (In the old days before computers, they added extra lead between lines to control vertical line spacing of type; hence the word, *leading*.) However, on the Web it's useful to select a percent so that the line differences look good on different size browser windows and monitors.

- ✔ **Font window:** Directly below the Font Family window is a Font window. Click the New button, and then you can type in the name of the font or click the pull-down menu (up/down arrow icon above the New button) to select the font you want from the menu. Below the Font window is another pull-down menu that shows the existing font families you defined. Whichever combination you select becomes part of the CSS font family for the current definition.

- ✔ **Style:** The font's style options are limited to unchanged, italic, oblique, or normal. Italic and oblique are similar in their appearance on the Web.

- ✔ **Weight:** The weight of a font pretty much refers to how bold it is. In the old days, if more ink were applied to a font, it weighed more. No color or tint change makes it "heavier." This option thickens the appearance of a font. Beside the normal and bold weights, there is a range from 100 to 900 and relative weights of lighter and bolder. Some of the variations of weights may not show up on your browser, so you'll have to check to make sure how the weights show up on the different browsers.

- ✔ **Decoration:** The decoration options include none (my favorite), underline (usually used for links), strike, overline, and blink (a conspiracy to drive us all mad).

After you name your class or tag, put some text on your page and select it. Apply the class or tag to the text by selecting the Style tab of the Text Inspector and then clicking on the style you want. Open the Style Sheet window to initiate the CSS Selector Inspector again and continue making changes. As you add and make changes to the class or tag, you can see them taking place in the selected text on the page. This technique enables you to get a better idea of what your CSS definitions look like and reduces development time.

Style Your Text

After you create a new class by clicking the class icon on the Style Sheet toolbar, you can do some interesting things with the text. Select the Text tab (third from left) of the CSS Selector Inspector and prepare to make your blocks of text do your bidding. The options available are as follows:

✔ **Text indent:** Instead of using block text (unindented paragraphs) or   (code used to create a blank space in HTML), you can simply and cleanly indent text. I generally use one em space for an indent, but you can choose from point, pica, pixel, ex, millimeter, centimeter, inch, percentage, or normal. (For HTML, normal means "do nothing.") In building text blocks, the indent is a wonderful addition to HTML page design because it's automatic for the whole paragraph. In pages with lots of text, the paragraph indent sure beats block upon block of text.

✔ **Word spacing:** As with text indent, you have several measures from which to choose, but I leave it unchanged or normal. If there's a problem with the spaces between words, select your favorite measure and make the necessary changes. Word spacing can come in handy when you're designing interesting headers.

✔ **Letter spacing:** For headers and special effects, putting spaces between letters can really make your page look great. For those who insist on using ALL CAPS to decrease communication, readability, and good sense, there's hope. Try dropping some extra letter spacing between ALL CAP (if you must) and some word spacing as well. Figure 10-2 shows a line of text in all caps (Top line) and one with 1ex space (the width of the letter "x" in a font) between letters and words.

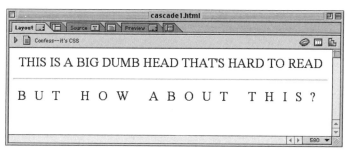

Figure 10-2:
Use of word and letter spacing in CSS.

✔ **Vertical alignment:** Vertical alignment sets the selected text higher or lower relative to the paragraph. Several options are available here, but be sure to try them out in different browsers to see what you get. For example, the sub (subscript) and sup (superscript) often don't appear in a browser; so if you use them, try and do it so that words like 1st and H2O are clear enough to understand even if the subscript or superscript formatting doesn't make it through a viewer's browser.

✔ **Font variant:** Only three exist: unchanged, small caps, and normal. Normal is the default font, while unchanged makes no changes in the current font's variant, if it has one. All this selection does is provide small caps as a variant for adding interest to a font. Small caps require Internet Explorer 5 (IE5) or Netscape Navigator 6 (NN6) or later.

- ✔ **Transformation:** The transformation option changes any text into one of three types: initial capitals (good for headers); all uppercase; or all lowercase.

- ✔ **Alignment:** CSS provides four alignments: left, center, right, and justified. Most browsers don't yet support justified text, but if CSS standards are met, they soon should.

GoLive's Preview mode may be overly generous when it comes to displaying some CSS features. In testing what shows in the Preview mode against what the browser shows, I find that the preview in GoLive shows both spacing and vertical alignment differently in the Preview mode than in the browser window. However, the Preview doesn't display small caps even though IE5 and NN6 do. Test it in the browsers before you put it on the Web!

Adjusting Blocks

The Block tab, the fourth tab from the left on the CSS Selector Inspector, works *something* like the `<BLOCKQUOTE>` tag, but as with everything else in CSS, you have far more control. The tag indents a block of text in the `<BLOCKQUOTE>` container, and each nested container indents the text block one more tab. The `<BLOCKQUOTE>` groups text into blocks with a common indent. In HTML each instance of the `<BLOCKQUOTE>` tab indents the block one more tab.

- ✔ **Margin:** The first four cells of the margin column set the text a specified number of units, or percentage of page, from each of the four sides of a box. A left margin of 10 pixels, for example, would set the text 10 pixels in from the side. The fifth window sets all the four margins to either multiple or specified number of units inside an invisible margin box.

- ✔ **Padding:** The padding sets the text in the specified number of units in from the border set up by the margin. Imagine a box with a specified margin around it. Inside the margin is a visible border. The offset inside the border is the padding.

- ✔ **Block:** The block elements set the outside boundaries and elements as a floating box. The Float setting from the pulldown menu gives options for wrapping text left and right, unchanged, or none. Practice with all of the block elements to get your text groupings looking the way you want on the page. (Floating boxes are independent blocks of text and graphics that can be moved on a page — they "float" to different positions. Chapter 16 describes how to work with these dynamic features.)

Stating Your Position

The parameters of the Position tab (the fifth tab from the left on the CSS Selector Inspector) apply to floating elements, primarily floating boxes. Floating boxes are like little Web pages that float around the main Web page. (The term *layers* is used, also.) Select text in an existing style sheet, fill in the positioning properties, and the text is gathered into a floating box. Imagine all of the position properties in terms of a smaller window superimposed on the Document window. The position of the box is relative to the top and left side of the window. So, for example, a position of 200 (left) and 500 (top) places the floating box 500 pixels from the top of the window and 200 pixels from the left side. The clipping properties refer to how the text and other objects in the floating box are to be cropped, scrolled, or wrapped. Chapter 16 fully covers floating boxes and their properties.

Picking a Border

Borders are visual boxes of color surrounding text. As with using the <BLINK> tag, you can ruin a good page easily by using the wrong border with CSS. However, used judiciously, text borders can make your page stand out just right. The Border tab (the sixth tab from the left on the CSS Selector Inspector) contains the following three columns:

- **Border width:** You can specify width of the four borders individually by typing in the first four fields or for the whole border by entering changes in the fifth field. Measure borders in point, pica, pixel, em (same as em dash), ex (width of letter "x"), mm, cm, or inch. Or, you can just select thin, medium, or thick.

- **Color:** The center column determines color. Drag and drop colors from the Color Palette or select one of the colors in the pop-up menu. Just for the fun of it, try using a different color for each side of the border.

- **Line style:** Save on graphic lines and choose from dotted, dash, solid, double, groove, ridge, and inset or outset style lines for your borders. Any box that you can create by using a graphic tool you can also create with the border. (Well, almost.)

Doing a Background Check

Background control in CSS far exceeds the background color or image available to define an entire page. When you select the Background tab (the seventh tab from the left in the CSS Selector Inspector), not only can you decide which background image you want, you decide which way you want it to tile!

Chapter 7 shows how to add background color and images to your page as a whole. CSS, however, allows you to add a background image to any selected text on the page. So if you want a single character on your page with a unique background image, you can do it! Here are the options:

- **Background image:** Add your background image as you would on a page by using the Page icon and Page Inspector as discussed in Chapter 7. The image you choose shows up only on the portion of the page you defined with the CSS tag or class. Simply choose the background image in the CSS Selector Inspector either by using the point and shoot line (as described in Chapter 2), by clicking the Browse button or by simply dragging the file from the Site window to the Background Image window.

- **Color:** Either choose from the 16 colors in the pull-down menu or grab your favorite color from the Color palette and drop it in the color box. Or, just click the Color well in the CSS Selector Inspector to choose the color you want from the Color palette.

- **Repeat:** The Repeat window refers to repeating a background image. The Repeat selection treats the background image like a normal background image on the page. Select Repeat x to repeat the tile horizontally and Repeat y for a vertical tile of your background image.

- **Attached:** The background image can either scroll or stay put (fixed).

- **Top:** Number of units the background image is from the top of the text block.

- **Left:** Distance the background image is from the left of the text block.

Loving Those Lists

If you use lists in your HTML, you'll be delighted to learn that you can change both bullets and numbers — including ones you make yourself. The List and Other Properties tab, the last tab on the right of the CSS Selector Inspector, lets you customize your lists and get ready for future browsers that implement new CSS properties. Look at everything you can do on this tab:

- **Bullet Image:** Make a little red heart GIF (one of the Web-safe graphics file formats), drop it into the Image window and send a Valentine list to your sweetie! Those dots, circles and squares get boring.

- **Style:** Change the boring dots to boring discs or squares! Choose your style based on your page design.

- **Position:** This is cool. Put the bullet on the left or the right of the text in the list.

✔ **Other Property:** This is the CSS wish list. Visit `www.w3c.org` to look at the options available for CSS that have not yet been implemented on the browsers. For example, text-shadow promises to provide a shadow with colors. Figure 10-3 shows how to put an as-yet-undeveloped option into a style sheet. You just write it in, and if the feature is implemented in a browser, it shows up on the Web page in the browser. (Be realistic about using this feature. If a property has not been implemented, the chances of people seeing it on your page aren't so hot.)

Figure 10-3:
Placing future CSS options in the CSS Selector Inspector.

Applying Style Sheets to Your Page

Applying CSS styles to your Web page is simple. In fact, I find it less difficult than wandering through all the formatting menus in the Menu bar. So, after you've created your own style sheets, getting them on your Web pages is a snap. Follow these steps:

1. **Open a page by choosing File⇨New from the menu bar or by pressing Ctrl+N (in Windows) or Cmd-O (on the Mac).**

   An untitled page appears in the Layout view of the Document window.

2. **Type** This is genuine CSS formatted text **on the page.**

   The text line is simply something to select. You can write anything you want.

3. **Create some style sheets by following the steps in the section, "Making Your First Style Sheet the Easy Way."**

   Use as many options as you want. Start by creating something simple such as a class that generates a big colored font, or change a tag so that the text has a colored background.

4. **Choose Window⇨Inspector or undock the Inspector by clicking the Inspector tab at the side of the screen.**

   The Inspector appears.

5. **Select the text on the screen.**

   The Inspector becomes the Text Inspector.

6. **Click the Style tab on the Text Inspector.**

   The Style tab appears. The Style column lists the names of the various styles you have created; the Inline, Paragraph, Division, and Area columns (with their check boxes) let you control what portion of your Web page gets the new style.

7. **Check the Inline box for one of the styles.**

   Kazaam! Your text changes to the style sheet you created.

Besides Inline, other options are available in the Style tab of the Text Inspector. Read on to see how to use each one.

Inline

When you need to apply CSS to a little part of your paragraph, a single word, or even a single letter, select Inline. The HTML tag <SPAN> provides the container.

Paragraph

You can paint an entire paragraph with CSS. Select text in the paragraph and check the Par. column. In HTML the `<P>` provides the parameters.

Division

Selecting the Div column provides CSS effects over all the text in the DIV block. Not surprisingly the `<DIV>` tag provides the container in HTML for this selection. If you select the Div column, GoLive sets up the `<DIV>` tags in the HTML for the selected area automatically. So when you select a block of text for CSS and select the Div column, GoLive effectively creates a Div container. However, if you select some of the text in the Div container, and de-select the CSS style, the selected text only is removed from the Div container.

Body (Area)

To affect the whole page, check in the Area column. The CSS is placed in the `<BODY>` tag in HTML.

Varying Style Sheets

Suppose that you want to use two different style sheets on the same text. Is it possible? Yes! Not only can you use more than a single style on selected text, you can use more than a single Style column selection. For example, suppose that you want part of a paragraph in reverse text (white text on a black background), but you want the entire paragraph in a big font. No problem. Just select text and check the boxes in the Text Inspector's Style tab as shown in Figure 10-4.

Figure 10-4:
Select more than one style at the same time.

You can cause conflict if you use two styles with different properties. For example if one style defines the text color as red and another style applied to the same text defines the text color as purple, you have a conflict. Such conflicts are especially evident in cases where the different levels of the page (such as Inline or Paragraph) are selected to be styled. However, CSS wisely gives the smaller level precedence over the larger level. Therefore, Inline takes precedence over Paragraph, Paragraph over Division, and Division over Area.

External Style Sheets

After you go to the considerable work of creating the style sheet you want, you probably don't want to repeat the process for every page in the Web site. Fortunately, GoLive provides an easy way to store all of the style sheets in files that you can use on the page as external file sheets. Not only do external style sheets relieve your burden of redoing the work, you can use a single style sheet in as many pages as you want. And because you save external style sheets as .css files on your system, you can use them again on other sites.

When you create a style sheet in GoLive, CSS script is generated automatically and put into the HTML tags in the Head area of the page. With external style sheets, there is a single tag line that calls up all of the styles created on the external sheet. You can save a single style in one .css file or several. A .css file is a text file with all the CSS information to format the material on your page, and you can use it on any page in any site.

Creating external style sheets

The first step is to create an external .css file. The process is exactly the same as discussed above for creating style sheet, but you have a couple of extra steps to preserve the style sheet in a file. Here's how:

1. **Open the Site Window and Layout view of the Document Window active.**

   The Layout view and page should be on top of the Site window.

2. **Choose File⇨New Special⇨ Style Sheet Document.**

   An untitled Style Sheet window appears. Click it to activate the CSS Toolbar. This is the crucial step for creating external style sheets.

3. **Click the class, tag, or ID button on the toolbar to get started creating as few or as many tags, classes, and IDs as you want.**

   Use the same techniques for creating classes and tags as discussed above in this chapter beginning with the section "Discovering the CSS Window, Toolbar, and Style Tab". See the section, "ID, Please" later in this chapter, to find out how to create IDs.

4. **Choose File⇨Save or press Ctr+S (Windows) or Cmd-S (Macintosh).**

   A special Save CSS dialog box appears, as well as a pull-down menu in the upper-right corner of the screen.

5. **Click the arrow near the top of the dialog box to scroll through the menu and select Root Folder to open your site's main folder, as shown in Figure 10-5.**

   The other selections in the pull-down menu are Stationeries and Components. Ignore them.

6. **Click the Save button after making sure you included the name of the file in the Save As window at the bottom of the dialog box.**

   Double-check to make sure you leave the ".css" extension on the file name you use. (See Figure 10-5.)

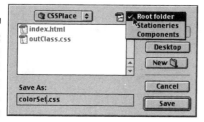

Figure 10-5:
Saving
external
cascading
style sheet.

Using external style sheets

After you save an external style sheet to the root folder of your site, you can use it whenever you want. (It's important to get the external file into the root folder of your site so that it can appear in the Files tab of your Site window.) Follow these steps to get your text wearing the latest external style sheet — straight from Paris:

1. **Open the Site Window and in the Files tab double click a page icon to launch it into the Layout view of the Document Window.**

   The Layout view and page should be on top of the Site window.

2. **Choose Window⇨Inspector or undock the Inspector by clicking the Inspector tab at the side of the screen.**

   The Text Inspector appears.

3. **Click the CSS Button (it looks like a staircase) on the upper right corner of the Layout view of the Document window.**

   The toolbar changes to the CSS Toolbar and the Style Sheet window opens.

4. **Click the New Item icon on the CSS Toolbar (it's the one that looks like a staircase).**

   A Page icon labeled (Empty Reference!), a Warning icon, and an External Folder icon appear in External Style Sheet Window. The Inspector becomes the External Style Sheet Inspector, and (Empty Reference!) appears in the link box, along with the Browse and the Point-and-Shoot button.

5. **From the External Style Sheet Inspector, drag the point-and-shoot line to select the external style sheet file from the Site window, as shown in Figure 10-6.**

   Remember, the external style sheet file has a **.css** extension.

Voila! You've done it. You now have an external style sheet in your page. So now your are ready to use your external style sheet. Just select the text, click the Style tab of your Text Inspector, and you will see your external style listed. Figure 10-7 shows plain vanilla text transformed into a reverse pattern (light text on a dark background) by an external Cascading Style Sheet.

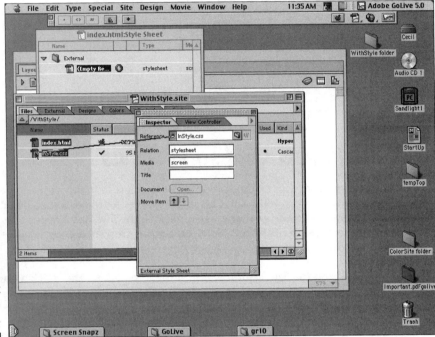

Figure 10-6:
Importing an
External
Style Sheet
file into a
page.

ID, Please

IDs are a special type of CSS used for a limited and unique kind of style sheet. When you require special formatting for a small part of your page for a dramatic effect, IDs can produce the appropriate style. (There's no style you can produce with IDs that can't be done with classes, but IDs don't show up in the Text Inspector's Style tab because they are for very limited use.) Unlike tags and classes, you have to go into the Source view and get your hands dirty in code! You create IDs just as you create classes only you start by selecting the ID (#) symbol from the CSS Toolbar instead of the class icon (•). IDs, though, are for limited use. For example, Figure 10-7 shows a background splitting a line of text using IDs. Use the following steps to see how easy it is to create your own ID.

1. **Open a new page by selecting File⇨New from the menu bar.**

   The Layout view and page should are on your screen.

2. **Choose Window⇨Inspector or undock the Inspector by clicking the Inspector tab at the side of the screen.**

   The Text Inspector appears.

3. **Click the CSS Button (it looks like a staircase) on the upper right corner of the Layout view of the Document window.**

   The toolbar changes to the CSS Toolbar and the Style Sheet window opens.

4. **Click the ID icon on the CSS Toolbar (it's the one that looks like tic-tac-toe — #).**

   A new #ID appears in the CSS Selector Inspector. Give it a name, but leave the pound sign (#) were it is. You might name it #Henry or #Shift or whatever you want as long as you keep the pound sign in place.

5. **Create a Cascading Style Sheet using the techniques discussed above in this chapter.**

   Use the same techniques for creating classes and tags as discussed above in this chapter beginning with the section "Discovering the CSS Window, Toolbar, and Style Tab."

6. **Select File⇨Save or use Ctrl+S (Windows) or Cmd-S (Macintosh) to save your page to your disk drive.**

   In the directory window, click the disk and directory you want to save your file in and give it a name with the .html extension.

You have now created a Cascading Style Sheet ID. The next step is putting the ID to work on your page. The following section explains how to do so.

I'm not crazy about using IDs because ambiguities exist in CSS specifications for their use. About the only thing I find them somewhat helpful for is making unusual formatting that's used once in a site and, because the IDs are not stored on the Style tab of the Text Inspector, I won't accidentally click the unusual style when using the Style tab instead of a commonly used one. IDs require hand coding (see below) to insert them into a page. For the most part, I use classes or tags with CSS and don't bother with IDs.

Putting IDs into a page

After you define and name an ID in the CSS Selector Inspector, you can put it into your HTML. Doing that requires opening the Source View of the Document Window or using the Source Code palette and typing in the ID and associated tags. The simple <P> tag is used in the following example. The following lines of HTML show how two IDs are used together to create a line of text split by a color block. Your CSS Window has a list of all the IDs you created.

```
<P id="topdog">   </P>
<P id="underdog"> Split Line </P>
```

When GoLive generates the CSS code in an ID, it precedes the name of the ID with a pound (#) sign. However, when you place the ID in a paragraph, drop the pound sign. Optionally, use double quotation marks around the tag names in containers, as shown in Figure 10-7.

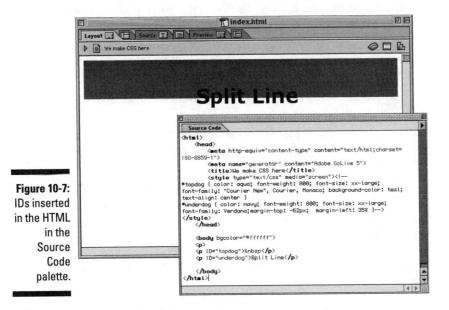

Figure 10-7: IDs inserted in the HTML in the Source Code palette.

Previewing CSS

As time goes by, fewer and fewer people are going to be using their Civil War era browsers (for example, Version 3 and earlier) and previewing pages containing CSS will not be as critical. However, for the time being, what you see in GoLive may not be what you expect. To prepare for different views of your page using CSS, check out the page with the different browsers *and* different versions of the Browsers. Version 5 of Internet Explorer and Version 6 of Netscape Navigator (remember Netscape went from NN4 to NN6 and skipped NN5) handle CSS pretty well and similarly. However, check with *some* of the earlier versions of both major browsers and Windows and Macintosh platforms.

Some designers are putting in messages indicating that older browsers will not be able to see many of the features of the Web sites they create. (Come on guys! Browsers are free!) Using CSS is becoming less and less of a problem as users adopt the latest versions of browsers. While designers are encouraged to keep in mind that older systems and browsers may not see the updated elements in newer browsers, there's a limit. If you try to appeal to the guy with a computer whose system runs on charcoal briquettes instead of electricity, you may lose the rest of the audience who is expecting more interesting Web designs and sites.

If you experiment enough with CSS, you can create some great-looking headers, styles, backgrounds, and other effects without having to import graphics into a Web page. There's nothing wrong with graphics, but compared to CSS, they're slower to load and can actually be more time-consuming going from page to page.

Part III

A Site for Sore Eyes: Caring, Feeding, and Organization of Web Sites

The 5th Wave   By Rich Tennant

PLEASE

NO WEB PAGE

In this part . . .

Part III shows you how to rule the world and then clone it! Taming a Web site used to be about as easy as herding cats, but you're going to have those sites as docile as a flock of sheep. In this part, the World Wide Web is at your beck and call because you find out how to use GoLive 5's considerable power to organize pages in a site and keep them that way on your desktop and on a server as well. What's more, you can see how to clone your work so that when you develop a great site component or template, you can stash it where you can bring it out and use it again and again. Find out how to put up your Web site on a server and then make changes to it. GoLive 5 makes it all behave!

With GoLive 5's new Design window, you can style your sites with all different types of arrangements. After you get the one you want, GoLive 5 automatically turns a set of pending icons into a set of pages ready and organized for content, sitting right in front of you in the Site window. With the Navigation window, you can globally change pages and images so that daily, weekly, or monthly updates of your site are a piece of cake rather than a tangle of Web pages.

Ever create a really great page, and you wish you could do other pages in your site almost the same without having to start over? Using GoLive 5's stationeries and components, you can have little icons stored in your site totally recreate an entire page or an essential component (like your graphical navigation system) just by using the drag and drop feature.

Finally, Part III tells you everything you need to know about using GoLive 5's great File Transfer Protocol (FTP), built right into the Site window. When you're ready to post your site on the Web, you just give GoLive your host's URL, your ID and password, and GoLive does the rest. You can send your entire site with a single click of the mouse, and when it comes time to update your site, GoLive knows which pages have been changed and which haven't, and it just sends those pages with changes. Talk about saving time and sanity . . . .

Chapter 11

The Site Window of Opportunity

● ●

In This Chapter

▶ Designing your site

▶ Looking at the site files

▶ Generating a table of contents

▶ Making global changes

▶ Reorganizing existing sites

▶ Organizing external links

▶ Site color control and inspection

▶ Organizing fonts for a site

▶ Cleaning up your site

▶ Getting site statistics

● ●

*C*hapter 4 introduces the many and varied ways to deal with links in GoLive and how to use the Site window to help with your links. This chapter extends your understanding of the Site window and tells you how to get total control of your site.

GoLive 5 not only helps you design your site, it provides assistance in maintaining it as well. The new Design window and tab in the Site window provide a way of "blueprinting" your site and developing your pages and their hypothetical links before you put in actual links. You can build and name all your pages in the Design window, and then *submit* them so that they exist on your Site window before you add content. The term "submit" is used in a special way in the Design window. *Submit* means to transform the design into actual pages available in the Files tab of the Site window.

After your site is designed and implemented, it need not be a chore to change it periodically or fix it when needed. This chapter shows you how you can make changes that affect *all of the pages in your site*. Suppose, for example, that you have a graphic logo on all the pages in the site. Then you find a great new logo that you want to put on all your pages. With GoLive, all you need to do is to make one change and all of the old images are replaced with the new one. It doesn't matter if you have 10 or 100 pages; with just one change, all the pages are changed.

For a site to look like a site and not an odd collection of pages, you need to think in terms of common design features. This chapter shows you how using the Site window can help you coordinate many of the common design elements that go into your Web site. For example, a color scheme and choice of fonts tell the viewer whether your page is serious, playful, businesslike, or even bizarre. If you try to gather up design elements page by page, not only are you going to be in for more work, you're less likely to have a consistent design. So let's get lazy and deal with the site the easy way with GoLive 5.

Designing Your Site

In Chapter 3, I suggest that you get some graph paper and outline your site, including all the links and pages, as a first step in designing your site. Now, however, I introduce you to a new GoLive 5 feature that may make the paper step unnecessary and further increase your ability to create great Web sites. The new feature resides in the Design tab and menu bar of the Site window. Here's how it works:

1. **Create a new site by choosing File⇨New Site⇨Blank or by pressing Alt+Ctrl+N (Windows) or Option-Cmd-N (Macintosh) and give it a name in the Create New Site dialog box.**

   A new Site window appears. You don't need to do anything in the Document window or Layout view to create several Web pages and a Site outline.

2. **Choose Window⇨View Controller or undock the View Controller by clicking the View Controller tab at the side of the screen.**

   The View Controller (along with its roommate the Inspector) appears on the screen.

3. **Click the Designs tab of the Site window.**

   An empty Designs tab appears.

4. **Choose Design⇨New Site Design from the menu bar.**

   An Untitled Design icon appears on the Design tab of the Site window.

5. **Click the file to select it and then rename it (Macintosh) or right-click the icon and select Rename (Windows).**

   The name of the design need not be the same name as the site. In fact, using different names is a good idea so that you can try out several different designs and not confuse them.

6. **Double-click the Design icon in the Designs tab of the Site window.**

   An empty Design window appears.

7. **Click the Files tab of the Site window and drag the file index.html to the Design window.**

   A Design icon appears in the Design window with an anchor next to it and a point-and-shoot button on or below the icon. (Depending on what kind of design icon you use, the point-and-shoot button is either on or below the icon.) To change the icon's appearance, select the radio buttons in the Display tab of the View Controller. I prefer the oval shape in the Design window to distinguish it from the Navigation and Links view windows. See Figure 11-1.

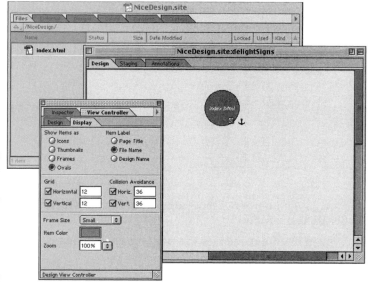

Figure 11-1:
The Design window after dragging the index.html page into it.

The first page the viewer sees is the *anchor page.* In the context of designing a site, the anchor page establishes a point in the site hierarchy. With either the entire site or a portion of the site, the anchor page typically sits at the top of the hierarchy. It can be an entry page into the site, a home page, a core page, or some key page in a section of the site. However, you *do* need an anchor page in the design for later transition into live pages, as I discuss in the section, "Submitting a site."

Adding pages to the design

Okay, now that you've got your anchor page, it's time to add new pages. Adding new pages to a Design window is a little different than adding pages to the Site window from the Files tab. The pages you add are planning pages. They are not real pages that are part of your site yet, but rather *pending* pages that you work with, adding and deleting, until you get the site organization you want. You can see what your pages look like and get a look and feel for how the site will flow before actually adding new pages and links. The process is something like sketching a design on paper before you actually put the pages and links in place. They're not real pages, just a mock up of what you *may* want to put into your site. Later, you find out how to turn the mock-ups into actual web pages. (Try that with graph paper!) Here's how to add pages, picking up from the previous six steps in the last section.

1. **Select Design⇨New Pages from the menu bar.**

   The New Pages dialog box appears. (See Figure 11-2.)

Figure 11-2: Add pages and pending links to design in the New Pages dialog box.

2. **Type in the number of new pages you want in the Number of Pages to Create text window.**

3. **Type in the file names for the pages in the Filenames window.**

   The Filenames window generates a series of names beginning with the name you put in the window. For example, I enter name "Jeans" and GoLive 5 generates Jeans.html, Jeans1.html, Jeans2.html, and so on up to the number of pages you want to create. (See Figure 11-3.)

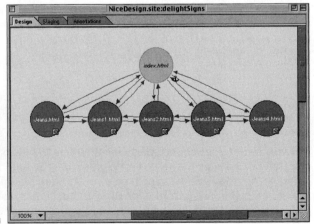

Figure 11-3: Pages added to the Design tab of the Design window.

4. **In the Generate Links section of the New Pages dialog box, select the type of link arrangements you want from the pull-down menus and then click the Create button.**

   First, in the Parent menu (refer to Figure 11-2), select either to link to each child, to each child and back, to the first child only, or none. Next, from the Sibling menu, select the pending links either to be to the adjacent sibling or none. You also have the option of using Stationery (pre-made page designs you have stored as stationery) or making the parent a section. A child refers to a page directly below the current page in the hierarchy, a sibling refers to a page on the same level in the hierarchy, and a parent is a page above the current page in the hierarchy. The hierarchy is a sequence of pages with the top being the first page that is viewed. When pages are on the same level of a hierarchy (siblings) they can be selected in no special order by the page or pages before them in the hierarchy since they reside in the same level. A parent page is a page that precedes the current page.

After you add new pages, each gets a name and Point-and-Shoot button. Figure 11-3 shows the pages you created by using the options in the New Pages dialog box.

You can add pages to your design easily by clicking one of the Add Page icons on the Design toolbar. An untitled page appears. However, I like choosing Design⇨New Pages from the menu bar, even if I'm adding a single page. As soon as you add a single page or multiple pages, name them. Naming a page right away helps you see what the page does. More importantly, there's no need to waste time later finding the page and renaming it. Choosing Design⇨ New Pages (not New Page) is the only way to name your page or pages immediately. By doing so, later on when she is attempting to remember what a page is supposed to do in relationship to other pages in the site, she won't be lost.

Adding pending links and annotations

The Point-and-Shoot buttons on the Page icons in the Design window exist to help you make any additional pending links you may want. For example, in Figure 11-3, if you wanted to create a link between **Jeans4.html** and **Jeans1.html,** you would pull a point-and-shoot line from **Jean4.html** over to **Jeans1.html.**

A more interesting feature of the Design window is its annotations. While building a design, you may have a special comment for a page or a link. Use the annotations feature to remind yourself why a particular link or page is important, unique, or just to insert a comment. (See the sections, "Designing Your Site," and "Adding pages to the design," earlier in this chapter.) Follow these steps to use annotations:

1. **Select Window⇨Objects or undock the Objects palette by clicking on the Objects tab at the side of the screen.**

   The Objects palette appears on the screen.

2. **Select the Site tab in the Objects palette and drag a Design Annotation icon onto a link or page in the Design window.**

   When the Design Annotation icon is properly positioned over the page or link, you see a "halo" effect. The pages get an outer ring around them, and the link arrows get fuzzy and wide. A yellow icon appears. Keep it selected.

3. **Select Window⇨Inspector or undock the Inspector palette by clicking the Inspector tab at the side of the screen.**

   The Inspector appears as the Annotation Inspector.

4. **Type in the Subject and Text of the annotation you want to make and click the Display Subject and Display Text check boxes at the bottom of the Inspector.**

   Your annotation now appears on the link or file you selected in the Design window. If you want to reposition the Text and Subject, use the Position pull-down menu at the bottom of the Annotation Inspector. (See Figure 11-4.) You also find that your annotations are now stored in the Annotations tab of the Design window.

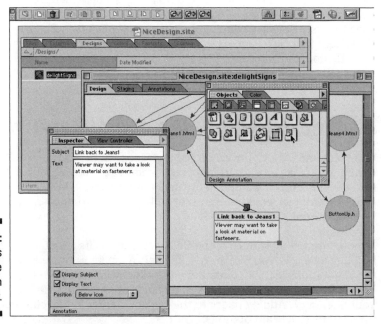

Figure 11-4:
Annotations added in the Design window.

If you want to remove any of the pending links or pages, just select the Page icon or Link Arrow line and click the Trash Can icon on the toolbar. Notice that when you select an arrow link, a little box appears in the middle of the line. You can drag the link to bow the Link Arrow to more clearly see the pending links between the pages.

If you're working on a big site, the Page icons can scroll off the screen and you end up pumping the scroll bars to see what you want. Clicking the Design tab of the View Controller when a design icon is selected lets you use a panoramic view to see where you are in relationship to the other pages in the design. Just select the Panorama check box and a red rectangle appears in a new pane in the Design window. Drag the rectangle around the page to effectively "back away" from the design elements and see more of them in a single pane. You can get the same effect, but in a smaller window, by selecting Window⇨Site Navigator to open the Site Navigator palette. Using the slider on the Site Navigator, you can zoom in and zoom out and move the red rectangle to adjust what you see in the Design window.

Submitting a site

Suppose that you complete your design, your pending links are dandy, the annotations make everything clear, and now you want to apply your design to your Site window. Remember that you're not dealing with real pages yet. You're just examining some designs. If you click the Staging tab of your Design window, you see all of the pages in the Design Pages folder, as shown in the left window of Figure 11-5. Design pages are like blueprints. The concept exists, but nothing is concrete yet. When you submit a design, you turn your design pages into live pages. All the live pages are shifted into the Live Pages folder in the Staging tab of the Design window. More importantly, the pages now appear in the Files tab of the Site window. That means they're all set for you to work with. Follow these next steps in creating a site design to turn your design into a set of pages you can begin filling with content and links.

1. **With the Design window on the screen, click the Check Design icon on the toolbar or choose Design⇨Design Staging⇨Check Design from the menu bar.**

   GoLive checks to make sure that all the pages are linked to an anchor page and no problems exist with files or folders when the design is submitted.

2. **Click the Staging tab of the Design window.**

   The contents of the Staging tab are displayed, as shown in the left side of Figure 11-5. If your page has no problems, you see check marks next to each of the pages in the Status column. Error or warning icons appear next to pages with problems or pages that have no content or links. Other than the index.html page, most will have warning icons. Warning icons are removed as soon as you add content to the pages. If an error icon appears (a green bug), open the page and see if the links conform to the design. If not, change either the links in the design or page so that they are the same.

3. **If no errors exist, click the Submit button on the Design toolbar or choose Design⊏>Design Staging⊏>Submit Design from the menu bar.**

   All of the pages in the Design window are now in the Live Pages folder in the Staging tab of the Design window. (See the right Design window in Figure 11-5.) The new pages also are in the File tab of the Site window as well now. However, you need to put all the links in the individual pages by following the design recommendations.

Figure 11-5:
The Design pages before (left) and after (right) being submitted. All of the live pages, including the anchor page, appear in the Site tab of the Site window as well.

Generating a Table of Contents

When you create a site in GoLive 5, it generates a *root folder* automatically. Everything in your site should go into this folder, or a subfolder within the root folder. (Using the Design window to create a site puts all of the files submitted into the root folder automatically.) By the time you've created a bunch of pages, added graphics, maybe a little JavaScript, made external links, and put in a kitchen sink, your site might be a little confusing — even to you. To make life a lot easier on yourself, you need to generate a Table of Contents or, as the pros say, a TOC. Use the following steps to get a grip on your site:

1. **Open your site by first choosing File⇨Open from the menu bar or Ctrl+O/Cmd-O and then opening a completed site from the directory dialog box.**

   Your site opens in the Files view of the Site window.

2. **Choose Design⇨Navigation View from the menu bar.**

   The Navigation View window opens, and you see icons of your site pages and link arrows. You can open the Navigation View window from any tab in the Site window.

3. **Choose Design⇨Create Table of Contents from the menu bar.**

   Sit back and wait while GoLive generates a TOC page, as shown in Figure 11-6.

Figure 11-6:
A table of
contents
automatically
generates
in GoLive.

The TOC page shows all of the pages in the root folder. They're organized in the hierarchy of links. The hierarchy simply refers to each page in relation-ship to other pages. A parent page is higher in the hierarchy than a child page (the page it links to downward) and a sibling page is on the same level in the hierarchy. To some extent, the concept of hierarchy doesn't make a lot of sense in a fully hypertext environment when everything is linked to every-thing else. It only makes sense when a site is designed in a sequence. A parent page precedes a child page, but a sibling can be selected in any order from a parent. Sibling pages on the same level may link to one another in any order. As a sequence, the hierarchy makes sense, but not as a wide-open hyperlinked site where any one page is linked to any other one. (The hierar-chy also makes sense to bureaucrats.)

Limiting the TOC page to those pages found in the root folder is both a good and bad feature. On the one hand, if you have a page sitting on your computer's desktop that you linked but didn't place in the root folder, it won't show up in the TOC or in the Site tab of the Site window. The good feature is that you can see that the page is missing from the TOC and get busy and put it into the root folder. The bad feature is that if you forgot all about the page, it won't be placed in the root folder. When you publish your page, the link goes, "Huh?" and doesn't have a clue where the page on your desktop is located. That's why you want to be sure all of your files are in the root folder. (At the end of the chapter I show you how GoLive saves you from even this problem!)

Making Global Changes

When you have to replace an image or set of images in a Web site, GoLive makes it easy with global image replacement. For example, suppose you have a ho-hum "Next page" arrow image. After putting the arrow image in 68 pages in your site, you find a great looking arrow you want. Instead of having to wade through all 68 pages, you can make one change and have all of the images changed in one fell swoop. (Once a swoop fell on me.) Here's how to perform a global image replacement:

1. **Open your site by choosing File⇨Open from the menu bar or Ctrl-O and then open a completed site from the directory dialog box.**

   Your site opens in the Files view of the Site window.

2. **Drag the new graphic file from where you have stored on your computer into the Files tab of the Site window or select Site⇨Finder/Explorer⇨Add files to get it placed in the root folder.**

   You should be able to see all your HTML files and media files and related folders in the Files view of the Site window.

3. **Choose Window⇨In & Out Links palette, click the In & Out Links button on the Site toolbar (the eighth button from the left), or undock the In & Out Links palette.**

   Unless you have a page or image selected, the In & Out Links palette is blank.

4. **In the Files tab of the Site window, select the image you want to replace.**

   Be sure to select the one you want to eliminate. It now appears in the In & Out Links palette with all of the links to it. Notice how many pages are linked to the same image. (See Figure 11-7.)

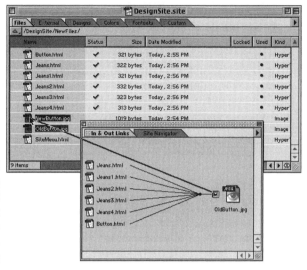

Figure 11-7:
Global
replacement
of an image
file.

5. **Pull the point-and-shoot line from the file to be eliminated in the In &
   Out Links palette to the new image file in File tab of the Site window.**

   In Figure 11-7, you can see the file "OldButton.jpg" being replaced by
   "NewButton.jpg." Notice that most of the Web pages in the site use the
   OldButton.jpg. Newbutton.jpg replaces all of them. As soon as you
   release the mouse button the point-and-shoot operation is complete,
   and the Change Reference dialog box appears. (See Figure 11-8.)

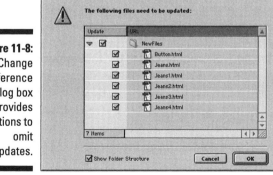

Figure 11-8:
The Change
Reference
dialog box
provides
options to
omit
updates.

6. **Click the OK button in the Change Reference dialog box.**

   If you intend to replace the image in all of the pages in the site, just click
   OK. However, if you want to leave the original graphic in any of your
   Web pages, uncheck the boxes next to the pages where you want to keep
   the original graphic. Figure 11-8 shows all the boxes checked, indicating
   that the new one replaces all of the original graphic files.

When a new image replaces an old one, the *old* height and width are maintained. If the images are identical in dimensions, there should be no problem. However, if the dimensions are different, the Resize Warning icon appears on the image in each of your pages in the Layout view. If that happens, you need to select each image, call up the Inspector (it appears as the Image Inspector), and then click the Image Resize Restore button on the Image Inspector to fix it. (If you have to resize the replaced graphics page-by-page on your whole site after a whiz-bang global change, you may wonder, "What's the point of a global change if I have to fix it page by page?" Reason enough to make sure that the old and new image have the same dimensions.)

Reorganizing Existing Sites

If you wish you could fix up some of your existing sites using GoLive 5, but you don't want to start from scratch, there's hope. Because GoLive handles just about every aspect of Web sites better than other tools, it comes as no surprise that GoLive has a way to take an old site constructed using some other Web site program and help you tweak it to perfection. If you have a site on your computer with major portions of it safely stored in one folder, you're in luck. However, even if your Web site is scattered all over your computer's folders, disks, and directories, you can still pull it together. Start by importing the folder with the site's root folder and index page.

1. **With GoLive 5 open, choose File⇨New Site⇨Import From Folder from the Menu bar.**

   The Import Site Folder Dialog Box opens.

2. **In the Import Site Folder Dialog Box, click the top Browse button next to the folder window.**

   The Choose a Folder Dialog Box opens. Shuffle through the files and folders until you find the folder you want to use as the root folder for your site. It may only have a few pages in it, but even so, you need a root folder. Your best choice would be a folder with the home page for your site.

3. **Click the Choose or OK button when you have selected the folder you intend to use for the root folder.**

   You return to the Import Site Folder Dialog Box.

4. **Click the second Browse button in the Import Site Folder Dialog Box next to the home page window.**

   An Open Dialog Box appears. You should find the folder you selected for the root folder and inside it the file you want to use for your index page.

5. **Click the Open button after you pick the file you intend to use as your home page.**

   The Import Site Folder Dialog Box reappears.

6. **Click the Import button at the bottom of the Import Site Folder Dialog Box.**

   Wait a little while GoLive generates a data folder. When GoLive is ready, the File tab of the Site window appears.

7. **Choose File⇨Save.**

   Provide a name for the site file and click the Save button.

That's it. Your old messy site is at least partially enthroned in a GoLive 5 root folder. You should now have two folders and a file:

- ✔ The Root Folder.
- ✔ The Data Folder. It has the same name as your root folder except it has a ".data" extension.
- ✔ The Site File. It has the same name as the root folder with a ".site" extension.

Create another folder and put the two folders and site file together. Otherwise, you soon have another mess on your hands because you have no single place for all these folders and files you just generated. After you have the Site window open, you can import all of the files not included in the root folder you created into your new site and again (or for the first time) have control over your site.

Organizing External Links

Your Web site may have several external links (such as links to other Web sites) that you want to use in your site. GoLive has a unique way of dealing with external site links in the Site window. Rather than trying to remember a long URL for an external link, GoLive can use your browser's own bookmarks. In fact, a good way to organize your Web site is to begin with your browser.

Bookmarks have long been a standard feature of Web browsers because they seem a natural and efficient way to store Web addresses for easy access. In Netscape Communicator, you bookmark a page by choosing Bookmarks⇨ Add Bookmark from the menu bar. With Internet Explorer, bookmarks are called Favorites. In IE, choose Favorites⇨Add to Favorites from the menu bar to bookmark a Web page. To put that efficiency to good use for handling the external links for your own Web site, start by bookmarking the Web addresses you need in one of your browsers. After you have all the bookmarks you need for your site, integrating them into the Site window is simple. Follow these steps:

1. **Open the Site window by clicking the Select Window button on the toolbar or by choosing File⇨Open on the menu bar.**

   The Site window opens in the most recently used view.

2. **Click the External tab of the Site window.**

   The External view of the Site window opens. You see four columns: Name, Used, Status, and URL.

3. **Open your browser.**

   Remember to open the browser that has the bookmarks/favorites you want in your site.

4. **In Netscape Communicator, choose Bookmarks⇨Edit Bookmarks from the menu bar to open the Bookmarks window and in Internet Explorer choose Favorites⇨Organize Favorites to open a Favorites window.**

   In both browsers, the Bookmarks/Favorites window opens.

5. **Drag the URL icon (an @ symbol in Internet Explorer 5 on the Macintosh or a stylized E on the Windows version of Explorer or a bookmark ribbon in Netscape Communicator) from the browser to the name column of the External Tab of the Site window.**

   Voila! You can now see all the external links you bookmarked in your browser in the External Tab of the Site window. Figure 11-9 shows how the Site window's External view looks like with installed links.

You can even drag a URL directly from a Web page. Just find the link on the page you like and drag and drop it in the External Tab of the Site window. That may save a step or two, but it's usually easier to organize the external links in your Favorites or Bookmark folders first.

Figure 11-9: You can drag external links from a browser's bookmarks to the External Tab of the Site window.

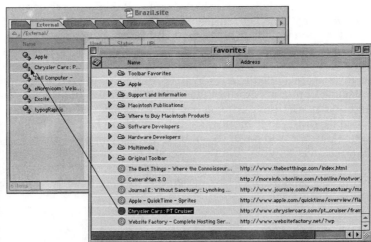

Changing links on the site

You can't create a link from the Site window, but you can replace an existing link using the In & Out Links palette. You use a similar technique for replacing links as you do for changing images on your site. For example, suppose that you have an external link that has changed addresses or you find an external link that you simply like better than a previous one. Making the change requires some tab flipping, so note the steps carefully:

1. **Open your Site window by clicking the Select Window button on the Toolbar or by selecting File⇨Open on the menu bar.**

   The Site window opens in the most recently used tab.

2. **Click the External tab of the Site window.**

   If no external icons exist on this page, follow the steps outlined in the previous section and add some. Select the external site that you want to change.

3. **Open the In & Out Links palette by clicking the In & Out Links palette button (the eighth from the left) on the Site toolbar.**

   You can also get the In & Out Links palette by choosing Window⇨ In & Out Links palette from the Menu bar or just undock it.

4. **In the In & Out Links palette, select the page linked to the external site you selected.**

   If you selected the link you wanted to change, the page shows up in the In & Out Links palette. By clicking it in the In & Out Links palette, it becomes the selected item.

5. **Pull the point-and-shoot line from the icon of the external link you want to replace to the External Tab of the Site window.**

   Figure 11-10 shows the point-and-shoot line making a connection to an external site.

6. **After you have the point-and-shoot line over the new icon, release the mouse button.**

   Whew! Actually, it's not that complex. Practice a few times and you'll find it to be a simple way to replace URLs on your site.

Organizing external links that you'll use throughout your site saves time and reduces typing errors if you key in your external URLs. Also, by using browser bookmarks, when you make the changes with the In & Out Palette, you're further assured that you didn't type in an incorrect URL by mistake.

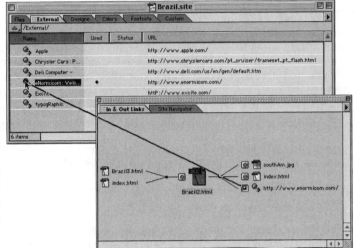

Figure 11-10:
Point-
and-shoot
change of
URL in the
Site
window.

Hold the phone! (Hold the e-mail!)

The External tab of the Site window is a great place to store URL addresses, but that's not the only kind of address you can store there; the External tab also lets you store any e-mail addresses you may want to use in your Web site. To make things even more convenient, e-mail addresses are stored in the External tab with the handy "mailto:" preface already attached, so that when you drag and drop them into a Web page, they're all set to bring up an e-mail page for a quick bit of electronic correspondence. For a big Web site, making it easy for the viewer to contact the organization is important; that means it's also important for the designer to have an easy way to place and change e-mail addresses in the site. The following steps show how easy it is:

1. **Open your Site window by selecting it from the Select Window button on the toolbar or by choosing File⇨Open on the Menu bar.**

   The Site window opens in the most recently used tab.

2. **Click the External tab of the Site window.**

   The External view may have some icons from external URLs or it may be empty, depending on what you've been up to.

3. **Choose Window⇨Inspector or undock the Inspector by clicking the Inspector tab at the side of the screen.**

   The Inspector becomes the Reference Inspector.

4. **Click the In & Out Links palette button (the eighth from the left) on the Site toolbar.**

Although the In & Out Links palette isn't actually used in this operation, it conveniently shows both the e-mail address and the Address icon (a picture of a face). Because you need to recognize the Address icon in future operations, it's good to have a peek at in the In & Out Links palette.

5. **Choose Window➪Objects from the menu bar or undock the Objects palette.**

   The Objects palette opens to the most recently selected tab or the Basics tab.

6. **Click the Site tab on the Objects palette.**

   The Site tab is the sixth tab from the left. A globe icon (Get it? Global?) identifies the tab.

7. **Drag the Address icon (picture of a face) from the Site tab of the Objects palette to the Name column of the External tab of the Site window.**

   An untitled address icon appears with that happy guy of a face.

8. **With the Address icon in the External tab of the Site window selected, click the Edit... button on the Reference Inspector.**

   The Edit URL window appears.

9. **In the Edit URL window, replace the untitled address with the full e-mail address.**

   Leave the "mailto:" alone. Just type in the e-mail address after "mailto:".

10. **Click the Change button in the Edit URL window.**

    Now your new e-mail address should appear in the Reference Inspector.

11. **Put the cursor in the Name window of the Reference Inspector; type in a name for the e-mail and then press Return/Enter.**

    The In & Out Links palette, the External tab of the Site window, and the Reference Inspector all should show the correct e-mail address.

When you organize a site for a company comprising many people with different e-mails, collecting the e-mails in the External view of the Site window makes it easier to use and reuse e-mail addresses and make sure they're consistent.

Site Color Control and Inspection

Chapter 7 introduces the Color tab of the Site window and shows how to create a color palette to give your site a cohesive and coherent color scheme. This chapter shows you that you can do more with your site colors, both when you create a site and when you renew it. From the Color tab of the Site window, you can inspect the colors in the site and find what pages use different colors. Color inspection uses the In & Out Links palette in conjunction with the Color Inspector, the Color tab of the Site window, and the Color Palette. (Image colors on media files, however, are not shown.)

If you have been using colors from the Web Name List on your pages, when they are transferred to the Color tab of the Site window, they are listed as "untitled" in the name column of the Color tab. However, they are named in the HTML name column. If the colors are not from the Web Name List of the Color palette, the name given to the colors in the HTML name column is the color's hexadecimal value. However, the Name column of the Colors tab *does* show a color swatch to show what the color looks like. To see which pages on your site are sporting a lovely shade of chartreuse or Dodger blue, do the following:

1. **Click the Color tab of the Site window.**

   For a developed site that has been saved or imported, you should see a list of untitled colors in a New Colors folder unless you have given them a name. Select a color. (If no colors are there, choose Site⇨Get Colors Used and they're placed in the Colors tab of the Site window.)

2. **Click the In & Out Links button (the eighth from the left) from the Site toolbar.**

   A block of color appears with links to the pages that used the color. If you selected black, there are probably lots of pages with links because black is the default text color.

3. **Choose Window⇨Inspector or undock the Inspector by clicking the Inspector tab at the side of the screen.**

   The Inspector becomes the Color Inspector, appearing with a color well showing the selected color from the Color tab of the Site window. You can change the untitled color name to something a bit more useful if you want.

4. **Choose Window⇨Color Palette or undock the Color Palette.**

   The Color palette appears. Okay, it's getting a little crowded, but all of the windows are working together (see Figure 11-11). With the color selected in the Color palette, you can now apply it to a page in the Layout view if you want.

Importing and exporting site colors

Copying the site colors to another site is simple. (The technical term for this is called, "Not reinventing the wheel.")

1. **Open the Color tabs of the Site windows of both the site that gets the colors and the one that has the colors you want to export.**

   You see two Site windows. One should have all the colors you want to export in the Colors view of the Site window.

2. **Drag some or all of the colors from one Site window to the next.**

   All the colors dragged from one site to the other now appear in the receiving site's Color view in the Site window.

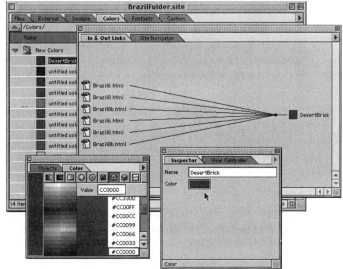

Figure 11-11:
The In & Out Links palette displays all pages with selected color.

 While you can make global changes in files, you can't make global color changes. In the global rearrangement of links, the old file names are replaced with the new. In GoLive, that's not possible with color names. However, you can make global changes to background *images*. Remember, a background *color* is not an image, and while a background image can be swapped for another one, the same is not true with colors. The reason is that a background image, like all images, is an independent file and must be linked to your page. Because links can be changed, the background images can be changed as well by using the global tools.

 If you want to make global changes with background colors in a site, you can use a solid block of color from a graphic. That is, use a background image for your background color. Create all the background color-block images you want and do global changes all you want. (If the idea sounds loopy, consider it an easy way to routinely change a Web site to maintain user interest.)

Organizing Fonts for a Site

Instead of going stark raving mad by fumbling through menus to find the font you want, organize them in the Fontsets tab of the Site window. Every single font you use in your site should be in the Fontsets tab of the Site window for easy access and design coordination. The first step is to get your fonts into the Fontsets tab of the Site window.

1. **Click the Fontsets tab of the Site window.**

   Unless you imported the site or chose Site⇨Get Fontsets used, the page will be blank. Otherwise, it shows the fontsets used in the pages that make up your site.

2. **Choose Window⇨Inspector from the Menu bar or undock the Inspector.**

   The Inspector becomes the Fontset Inspector and displays the fonts of any font set you select on the Site window.

3. **Choose Window⇨Objects from the menu bar or undock the Objects palette by clicking on the Objects tab at the side of the screen.**

   The Objects palette appears on the screen.

4. **Click the Site tab on the Objects palette.**

   The site has the globe icon on it, and when opened, 13 icons appear. Look for the Font Set icon. It has an italicized "A" on it. (I don't know why, either.)

5. **Drag the Font Set icon from the Site tab of the Objects palette and drop it in the Name column of the Fontsets tab of the Site window.**

   An untitled New Font appears in the Fontset tab of the Site window. The Inspector is now the Font Inspector.

6. **Select the New Font and open the pull-down menu located in the lower right side of Font Inspector right above the Delete and New buttons.**

   All of the fonts on your system appear.

7. **Scroll through the font list and select the font you want.**

   The font name appears in the Font Set column and in the Font window next to the pull-down menu.

8. **In the Name column of the Fontset tab of the Site window, enter a name for the font.**

   A font set can include several fonts or just a single font. With fonts like Verdana, it is probably a good idea to include Arial and/or Helvetica. That's because some computers may not have Verdana (very few), but to keep the font in a sans serif face, you need other fonts such as Arial or Helvetica that cover just about all computers.

Figure 11-12 shows a site with several fonts in the Site window. If you select a font with the In & Out Links palette open, all of the pages in the site using the selected font are displayed. You also can add individual fonts simply by dragging them from a page in the Document window and dropping them in the Font Sets tab of the Site window.

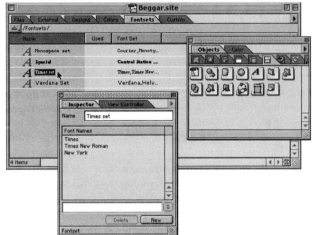

Figure 11-12:
Place fonts into the Fontsets tab of the Site window.

Getting the fonts in the Fontsets view

If you open an existing site created with another program to create a GoLive site file, all of the fonts in the imported site are placed in the Fontsets tab of the Site window. However, if you're working on a current GoLive site and haven't placed the fonts in the Fontsets tab, you can move all the fonts from all of the pages with a single operation.

1. **Click the Fontsets tab of the Site window.**

   The empty Fontsets view in the Site window opens. No fonts or sets are there yet.

2. **Choose Site⇨Get Fontsets Used in the menu bar.**

   All of the fonts used in the site appear in the Font Sets tab of the Site window. (That makes life easy.)

Using your site fonts

Applying fonts from the Fontsets tab of the Site window is a lot easier than using the menu bar. In Chapter 2, you found out how to select a font by rummaging through the menus. Using the fonts from the site, all you need to do is grab the font or font set you want and plunk it done on the selected text. Here's how:

1. **Select the text you want for the font in the Layout View of the Document Window.**

   The selected font is highlighted.

2. **From the Fontsets tab of the Site window, drag the desired font or font set onto the selected text and drop it.**

   Shazaam! You now have transformed the font to the one selected from the Site window. If you select a font set, the top font is selected for the actual style. In cases where the font is not in your system, the browser automatically selects the next font in the set until it gets one on the viewer's system. If none of the fonts are there, a default font used by the viewer is substituted.

Cleaning Up Your Site

When everyone gets busy, site work gets messy. (Dust bunnies are every-where.) Some of the internal link HTML pages may not have been put into the root folder, or maybe you've created a new image that somehow didn't placed where it belonged. Put all these oversights together and your site looks about as organized as a pillow fight. Take heart, for GoLive knows how to de-slob your site in one simple, yet effective, operation:

1. **Open the Site window to any tab.**

   This is easy because any tab in the Site window works.

2. **Choose Site➪Clear Site.**

   The Clear Site Options dialog box appears, as shown in Figure 11-13. The options fall into two categories: items you want added (Add Used) and items you want removed (Remove Unused). Remember that getting rid of objects you don't need is as important as bringing in those you do need. You may also want to consider checking the "do not show again" check box to save a little time in clean up operations. However, before you do so, make sure that the options you check are the ones you want for all your sites.

3. **Check those items you want moved into the Site window and root site and those you want removed and click OK.**

   The Clear Site dialog box appears, replacing the Clear Site *Options* dialog box. (The dialog boxes look very different but have similar names.)

4. **In the Clear Site dialog box, make sure that the files listed are the ones you want to be copied into your root folder and then click OK.**

The clear site operation is equivalent to a site spring-cleaning. What's more, all of the external links, colors, and fonts are placed under the appropriate tab in the Site window. (GoLive cleans sites created from existing sites automatically.)

Figure 11-13:
The Clear
Site Options
dialog box.

Instead of adding color, external links, and fonts to a site individually, use the
Clear Site option. One operation takes care of all the tabs, and it takes no more
time.

Getting Site Statistics

After slaving on your site, you don't want to find out that no one wants to
look at it because your pages take far too long to download. Although the
Document Statistics information in GoLive is not really a site operation, finding out how to put that information to work for you is a necessary part of
good site management. Slow pages impact your site, so it makes sense to put
your pages on the digital scale and weigh them as part of your site evalua-
tion. Here's how:

1. **Open a page in the Document Window.**

   Any of the views work.

2. **Choose Special⇨Document Statistics from the Menu bar.**

   The Document Statistics window appears with information about byte
   count, character count, and word count for the selected page.

Figure 11-14 shows a fairly light page, with a total byte count of 4.2 kilobytes.
With the slowest modem (9600 bps), the page takes 4 seconds to load. But
with a T1 line or faster connection, the page is up in a second. Notice that
both the text and graphics are included in the calculation of weight.

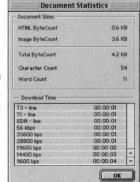

Figure 11-14:
Document
Statistics
window for
a single
page.

The times for the downloads are based on certain standardized times for optimal conditions. With more people spending more time on the Web, the Internet does get clogged up; during heavy usage periods such as the middle of the day, everything can slow down to a crawl. So, you have to take the time estimates with a grain of salt and realize that the times are relative estimates at best. Also the Document Statistics window doesn't measure movies and sound files; so if your pages have such files, you better get the old stopwatch out and time them yourself.

If your business depends in any significant way on your Web site, it's a good idea to open your pages at different times of the day to find out how long they take to open. During peak hours, you may want to consider a very light *text only* page to get the information to the viewer quickly.

Chapter 12

Creating and Maintaining: The Art of Templates and Cleanup

*S*tationeries and components are GoLive 5 tools for saving individual pages and page elements. If you spend all the time that you need to get the right look and feel for a particular page, you then can use that page as a stationery that you can apply to all the other pages on your site. As a result, all the pages on your site consistently display the same look and feel. In GoLive 5, the steps for creating such a template are pretty straightforward. And if you're careful to get the process right the first couple times, you end up with the results that you want. (The voice of experience is speaking here.)

Likewise, a major element in your page can be useful for several pages. Instead of redoing that element, you can make a component from it and re-use the component. Suppose that you have a set of graphic navigational tools you spent a lot of time creating. Instead of remaking the same set of navigation tools for every page, turn them into components and use them throughout your site.

Creating Clones

The basic plan in devising a Stationery is to create a page just the way that you want it, including all the images, colors, fonts, forms, and you-name-its that go into a Web page. Then you store the page as a so-called *Stationery*

Item (a fancy word for a template) in the Stationeries folder that you find in the Extras tab of the Site window. After you place a page in the Stationeries folder, it automatically appears in the Site Extras tab of the Objects palette, where you can use it as a template whenever you need it. Follow these steps to get a page into the Stationeries folder:

1. **Select File⇨New Site⇨Blank, provide a name for the site in the New Site Name window and click the Save button to open a new site.**

   The Site window appears. Click the Files tab of the Site window to open the Files view and note the single new file, index.html.

2. **Double-click the index.html file in the Site window to open it.**

   The page opens into the Layout view of the Document window. This is the page to use for creating a special Stationery page. Remember that this page is a special page, so watch all your design features carefully. For example, make sure that the colors look good together. (Chapter 3 describes kcy page design elements.)

3. **After you fully complete the page, choose Site⇨Clean Up Site from the menu bar.**

   You want to make sure that all the components for your page are in the root-site folder, and that's exactly what the Clean Up Site command does. Although such a move technically isn't necessary, you may easily regret not doing so later, as you use the Stationery Item as a template. Remember that the Clean Up Site command doesn't throw out good stuff. It simply moves files to your root-site folder that aren't already there, as I discuss in Chapter 11.

4. **Save the page by choosing File⇨Save or pressing Ctrl+S (in Windows) or ⌘-S (on the Mac). Then close your page by choosing File⇨Close or pressing Ctrl+W (in Windows) or ⌘-W (on the Mac).**

   The Document window containing the page disappears, but the page is still visible in the Site window.

5. **Click the Files tab of the Site window.**

   You can now see your file in the Files view of the Site window.

6. **If the right pane of your Site window isn't open, click the double-arrow button in the bottom-right corner of the Site window.**

   The right pane opens in the Site window. (Watch out that you avoid clicking the left and right horizontal scroll arrows down there. The correct arrow set is the one that's *farthest to the right* — right below the downward vertical scroll arrow.)

7. **Click the Extras tab in the right pane of the Site window.**

   The Extras view of the Site window appears. You see folders for components, Designs, Site Trash, and Stationeries.

8. **In the right pane of the Site window, use either Ctrl+drag (in Windows)
   or Option-drag (on the Mac) to pull the Page icon for index.html from
   the Name column of the Files tab in the Site window into the
   Stationeries folder in the right pane.**

   The Ctrl+drag/Option-drag operations make copies of the file. The idea
   is to make a copy of the page to store in the Stationeries folder — not to
   remove the page from the Files tab of the Site window. You then see a
   Stationery icon in the Stationeries folder as well as your original file's
   Page icon still in the File tab of the Site Window, as shown in Figure 12-1.

Figure 12-1:
The
Stationery
icon now
appears in
the
Stationeries
folder.

You did it! That's all you need to do to create a Stationery Item. Next, you
need to know about some ways to use the item as a template, which I
describe in the following sections.

Making Stationeries Work for You

Making and using stationeries are really two separate operations, and
so I treat them as such. You don't need to turn off your computer or close
GoLive 5, but after you create a stationery, putting it to use requires a different
mind set. To appreciate and understand why a template is a useful tool in
managing your Web site, consider the page shown in Figure 12-2. This page is
an example of a page that you can use as a Stationery. It displays a graphic
logo, graphic links with text labels, and a text box for making weekly and
monthly changes.

Figure 12-2:
A typical
Web page
that you can
use as a
Stationery.

The page in Figure 12-2 represents a page that undergoes regular updating in a Web site and that you can use as a template for other pages in the site. As a Stationery, however, you can store it in the Objects palette, and you need only to drop it onto a page for reproduction. Each week, a new page must update the Weekly Special, and each month, another must update the monthly ones. Obviously, you can just change the text window on a single page and resave it to reflect the updated materials. By using a template, however, you can quickly develop any other page containing the same components. To use Stationeries as templates, just follow these simple steps:

1. **Begin in the Files tab of the Site window.**

2. **Choose Window➪Objects from the menu bar to open the Objects palette or undock the Objects palette by clicking the tab at the side of the screen.**

   The Objects palette appears on-screen.

3. **Click the Site Extras tab (third tab from the right in the Objects palette).**

   After you select the Object palette's Site Extras tab, you see the Stationery Item icon on that tab. (If you don't see it, click the Stationeries Pad button at the bottom of the Site Extras tab to toggle it to components and then click it again to toggle it back to Stationeries Pad.) The icon sometimes requires that jump start to wake it up. If the Stationery icon's in the Stationery folder in the Site window, it's in the Objects palette as well. (You just may need to hunt for it a bit.)

4. **Drag the Stationery icon from the Site Extras tab of the Objects palette to the Name column in the left pane of the Site window (see Figure 12-3).**

   If you want the file to go into a folder or subfolder, you can drag the Stationery icon directly to the right pane of the Site window and onto the icon of the folder in which you want to place it. The filename then reads New from, with the filename following.

5. **Change the filename to the one that you want to use by clicking the icon and typing the new name to replace the current name.**

   The new name now appears on the Page icon.

6. **Click the Page icon to select it and choose File⇨Open from the menu bar (or just double-click the icon).**

   After the file opens, you see your template page. It looks identical to the page you saved as a Stationery.

Drag the Stationery icon from the Objects palette to the Site window.

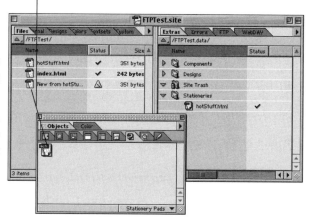

Figure 12-3: You can move the Stationery icon by dragging it from the Objects palette.

After your page is open, you can make any changes that you want and save the page. After you develop a template page for a site, the idea is to use that template to maintain the same design on your pages but to change certain key elements periodically. In Figure 12-4, for example, the text changes from its earlier version (refer to Figure 12-2), but the rest of the page remains the same.

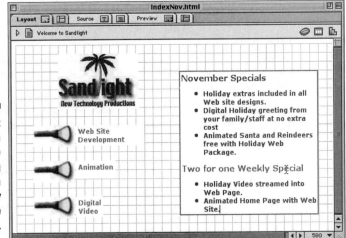

Figure 12-4:
Changes in
the page
resulting
from using a
Stationery
to update
the page.

Importing Stationeries

Beyond one that works for just a single site, you may find that a page can
serve as a template for a number of different sites. You can use Stationeries
that you develop on a given site in a number of different ways, but the sim-
plest way is to transfer the template page from the source site to the new
site. To do so, follow these steps:

1. **Open a new site in the Site window and click the Files tab of the Site
   window.**

   The site is the one that you want to receive a Stationery Item.

2. **If the right pane of your Site window isn't open, click the double-
   arrow button in the bottom-right corner of the Site window.**

   The right pane opens in the Site window. (Watch out that you avoid
   clicking the left and right horizontal scroll arrows down there. The
   correct arrow set is the one *farthest to the right* — directly under the
   downward vertical scroll button.)

3. **Click the Extras tab of the right pane of the Site window.**

   You see the Stationeries folder with the other folders in the right pane.
   You want your new Stationery Item to go in the Stationeries folder.

4. **Click the Stationeries folder to select it.**

   By selecting the Stationeries folder, the imported Stationery Item goes
   directly to the correct folder.

5. **Choose Window➪Objects to open the Objects palette or undock the Objects palette by clicking its tab at the side of the screen.**

   One way to check whether the import operation for the Stationery Item is successful is to check the Site Extras tab of the Objects palette. After you finish the import operation, you see the new Stationery icon waiting there for you. If you don't see it there, the import operation didn't succeed and you need to try again.

6. **Choose Site➪Explorer➪Add Files (in Windows) or Site➪Finder➪Add Files (on the Mac) from the menu bar to open the Add Files dialog box. In the dialog box, find and select the page that you want from the Stationeries folder of the source site.**

   This task may require a little digging. You must first find in the Add Files dialog box the folder containing the site with the Stationery Item that you want. After you find it, you need to open the folder and then look for the subfolder with the DATA extension. Inside the *SiteName*.data folder, you see the Stationeries folder. Select and open the Stationeries folder, and you find the Stationery Item that you want to import. This procedure is the same as any operation that adds files to a site, except that you need to know the names of the special folders (*SiteName*.data and Stationeries).

7. **Select the Stationery Item file, click the Add button, and then click the Done button to close the Add Files dialog box.**

   Because you selected the Stationery Item file in the import operation, you're all set. Check the Site Extras tab of the Objects palette, and you see your imported Stationery icon.

You can use an imported Stationery icon just as you use any other Stationery icon. The fact that you import it doesn't bear on its use at all.

Using an imported Stationery automatically launches an Update window as soon as you attempt to load it unless the element contains no links or images. (An Update window makes sure that the links are correct.) Depending on the nature of the page, such an update can add a lot of files that you don't want. Just deselect the ones that you don't want to import into your current site. Later, go in and change the links to the pages on the new site.

Working with Reusable Components

In some sites, the pages don't share a general template, but they do include several components that you painstakingly construct and need to reuse again and again. One of the more common elements that you see in use on several pages in a site, for example, is a graphic navigation system. This system can consist of an image map, images with rollovers (images that change as the mouse pointer moves over them), or several icons indicating the different major sections in the Web site. You don't need to rebuild these components for each page, but as is the case with Stationery Items, you can place them in a special folder in the Extras tab of the Site window. This folder, curiously enough, is known as the *Components folder,* and after you place a component there, it also appears in the Site Extras tab of the Objects palette.

To best understand how to use *components,* think of the process in two parts: The first part involves creating a single page containing the elements that you want to use on several different pages — for example, a navigation bar. You go ahead and create the page, but you put on the page only those objects (such as a graphic navigation system) that make up a component. The second part then involves creating the components for these selected objects.

You can't save background and text colors as component elements. Oddly, you can save far more complex elements, such as rollovers, as component elements. Go figure.

Constructing your components

The best way to think of creating and selecting components is in terms of what key feature are several pages in your site going to all need. It might be a special logo, a rollover action to remind the viewer that your products or services are the best, or it might be a set of buttons with rollovers run by a JavaScript script. You don't want to think in terms of creating entire pages to clone — that's the job of Stationeries. You want just reusable parts. To construct the components for your page, follow these steps:

1. **Select File⇨New Site⇨Blank, provide a name for the site in the New Site Name window, and click the Save button to open a new site.**

   The Site window appears. Click the Files tab of the Site window to open the Files view and note the single new file, index.html.

2. **Double-click the index.html file in the Site window to open it.**

3. **Create a page containing just those elements that you want to place on several different pages, such as a navigation bar. (See Chapters 2 and 3.)**

   Don't worry about fancy components using tables, images, rollovers, and links. Figure 12-5 shows one example of the kind of thing that you can set up as a component. Make sure, too, that you drag all the linked media files into the File view of the Site window (or choose Site⇨Clean Up Site to get GoLive 5 to do it for you automatically).

4. **Save the page by choosing File⇨Save or pressing Ctrl+S (in Windows) or ⌘-S (on the Mac). Then close your page by choosing File⇨Close or pressing Ctrl+W (in Windows) or ⌘-W (on the Mac).**

   Because you open the page from the Site window, it automatically goes into the site's root folder after you save it.

Figure 12-5:
You save
only the
elements for
the compo-
nent as a
page — in
this case,
the
navigation
bar
composed
of a
window,
graphics,
and links.

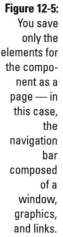
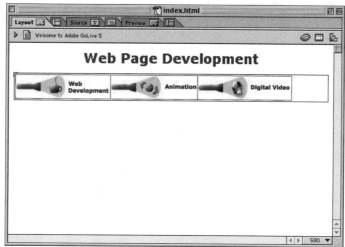

Figure 12-5:
You save
only the
elements for
the compo-
nent as a
page — in
this case,
the
navigation
bar
composed
of a
window,
graphics,
and links.

Turning your page items into components

In the preceding section I put together a little navigation bar to create a ter-
rific component. Now I don't want to have to make the same navigation bar
again. Since I have it in a component, I'll just grab the component and use it
on my page. To turn your page items into components, follow these steps:

1. **Begin in the File tab of the Site window where you saved the page that
   you want to turn into a component.**

   See the steps in the preceding section for details on this procedure.

2. **If the right pane isn't open in your Site window, click the double-
   arrow button in the bottom-right corner of the Site window.**

   The right pane opens in the Site window. (Watch out that you avoid
   clicking the left and right horizontal scroll arrow down there. The correct arrow set is the one that's *farthest to the right* — right below the
   downward arrow on the vertical scroll bar.)

3. **Drag the page containing the component from the Name column of
   the Files tab to the Components folder in the Extras tab of the Site
   window.**

   Note that you drag the whole page. So be certain that only the elements
   you want in the component are on the page. Essentially, your whole page
   becomes the component.

4. **Rename the page in the Components folder by clicking on it and typing in a new name.**

   I renamed the component page "FineParts.html" to remind myself that this page contains only parts (components) and not the whole page (stationery). You don't have to rename the component, especially if the name of the page you dragged into the component folder has a name that fits your purpose.

5. **Choose Window➪Objects to open the Objects palette or undock the Objects palette by clicking the tab at the edge of the screen.**

   The Objects palette appears, as shown in Figure 12-6. The file FineParts.html now appears in the Components folder.

The process is now complete. You see a component element in the Site Extras tab of the Objects palette. You also see an icon showing some graphic element of the page that you placed in the Components folder.

Figure 12-6:
Files in the Components folder of the Extras tab of the Site window and Site Extras tab of the Objects palette.

Putting Components to Work

Components are interesting little critters. You place a Web page in the Components folder, and then you put the component elements into another Web page from the Objects palette. It sounds strange, but the process works just fine and saves a lot of time. Even if your components contain JavaScript, the component elements place what you need into your Web page correctly. Check it out for yourself by following these steps:

1. **Open an existing page by selecting File➪Open from the menu bar or create a new page in the Layout view of the Document window by selecting File➪New from the menu bar or typing Ctrl+N (Windows) or ⌘-N (Macintosh).**

Ideally, select a site with a component you already stored away. Otherwise, see the preceding section for information about creating a component.

2. **Choose Window⇨Objects from the menu bar to open the Objects palette or undock the Objects palette by clicking the tab at the side of the screen.**

   The Objects palette appears on-screen.

3. **Click the Site Extras tab of the Objects palette (the third tab from the right).**

   You see your component on the Site Extras tab. If you don't, toggle the little Stationeries/Components button at the bottom of the Site Extras tab until it appears.

4. **Drag the Component icon from the Objects palette to the page in the Layout view of the Document window.**

   If there's more than one component, select the one you want and the component name appears at the bottom of the Extras tab window. You can drag a component onto a grid, into a window, or anyplace else where you can put a Web-page object, as shown in Figure 12-7.

If you look closely at a component in the Layout view, you can see a tiny green corner in the upper left of the box surrounding the component on the Web page. (That corner isn't visible in browsers.) The green corner tells you that what you're seeing is a component. That information is handy if you're editing the page later.

Drag component to page

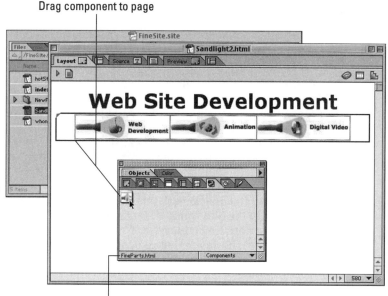

Figure 12-7:
Placing a
component
on a Web
page.

Component name

Getting the Bug Out

In addition to the Extras tab, with its Stationeries and Components folders, the set of tabs in the Site window includes an Errors tab. The Errors tab is the gateway to the many different ways in which GoLive 5 helps you make sure that your site is clear of flaws. The Status column of the Site window Files tab contains different icons representing degrees of problems, and GoLive 5 provides mechanisms to help you fix the problems that these Error icons indicate.

To understand all the errors that can show up on the Errors tab and in the Status column of the left pane of the Site window, Figure 12-8 shows a "wounded site" suffering from all the bugs that a willful designer can apply. It serves as a reference point to the different bugs and how to fix them in GoLive 5.

Figure 12-8: Error icons in the Errors tab (right pane) and Files tab (left pane) of the Site window.

A rogues gallery of trouble

First, you need to know that getting into trouble in GoLive 5 isn't an easy task. Making the errors that appear in Figure 12-8 is very difficult, because GoLive 5 keeps opening up helpful windows to update files and perform other good deeds to keep the site bug-free automatically. Bugs *can* creep in, however, and you need to know how to recognize them and rid yourself of them. The following list describes the various Error icons that I show in the figure and that GoLive 5 uses to identify problems on your site:

 ✔ **The Check icon:** The check mark that you may see in the Status column in the left pane of the Site window means that everything is okay with a file. Let sleeping dogs lie in this case. You need to do nothing to the file. That doesn't mean, however, that the connection *to that file* is working. Elsewhere in the site may lurk a bug connecting to the file because of an incorrect link name.

✔ **The Bug icon:** A Bug icon appearing in the Status column tells you that some kind of error is in the file, but it doesn't elaborate on what kind of error. Clicking the Errors tab provides more information about the bug.

✔ **The Alert icon:** Nothing is wrong if an Alert icon (the yellow triangle) shows up in the Status column. It simply means that a page is a new one with nothing on it. If a closed folder contains a page with nothing on it, you see the yellow-triangle icon next to the folder. If the folder itself is empty, however, no Alert icon appears.

✔ **The Stop icon:** A Stop icon in the Errors pane of the Site window means that a link lost its connection with the file. Usually, this icon means that the file was formerly in the root folder and that you deleted it or that you used an incorrectly written external URL in the original link. For example, if you typed in the URL for the external link without the `http://`, the page would be expected to be in the root directory. Since it would not be there, the Stop icon indicates that fact.

✔ **The Question Mark icon:** An icon associated with the Stop icon is the Question Mark icon. If GoLive 5 simply can't find a file at all, both the Question Mark icon and the Stop icon appear in the Errors pane of the Site window. Usually, that combination means that you wrote the wrong URL in the URL window of the Link Inspector as you were defining a link.

✔ **The Orphan File icon:** If a file lies outside the root folder, the Orphan File icon (a folder with an *X* on it) appears in the Errors pane of the Site window. Don't overlook this warning! As you publish your site on a server, you want all the files associated with the site in the root folder. In testing your page, the link may work fine because the link resides on your computer and your browser just follows the path. If you don't make the necessary changes, however, no one can find the file after the site is on the server.

To catch spelling and grammar errors, you must use the spell-checking feature of GoLive 5. The bug-catching feature of GoLive 5 doesn't extend to spelling or other inaccuracies in your page. (See the section "Spell checking," later in this chapter.)

Elementary bug squashing

Getting rid of bugs usually depends on what the bug is. A generic procedure, however, works for most of the bugs you're likely to encounter. Virtually all the bugs you encounter involve a link to another page or a graphic image file with a poor link. Following are a few basic steps to take if you want to play bad-link exterminator:

1. **Begin in the Files tab of the Site window and click the Errors tab (if it's not already selected) as described in the previous section.**

   If you don't have a site with lots of bugs, open one of the pages in the site and put in a bad link. Just follow the instructions for creating a link in Chapter 2 and use xyz or some other name not in the site's root folder. You'll get a bug as soon as you save the page. All the site's errors appear on-screen.

2. **Choose Window⇨Inspector from the menu bar to open the Inspector or undock the Inspector by clicking its tab at the side of the screen.**

   If none of the files are currently selected, you see the generic Inspector.

3. **On the Errors tab of the Site window, click the Stop icon for one of your problem files.**

   Each Stop icon is associated with a particular file. The Inspector becomes the Error Inspector. In the Error Inspector, you see a single URL text box for entering in a corrected URL for the target of your file's link.

4. **In the URL text box in the Inspector, type the correct URL name, pull the point-and-shoot line from the Point-and-Shoot button (the one with the spiral to the left of the text box) to the correct file in the File tab of the Site window.**

   Or you can click the Browse button — the one displaying a Folder to the right of the text box — to search for the missing file by selecting different directories that appear in the Directory window until you see the file you want.

   Entering URLs is not a good place to have typos. If you place an incorrect name in the URL text box, the link never works right. So make sure that you check that the URL name corresponds to the name of the target file for your link.

 If a URL consists of a long name, GoLive 5 offers a trick that enables you to expand the URL text box in the Error Inspector. Press and hold Ctrl+Alt (in Windows) or ⌘-Option (on the Mac) until you see a Pencil icon replace the Folder icon on the Browse button next to the URL text box. Click the Pencil icon and a larger URL text box opens so that you can enter a very long URL.

Orphans in the storm

If the Orphan icon appears, the procedure is a little different, but all orphans you can fix with a single operation. Just follow these steps:

1. **Begin in the Files tab of the Site window with the Errors tab selected in the right pane, as described at the beginning of the previous section.**

You see the Orphan File warning icon — the one with an *X* mark over a folder icon — in the Errors tab pane. If you don't have an orphan, you can easily make one by opening any page and establish a link with a file outside of the root folder. (If you don't see the file in the Files tab of the Site window, it's outside of the root folder.) See Chapter 2 for creating links that *are not* orphans.

2. **Choose Site⇨Clean Up Site from the menu bar.**

   GoLive 5 gathers all the linked files together into the root folder. If you're not sure exactly where you put your orphan file on your computer, using Clean Up is the easiest course is for GoLive 5 to go after all of them.

3. **After GoLive 5 prompts you to update all the file links, click the OK button.**

   Generally, I just click the OK button. If problems exist in your orphan file (like it has a bad link), you'll find out when it's in the Site window.

4. **After GoLive 5 prompts you to copy files to the root folder with the Clear Site dialog box, click the OK button.**

   GoLive 5 brings the orphan file into the root folder. That procedure usually does the trick. Magically, all the orphan icons disappear.

Remember that GoLive 5 is on your side. If you have something that's not quite right, GoLive 5 tries to make it right. Probably the most important items to keep in mind to avoid bugs on your Web site are as follows:

- ✔ Keep all the files in the root folder so that you can see them in the Site window.
- ✔ Use the Point-and-Shoot or browse-and select-methods of making all your links. That way, you avoid typos when keying in URLs or filenames.

Spell checking

A final kind of troubleshooting that GoLive 5 helps out with is spell checking. As is typical of GoLive 5, the spell checker works by checking an entire site. You may, however, spell check individual pages or even selected text. GoLive 5 provides several options for checking your spelling as well. Just follow these steps:

1. **Begin in the Files tab of the Site window for the site that you want to spell check.**

   You need to see all your files. The spell checker *doesn't* check for misspellings in graphics. (That's where I like to make all mine.)

2. **Choose Edit⇨Spell checking from the menu bar or type Alt+Ctrl+U (Windows) or Option-⌘-U (Macintosh).**

   The Check In dialog box appears.

3. **Select the language or version of language to check with from the Language drop-down list.**

   American English and English English are different. The English tend to use an *s* where Americans use a *z*, such as in *Organisation* and *Organization*. (And don't forget the British spelling of *luv*.)

4. **Click the Start button to begin checking for errors.**

   Your first typing error appears unless you have none, as is the case with my sites. (Yeah, wright!)

The spell checker goes through your site page by page until it finds an error. After an error appears, the page opens on-screen with the possible misspelling highlighted, and the spell checker provides several options for dealing with the possible misspelled word, as shown in Figure 12-9. The following list explains each option in some detail:

- ✔ **Delete:** This option is useful if you inadvertently put double words in the text next to one another. Click Delete to get rid of one of the double words.

- ✔ **Change:** If the spell checker doesn't recognize a word, one or several words appear in the Suggestions list box. In Figure 12-9, the word *staff* is misspelled *asdfa*. The suggested word appears both in the Suggestions list box and in the text box directly below the misspelled word. Click the Change button to change the misspelled word to the one in the text box directly below where the misspelled word appears. You may also type the correct word in the text box directly below the misspelled word if the suggested one isn't correct.

- ✔ **Ignore and Ignore All:** The spell checker doesn't recognize proper names such as Hinkelbump or some other surname, and so you can skip such "misspellings" by clicking the Ignore button. If you expect several such instances of a word that you want to skip, just click Ignore All, and the spell checker no longer stops and asks if it encounters that particular word.

- ✔ **Learn:** Clicking Learn adds the word to your dictionary. Your site may use words such as *e-commerce,* for example, and you plan to use the term often. Just click the Learn button to add to the spell checker's dictionary. The spell checker never stops on that word again.

- ✔ **Stop:** During the middle of checking your words, you can stop the checking process, go do something else on your page, and then come back and resume checking the spelling. As soon as you click the Stop button, the Start button replaces it. When you are ready to resume your spell checking, click the Start button, which changes to the Stop button again.

- ✔ **Next File:** If you're checking a site and you don't want to continue spell checking the current page, just click Next File to close the current page and open the next one that contains a spelling error.

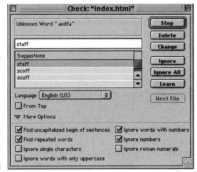

Figure 12-9:
The spell
checker at
work on a
Web site in
GoLive 5.

I found one rattling feature in the spell checker. If multiple occurrences of the same word are encountered back to back, the spell checker gives you the option of deleting one. So if one page ends with "Aloha" and the next page begins with "Aloha," the spell checker asks if you want to delete it. It is not unusual for sites to begin and end each page with a common word, such as a company's name. So careful! careful! when checking for multiple occurrences using the *site* spell checker.

In addition to the button options, the spell checker in GoLive 5 offers seven additional options in the lower part of the Spell checking dialog box that you may select by clicking a check box next to the option that you want. These options, such as Find Repeated Words and Ignore Numbers, are self-explanatory and provide more flexibility to your spell-checking chores — and do a bit of grammar checking as well (refer to Figure 12-9).

Chapter 13

Servers with a Smile — Moving Files to and from Servers

*A*fter your site is complete, it's time to put your work on a Web server. It helps to think of the server as a computer that mirrors your own. A Web server shows the rest of the world exactly what you see when you open your site and use all your pages on your PC. If copies of all the folders and files are transported together to the server, all of the relative links are maintained.

To get to a server, you need a Web hosting service. Such a service may exist at your place of business, educational institution, or government office. If you're starting up your own e-business, you need a Web host service. You can locate a host service through your ISP (Internet Service Provider) or by using a search engine in your browser. For example, if you type the words **Web Hosting** in a search engine such as Excite, Yahoo!, StarMedia, Lycos, or one of the other sites that provide ways to locate services on the Web, you find competitive deals for getting you online for some serious e-commerce.

While you're thinking about getting on the Web, you should also think about getting a domain name. A server has an address (made up of unique sets of numbers such as 24.3.129.174) that's about as easy to remember as a combination to a safe. A domain name replaces the server name with something like `www.adobe.com` that's easy to remember and associate with a product. A surprising number of free hosting services exist, but they usually restrict what your page can look like and put ads on your page. However, you can get inexpensive Web hosting services without any restrictions if you shop around on the Web. (Search the Web with the words, "Web Hosting" and you'll find plenty.) Start off with an inexpensive Web hosting service and then upgrade as your needs increase.

Using FTP to Transfer Files to a Web Server

Before heading for the Web with your pages, you need to know a little about File Transfer Protocol or FTP. Using FTP to put pages on the Web is like copying files from your hard disk to a floppy or high capacity disk. All you're doing is moving your Web pages and associated files from your computer's disk storage to another computer's disk storage. If all the connections are established correctly, it's a piece of cake to transfer files. GoLive has two different built-in FTP programs that you can use. However, several good and free FTP applications are available on the Web. Both of the following are free:

✔ **For Windows computers:** WS_FTP LE is a popular file transfer program. Available from `www.csra.net/junodj/ws_ftp.htm`, the program is easy to use and works great.

✔ **For Macintosh computers:** Fetch is a simple and effective FTP program. Using Fetch, you can drag and drop your files and folders into the Web server quite easily. It's available from `www.dartmouth.edu/pages/softdev/fetch.html`.

If you think of FTP as putting files on another disk that just happens to be in another room, the prospect of loading your pages on a Web server isn't so daunting.

People bandy about the term *server* without distinguishing between types of servers. Actually, any computer with server software can be a server. However, some specialize in certain functions. A file server stores files, a Web server delivers Web pages, and an e-mail server sorts and sends e-mail. An enterprise server is usually just a big computer that has different server software so that it can be all different kinds of servers. But remember that all of the servers and the computer on your desktop are close relatives and what you put on your computer is just being placed on another computer when you publish your pages on the Web.

Initial FTP Setup

The first step in GoLive 5 to get your pages from your computer to a Web server is to set up your FTP addresses in the Preferences menu. GoLive 5 has a two-step process in which you put in any FTP addresses you're using — and there may be several — and the second step is to select and use the address you want for a particular site. Follow these steps:

1. **Start GoLive 5 by launching it from your computer.**

   You see a blank untitled page in the Document window. It doesn't matter what's there as long as you can access your menu bar.

2. **Choose Edit⇨Preferences from the menu bar.**

   The Preferences dialog box appears with two columns. The column on the left has a number of icons and labels.

3. **Select Network⇨FTP Server from the left column.**

   The FTP pane appears on the right. Space appears at the top of the pane for you to list all the different FTP addresses you enter, the username for that particular FTP site, and the port you're going to use. (Port 21 is the default. Your system administrator may have another one for you to use, but usually it's 21.)

4. **Click the New button and enter the FTP address of your Web server in the Server text field in the lower part of the FTP pane.**

   The address can be either words or numbers. Usually, an FTP address looks pretty much like a Web address and URL. Sometimes you see an FTP address preceded by "FTP," but otherwise all else is the same. Figure 13-1 shows some examples in the top-right pane.

5. **Type a directory name, if necessary, in the Directory text field.**

   Depending on how the system administrator has the FTP set up, you may or may not be required to enter a directory name.

6. **Type the user name and password in their respective text fields.**

   The user name and password are like those used in e-mail. In fact, in some sites you use the same user name and password for e-mail as for FTP. It all depends on how the Web host administrator has the site organized. With several FTP sites, you may have more than one user name and password.

7. **Click the Advanced button to bring up the FTP Options dialog box.**

   The FTP Options dialog box opens as shown in Figure 13-1. Usually, you don't change your port number, but you may want to select the check box for what's known as the *passive mode*. Certain firewall conditions require the passive mode. Check with the system administrator to see whether it's required.

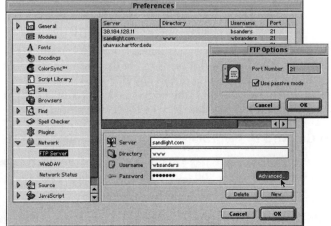

Figure 13-1:
Set up FTP
preferences
in this
window.

Moving from Site to Server

Now you're all set to put your beautiful pages on a server. GoLive has three different ways to use FTP for getting your site onto a server, and I explain each separately. (If you can't stand the suspense, I'll let you know right now that the first method uses the Site toolbar, the second method involves your dragging files from the left pane of the Site window to the right pane, and the third method makes use of GoLive's menu bar.)

Whichever method you use, it's wise to choose Site➪Clean Up Site from the menu bar one last time to get everything into the root folder. (See Chapter 11 for more on the Clean Up Site command.) The root folder is the source of the FTP process; if your files aren't in that folder, one of the methods I describe gets the files and folders to the Web server.

FTPing from the Site toolbar

To get your site onto a server by using the Site toolbar, follow these steps:

1. **Open the site you want to mount on a Web server in the Site window.**

   The Site window appears on the screen. Generally, you don't need your Document window open when moving files from your computer to a Web server.

2. **Click the Files tab in the Site window.**

   All your files and folders for your site appear.

3. **If the right pane isn't open in your Site window, click the double arrows in the bottom-right corner of the Site window.**

   The right pane opens in the Site window. (Avoid clicking the left and right horizontal scroll arrows down there. The correct arrow set is farthest to the right.)

4. **Click the FTP tab in the right pane of the Site window.**

   The tab should be blank. When you connect to an FTP site, you see the files on the Web server in this window.

5. **Choose Site⇨Settings or press Ctrl+Alt+Y (Windows) or Option-Cmd-Y (Macintosh).**

   The Settings dialog box opens. This is where you put in your server settings.

6. **In the Settings dialog box, click the FTP & WebDAV Server icon in the left column.**

   The FTP Server pane appears in the upper half of the right side of the Settings dialog box, as shown in Figure 13-2. (Later in this chapter, you find out how to use the bottom half to set up connections to a WebDAV server.)

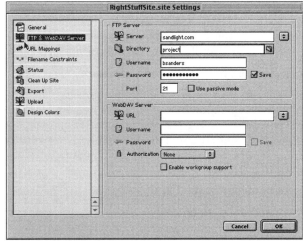

Figure 13-2:
The FTP Server Pane in the Settings window.

7. **Type the name of your server in the Server text field of the FTP Server pane.**

   Your Web host provides a name for the major domain of your site. Simply enter that name in the Server text field (refer to Figure 13-1). You may enter a series of numbers indicating the Web sites address as well — 37.182.128.15 is an example of a perfectly valid address. You may have to contact your technical guy (the one in the basement with the mushrooms) for the setup parameters. These include the address, directory, username, and password.

If you have put in your FTP information in the Preferences dialog box (see the previous section) you need only select your server from the pull-down menu to the right of the Server text field. Select the server you want, and all the rest of the information is filled in for you.

8. **In the Directory text field, type the name of the server directory, if any, to which your site is to be uploaded.**

   Remember that a server is just another computer. The arrangement of directories can be anything the computer's owner wants. On your own computer, you have directories and subdirectories, and you may have been assigned a certain directory on the server you need to enter at startup. Sometimes the directory window is automatically entered and sometimes you have to put in the directory name yourself. You may have to check with your network administrator to get this right. If you enter a directory name while your server software does it for you automatically, you receive an error because the computer duplicated the directory you just entered. For example, if your site is to go into a directory named "hotstuff" and you enter "hotstuff" in the directory name, the computer thinks you want a directory called "hotstuffhotstuff." (Unfortunately, the directory name you've been assigned will *not* show up in the directory window.)

9. **In the Username text field, type your User ID.**

   Sometimes the User ID is the same as your e-mail User ID if you're using your organization's Web server. If you set up your pages with a Web hosting service, your User ID is the one the service provides.

10. **In the Password text field, type your password.**

    If you have a secure computer (one that no one else can get their mitts on) you can save some time by checking the Remember Password check box. However, if others can get to your computer and you don't want them goofing with your site, keep the Remember Password check box clear. Your password is assigned by the Web hosting service or your company's Web administrator.

11. **Type the port number in the Port text field.**

    Port 21 is commonly used, but it may not work with your system. (Other ports on your computer go to your printer, mouse, or other devices.) Check with your system administrator or Web hosting service if Port 21 fails to connect you to your Web server. Sometimes a Web host will suggest a port number when you sign up for the service; so go through any materials you were e-mailed by your Web host service and check.

12. **If required by the FTP you are using, select the Passive mode check box.**

    Check the check box only if your system administrator or Web host has suggested you do so. Certain types of firewalls (electronic walls to keep out unwanted guests) require a passive mode.

13. **Choose Window⊅Toolbar or undock the toolbar by clicking its icon at the side of the screen.**

    The toolbar appears as the Site toolbar. Usually the toolbar is on the screen, but just in case it was taking a nap, I wanted to remind you.

14. **Click the FTP Server connect/disconnect button (10th from the left) on the Site toolbar.**

    At the bottom of the FTP pane in the Site window, the word "Connected" appears. However, if a problem occurs, a warning window comes into view to inform you that the connection has not been established. Check your settings and try again.

15. **Click the Incremental Upload button (11th from the left) on the Site toolbar.**

    The Upload Options dialog box appears.

16. **Leave the default checkboxes selected and click OK.**

    Leaving Files and Folders checked is a good idea to ensure that the folders and files arrive at the Web server in the order GoLive 5 has made for them.

17. **Click the OK button.**

    The Upload Site window appears. Make sure that all the pages you want uploaded are in the window and that the check boxes next to them are checked. If you have a page in the batch you do not want uploaded, just deselect the box next to it.

18. **Click the OK button in the Upload Site window.**

    If no errors are detected, your files are successfully uploaded and put on your server. In other words: You're on the Web!

After your files have been transferred to the target server, they appear in the FTP pane of the Site window. Figures 13-3 and 13-4 show the before and after views of an FTP operation. If you make changes to a file or two and upload the site again, only those files that have been changed are transferred. That saves a lot of time. GoLive makes sure that all links are updated before you send in the changes.

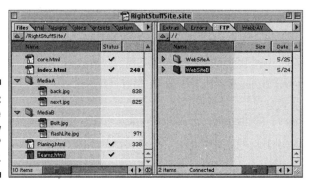

Figure 13-3:
The Site window before FTP transfer.

Figure 13-4:
The Site
window
after FTP
transfer.

Dragging and dropping in the Site window

A second way to load your pages with GoLive is by dragging the files from the left pane to the right pane in the Site window. Up to a point, it's similar to uploading by using the Upload Site window. After you follow Steps 1 – 12 in the previous section to connect to the FTP server, drag files or folders from the left pane (Files tab) to the right pane (FTP tab) of the Site window.

A loading window appears, showing the progress (or lack of) in loading the pages dragged into the FTP pane of the Site window. This method is more visual, but when loading an entire site, it might be easier to go through the steps using the Site toolbar's Incremental Upload button. Using the drag-and-drop method is a little easier for picking and adding or replacing individual folders and files.

FTPing from the menu bar

The final method for getting a site, a file, or a folder from your desktop to the server involves using the FTP Browser command on the menu bar. You don't need to open the Site window to put a site or a couple of pages or files on the server quickly; this method can be a simple solution:

1. **Open GoLive if it isn't already open.**

2. **Close any open pages as well as the Site window.**

3. **Choose Window⇨Inspector from the menu bar.**

   The Inspector appears on the screen. You use the Inspector to inspect the files and folder on the remote site as well as those on your own computer.

4. **Choose File⇨FTP Browser from the menu bar.**

   The FTP Browser window opens, as shown in Figure 13-5.

5. Type the name of your server in the Server text field or select it from the pull-down menu to the right of the Server text field.

Your Web host provides a name for your site's major domain. Simply enter that name in the Server text field, as shown in Figure 13-5. You're able to select a server from the pull-down menu only if you have established the server in the FTP Preferences. (See the section, "Initial FTP Setup" earlier in this chapter.)

6. In the Directory text field, type the name of the directory, if any, to which your site is to be uploaded.

Either leave the Directory window blank or put in the name of the directory you want to put your files into. Click the folder icon to browse the folders at your site on the server. In some cases, the server handles the directory automatically, and leaving it blank usually is a safe bet unless the system administrator has instructed you do otherwise.

7. In the Username text field, type your User ID.

If you set up your pages with a Web hosting service, your User ID is the one the service provides. At an organization with its own server, get your User ID and password from technical support.

8. In the Password text field, type your password.

Use the password provided by the hosting service or your Web administrator.

9. Click the Connect button.

If all your settings are correct and everything on the server end is working, you see "Connected" appear in the Status window and the Disconnect button come to life. Be patient as all of the files and folders on your server site appear in the bottom portion of the window, as shown in Figure 13-5. (If you have no files or folder on the Web site yet, you'll get a blank pane where files are displayed.)

10. Drag the files and folders you want to add to your Web server from the desktop or folder onto the FTP Upload & Download window.

The files and folders are sorted automatically and are added to the FTP Browser window when successfully uploaded. Select a file or folder and you can see information about it in the Inspector that now appears as the FTP Folder Inspector.

You can place non-viewable files on the Web server. *Non-viewable* files are those that can't be viewed by a Web browser that are placed there for users to download from your Web site. How do you download them? Just establish a link to the file from any Web page and it will be downloaded to the client computer when he or she clicks the link.

Figure 13-5:
The FTP
Browser
window.

If you plan to put files on your site for others to download from their browser, condense them first. Use programs such as ZipIt or StuffIt to reduce the size of the file. Not only does that save in terms of file space on the server; it saves in the amount of time it takes to download the file as well.

Making the AppleShare Connection

If your server is set up with an AppleShare connection to your computer, you can bring up the server onto your desktop. After it's on your desktop, you can treat the server just like another disk on your computer. From GoLive, you save your site directly to the server just as you would save it to your own computer by using the Save command. (No need to even bother with FTP!). Here's how it's done:

1. **Choose Apple Menu⇨Chooser from the Macintosh desktop.**

   The Chooser appears on the screen with different icons.

2. **Click the AppleShare icon.**

   The AppleShare icon has a globe and files on a platter and is labeled "AppleShare."

3. **In the AppleShare window, select the server you want to use.**

   Depending on the setup, enter the user name and passwords required. Some connections are set up to remember your password like GoLive does, and it may be only a matter of selecting the server in AppleShare.

4. **Note the name of the server's name (in an icon) when it appears on your desktop.**

   The server icon resembles the AppleShare Icon.

5. **Create a GoLive site and save it to a folder on your computer by choosing File⇨Save.**

6. **After you save the site, choose File⇨Save As from the menu bar.**

   Locate the server name in the Save As window, select it, and then select the folder you want to save your site in. It's just like locating any other folder or drive on your computer.

7. **Click OK.**

   That's it. It's the easiest way to upload files to a server because the process is identical to saving your site to your PC from GoLive.

8. **When you finish using the server, throw the server icon into the trash.**

   That breaks the connection between your computer and the server. Sometimes when more than one computer has the server open on its desktop at the same time, conflicts arise; so be sure to dump the server connection when you're finished using it.

Bringing 'Em Home: Downloading from GoLive

Generally, you don't want to download your files from the Web. To update your site, all you need to do is replace the existing files with the new ones. That way you know that the files on your computer are the same as those on the server. Downloading an old file, fixing it up, and then putting it back on the server is a needless waste of time. Besides, you run the risk of mixing up your files. The old ones downloaded from the server duplicate the ones on your disk. Usually, the need to download a file occurs when you lose the files on your computer (You mean the drive I just formatted erased all my files?) or you're downloading someone else's files in a cooperative effort. (To find out more, see the section, "Working with WebDAV," later in this chapter.)

Bringing files and folders to your computer

If disaster strikes and you do need to download a few files from your site, the FTP Browser command from GoLive's menu bar can save the day. Getting a few files from your site to your computer is the reverse of uploading by using the FTP Browser. All you have to do is follow the steps in the section, "FTPing from the menu bar," and when the server site appears, just drag the files and folders you want from the FTP Browser to your desktop.

Creating a GoLive site from an existing site

If you want to pull sites from the Web into GoLive for editing and you don't have copies of the files on your PC, you need to create a GoLive site on your computer in order to store the downloaded site materials. For example, if you have clients with old sites that need fixing up, you'll have to download them. Fortunately, GoLive has a great way of creating a GoLive site from an existing site on the Web. It downloads the site into a GoLive 5 site right on your computer. Follow these steps to create a GoLive site from an existing site:

1. **Launch GoLive.**

2. **Choose File⇨New Site⇨Import from FTP Server.**

   The Import Site from FTP Server dialog box pops up, as shown in Figure 13-6.

3. **Type the name of your server in the Server text field of the Import Site from FTP Server dialog box.**

   Your Web host provides a name for the major domain of your site. Simply enter that name in the Server text field. If you placed the server name in the FTP preferences as described in the section, "Initial FTP Setup," earlier in this chapter, you can select the server from the pull-down menu.

4. **Type a directory name, if necessary, in the Directory window.**

   Depending on how the system administrator has the FTP set up, you may or may not be required to enter a directory.

5. **Type the user name and password in their respective windows.**

   The username and password are like those used in e-mail. In fact, in some sites you use the same user name and password for e-mail as for FTP. It all depends on how the Web host administrator has the site organized. With several FTP sites, you may have more than one user name and password.

6. **Click Browse to find the home page for the site.**

   The Select Home Page dialog box appears on the screen displaying all the file items stored on the connected server. Usually, an existing site has a home page, but if you don't know the home page, go back and look at the site through a browser. Note the name of the home page and then enter it by clicking the Browse button so that you can find the page in the right folder. A home page may have a name like "index.html." However, in a given site, several pages named "index.html" may exist in separate sub-folders. Using the Browse button allows you to locate the correct one.

7. **After the home page is selected, click OK.**

   The Select Home Page dialog box closes and the Import Site from FTP Server dialog box reappears on the screen (see Figure 13-6).

8. **Click the Import button in the Import Site from FTP Server dialog box.**

   At this point, the operation looks exactly like setting up a standard Web site with GoLive 5. (See Chapter 2.) A window appears requesting a site name and you select a drive or directory along with a site name. Click OK, and your site is set up for you.

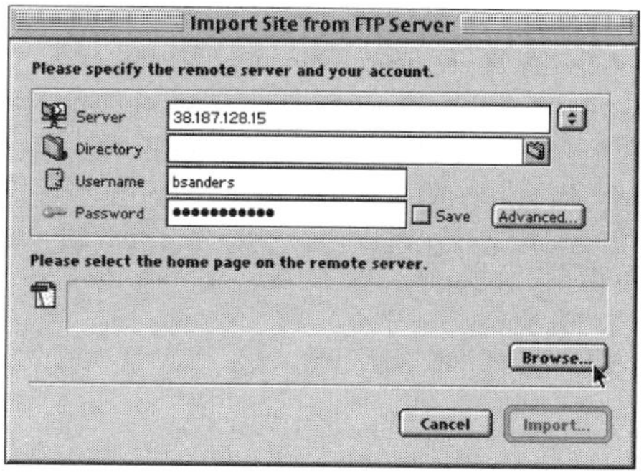

Figure 13-6: Use this window to import a site from an FTP server.

After this operation is complete, you have a full site with all of the pages integrated into a root site. When you load the site by choosing File⇨Open from the menu bar and supplying the site name, all the files you just imported appear in the Files view of the Site window. From that point on, just use all the GoLive 5 tools to edit and update the site. Later, you can re-export it by using the FTP tools in GoLive.

Working with WebDAV

Web site development is often a collaborative activity, with artists, designers, content suppliers, marketers, programmers, and a whole host of others working together to get a Web site up and going. What's more, these people are often in different places. By using WebDAV, people from all over can work on the same Web site collaboratively. You need to be connected to a server with WebDAV working, but otherwise, the process for connecting to WebDAV is much like connections through FTP.

Setting up WebDAV in GoLive

The first step in working with WebDAV is to set up the preferences so that your computer knows where to make a connection. Passwords and user names are involved just like e-mail or FTP described earlier in this chapter. To set up WebDAV in GoLive, follow these steps:

1. **Open an existing site or create a new site by choosing File⇨New Site⇨ Blank.**

   A new Site window appears on the screen.

2. **Choose Edit⇨Preferences from the Menu bar.**

   The Preferences dialog box appears with two columns. The column on the left has a number of icons and labels

3. **Select Network⇨WebDAV Server from the left column.**

   The WebDAV pane appears on the right. At the top of the pane is space for listing all of the different WebDAV addresses you enter, the user name for that particular WebDAV site, and the port you're going to use. (Port 21 is the default. If Port 21 doesn't respond, contact your system administrator.)

4. **Click the New button and type the address of your WebDAV server in the Server text field in the bottom half of the pane.**

   The address can be words or numbers. Usually, a WebDAV address looks pretty much like a Web address and URL. (If you went through the previous FTP sections, the procedure is almost identical.)

5. **Type the user name and password in their respective windows.**

   The user name and password are like those used in e-mail and FTP. Other times a common user name and password is given all of those working together on the WebDAV server. The common user name is essentially a group name that anyone in the group may use.

6. **Select the authorization level from the pull-down menu.**

   The authorization level can be *None* or *Basic.* The Basic level means that you have to have a password. "None" means you do not require a password. (I don't need no stinkin' password!)

7. **Click the OK button, and you're all done.**

   The Preferences window disappears. Your WebDAV configuration is complete. Later, you can return to the WebDAV preferences and edit any of your old settings.

Setting up the WebDAV connection for your site

After you establish your basic preferences for WebDAV, you need to make a similar setting in your site settings. Figure 13-2 shows FTP settings configured. In the lower portion of the window you can see the area where WebDAV settings go. Follow these steps to establish your WebDAV site settings:

1. **Open an existing site or create a new site by choosing File⇨New Site⇨ Blank.**

   A new Site window appears on the screen.

2. **Choose Site⇨Settings.**

   The Settings window appears. A column of icons for making the settings is in the left pane, and depending which icon you select, the right pane provides different options.

3. **Click the icon for the FTP & WebDAV server in the left pane.**

   The FTP & WebDAV selections appear in the right pane. The bottom portion of the pane is where you enter the information for WebDAV. (Refer to Figure 13-2).

4. **Click the arrow to open the pull-down menu on the far right and select the WebDAV server you want to use.**

   Unless you put more than one WebDAV address in your Preferences, only one appears in the window. When you select the address, all the information you need appears in the window automatically. (You can do it the hard way by typing the address.)

5. **Select the Enable workgroup support check box if desired.**

   Enhance your group efforts by using Workgroup Support in GoLive 5. You can simultaneously lock and download a file with Workgroup Support enabled. If you do use Workgroup Support, synchronize your files first. (See this chapter's section, "Synchronizing your sites" for more on this.) The major advantage of Workgroup Support using WebDAV and GoLive 5 is that many of the synchronizing and locking features are done automatically rather than manually, and you also get metadata information on files. (Metadata information is the information in the header that tells you about the file.)

6. **After you make your selections, click OK.**

   Your settings are complete and the dialog box disappears.

7. **Click the Files tab of the Site window.**

   On newly-created sites you see only the single file named "index.html."

8. **If the right pane isn't open in your Site window, click the double arrows in the bottom-right corner of the Site window.**

   The right pane opens in the Site window. (Avoid clicking the left and right horizontal scroll arrow down there. The correct arrow set is the farthest to the right.)

9. **Click the WebDAV tab in the right pane of the Site window.**

   Until you're connected, all you see is a blank pane. (That will change!)

10. **Choose Site⇨WebDAV Server⇨Connect from the menu bar or click the WebDAV Server Connect/Disconnect icon (thirteenth from the left) on the toolbar.**

The files on the WebDAV server appear in the WebDAV tab of the Site window. Some files have lock or pencil icons next to them. The lock icon means that only certain users can open the files, and the pencil means that *only* you can edit the files. (The others will *not* see the pencil icon because they cannot edit the files.) In effect, the files are locked except for you. (See Figure 13-7.) You can unlock your files so that other people can work on them by selecting the file and right-clicking (Windows) or pressing Control-Click (Macintosh) and selecting Check In from the context menu that appears. Later, you can reverse the process by selecting Check Out from the same context menu.

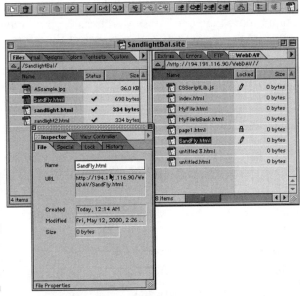

Figure 13-7: WebDAV and root folder files in the Site window.

Synchronizing your sites

After you make the connection with the WebDAV server, you're all set to upload and download files. In addition, you can synchronize your files. That means that all the files on both your site and the WebDAV server are the same. When you perform synchronization, GoLive 5 automatically uploads and downloads files so that the WebDAV pane and the Files pane are identical. With your Web site open and your connection to the WebDAV server made (see previous section), you're ready to work with a team on WebDAV. All of this takes place in the Site window. Here's how to synchronize all your files, or upload and download individual files:

1. **With the WebDAV and Files tabs selected in the Site window, click the WebDAV Synchronize All icon on the toolbar or choose Site➪ WebDAV➪Synchronize.**

   The Synchronize window appears, as shown in Figure 13-8. Four buttons below the main pane provide options for (from top to bottom) Skip, Upload, Download, and Delete. In the unlabeled column between the Site and Server columns are boxes where the chosen options are displayed. Full synchronization automatically inserts those files that have been changed and need to be uploaded or downloaded. (This is how to get *everybody* on the same page!)

2. **Make any changes by selecting individual files and clicking on an option button. Then click the Synchronize button at the bottom of the window.**

   The Synchronize window disappears and all the files are either up- or downloaded. Initially, the uploaded files may not appear in the WebDAV pane, and I found that disconnecting and reconnecting helped to get them in the WebDAV pane of the Site window.

Figure 13-8:
The
WebDAV
Synchronize
window.

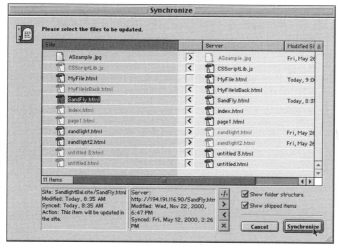

Upload and download individual files

To upload and download individual files or modified files, you need not synchronize everything. (With great big sites, synchronization can take a while because all the files have to be up- and downloaded.) Here's how to upload and download files:

1. **With the WebDAV and Files tabs selected in the Site window, select the individual file or files you want to upload or download by clicking the files in either the WebDAV or Files pane.**

   When you want to select more than one file simultaneously, press Shift-Click and select all the files you want.

2. **Choose Site⇨WebDAV⇨Upload Selection from the menu bar to send files from your site to the WebDAV server or choose Site⇨WebDAV⇨Download Selection to send the file or files from the WebDAV server to your site.**

   GoLive sends your files to the server from your computer and they appear in the WebDAV or Files pane of the Site window. Alternatively, you can select just those modified files by choosing Upload Modified Items or Download Modified Items from the toolbar or by choosing Site⇨WebDAV⇨Upload/Download Modified Items from the menu bar.

For group work on a project, especially when people doing the work are scattered all over the world, the WebDAV connection through GoLive 5 is great. Using the synchronize option is a powerful way to keep everyone working on the same page and coordinating efforts without wasting time. Keep WebDAV in mind when you have a project where several designers, developers, and programmers may need to coordinate their efforts.

Part IV

Swinging Pages: Tapping the Power within GoLive 5

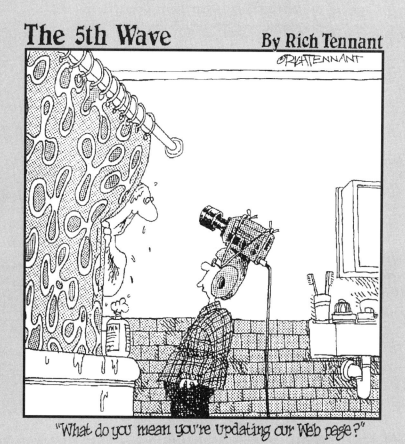

The 5th Wave   By Rich Tennant

"What do you mean you're updating our Web page?"

In this part . . .

You're going to have so much fun in Part IV, it should be illegal! Find out in this part how to use GoLive 5 to do everything from making buttons jump on-screen to hiding floating boxes. On top of that, GoLive 5 gives you your own movie editing studio that enables you to create special effects, add sounds and Hollywood-style transitions, and even combine animation from Flash movies!

When you want your site to get eye-popping attention from weary Web surfers who've seen too many flat, motionless sites, you're ready for Part IV. You're going to see how to make buttons that come alive by the surfer's simply passing a mouse over them. You'll have messages popping up to give a greeting or announce a special promotion. Likewise, you can integrate your digital QuickTime movies and edit them for interesting transitions and special effects right in GoLive 5. If that doesn't wake up an indifferent eye, then have a herd of floating boxes fly around the screen with text, graphics, or both by using Dynamic HTML. GoLive makes both the creation of the floating boxes and their motion as easy as dragging an object around the screen while GoLive records the path and then re-creates it on a Web page.

Chapter 14

Making Those Buttons Jump and Jive

· ·

In This Chapter

▶ Adding rollovers

▶ Triggering action on Web pages

▶ Achieving actions with a mouse click

▶ Boiling down JavaScript

▶ Putting a movie on your Web page

▶ Translating Photoshop files into Web graphics

· ·

*W*eb page designers use *actions* to make Web pages more interesting and take advantage of the computer's power to make rapid changes. An action is a change that happens on a Web page when the viewer makes certain moves. So, actually, an action on a Web page is a reaction to what the user does. One of the most popular actions is the *rollover*. As the Web surfer moves her mouse over the page, changes occur depending on where she moves the mouse. A rollover occurs when the mouse passes over those parts of the page where the designer placed an *action*. (I use the term *hotspot* elsewhere in this book to indicate a spot that responds to a mouse click used as a link. An action is one type of hotspot.)

To make an action, GoLive 5 provides special palettes that create JavaScript code. So instead of having to spend a good deal of time writing JavaScript code, the designer can now concentrate on where he wants the actions to be placed and on the overall look and feel of the Web page.

Swapping Images with a Rollover

A Web page is fundamentally different from a paper page in several ways. Images on a Web page can change when you place your mouse over them. For example, to get a viewer's attention to a text selection, many designers use a *rollover*. A rollover means that images swap when you place your mouse pointer over their areas on the page. Often, rollovers are buttons that initiate linking, but other times they can be images that swap for other purposes, such as comparing views. After you do some preliminary work, GoLive makes creating rollovers simple.

To get ready for a rollover, you need some images. First, create at least two graphics (JPEG, GIF or PNG) with identical dimensions. (See Chapter 2 for details about graphic file types that may safely be used on the Web.) For example, two graphics that measure 20 pixels by 30 pixels are identical as far as the Web page is concerned. The images in the graphics can be as similar (or different) as you want as long as the dimensions are the same. You can add a third image as well. The third image is the "click" image and appears when you click the mouse button. It must have the identical dimensions of the first two.

A group of objects called "Smart objects" on the Objects palette constitute a special group of icons familiar to users of earlier versions of GoLive. The objects on the Smart tab of the Objects palettes are a mixed bag of HTML tags and JavaScript functions that can be placed in the head or body of your Web page in the Layout view of the Document window. A class of Smart objects new to GoLive 5 act as placeholders for non-Web graphics such as Photoshop formatted ones. When the Photoshop file is dragged and dropped on top of the placeholder, a "Smart link" is established between the Photoshop image and a new Web-safe file generated by the Smart object. This chapter covers the Smart objects; they play an important role in livening up your Web site.

After you create images, you're ready to impress your friends and dumbfound your critics. Here's how:

1. **Choose File⇨New Site⇨Blank from the menu bar.**

   The New Blank Site dialog box appears.

2. **Type a name for the site in the New Site text field; then type a folder destination in the In Folder text field. Click OK.**

3. **When the Site window appears, click the Files tab.**

   The Files view of the Site window appears. You will see one new file named index.html.

4. **Choose Site⇨Finder/Explorer⇨Add files and add all the graphics you created to the root folder.**

   Click the Files tab of the Site window to make sure that you have all the graphic files you want for your rollovers.

5. **Choose Window⇨Inspector or undock the Inspector by clicking the Inspector tab at the side of the screen.**

   The Inspector appears on your page.

6. **Open the Index page in the Layout view.**

   Just double-click index.html in the Files view of the Site window. A blank page appears in the Layout view of the Document window.

7. **Choose Window⇨Objects or undock the Objects palette by clicking the Objects tab at the side of the screen.**

   The Objects palette appears. (Sometimes the Color palette sits on top of its roommate, Objects. If that's the case, just click on the Objects tab.)

8. **Click the Smart tab of the Objects palette.**

   The Smart tab is the second from the left. (For those of you who are used to GoLive 4, the Smart tab replaced the CyberObjects tab in GoLive 5.)

9. **Click and drag the Rollover icon from the Smart tab of the Objects palette and place it on the page.**

   The Rollover icon is the third from the left. The Rollover placeholder appears on the page with a question mark on the icon and the Inspector becomes the Rollover Inspector. You see three windows in the Rollover Inspector with question marks on them and Point-and-Shoot buttons next to each.

10. **With the Rollover placeholder selected on your page, click on the question mark icon labeled Main in the Rollover Inspector.**

    The Point-and-Shoot button is focused and ready to use in the Rollover Inspector.

11. **Place your main image on the Web page either by dragging it from the Files view of the Site window onto the Rollover placeholder or by using the Point-and-Shoot line of the Rollover Inspector to select the image from the Site window.**

    The image you select appears both in the Rollover placeholder and as a thumbnail image in the Main window of the Rollover Inspector. The main image is the default image, the one you see when you're not pausing over the image area. Any image can be the top one. Because this is just a practice run, use any image you like.

    When you use your Point-and-Shoot line, you can bring up the Site window by pulling the line to the Select Window toggle icon on the toolbar. The icon is the third from the right on the toolbar.

12. **Type a name for the button in the Name window of the Rollover Inspector.**

    Use any name you want or leave it as the default name *button*. If you add another Button image, GoLive gives it another name, like *Button2*. If you plan to have several rollovers on a page it's a good idea to name the buttons in relation to how you'll use them. For example, you might want to name them relative to the link they're connected to.

13. **In the Rollover Inspector, select the Over image box, as shown in Figure 14-1, and repeat Steps 8 through 10.**

    The Over figure is the one you want to appear when the mouse pointer is *over* the image. (That's why it's called *over*.)

14. **Click the Preview tab of the Document window.**

    The Preview window appears with the main image showing on the page.

15. **Move the mouse over the image and watch it change to the second image.**

16. **Pull the mouse away from the image area, and the original image reappears.**

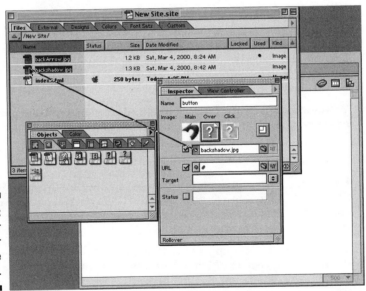

Figure 14-1:
The Rollover
Inspector
adds the
Over image.

Tools such as Photoshop, ImageStyler, or Fireworks make it easy to create images for rollovers. Simply create an image, save or export it, add a drop shadow to the same image and save or export the image with a different name. In ImageStyler, the image size is maintained when different styles of the same image are exported.

If you don't have the images the same size, the Over and Click images will be constrained to the dimensions of the Main image.

Adding a Message to Your Rollover

Besides making the images swap in a rollover operation, you can also make a message appear at the bottom of the browser window whenever you move the mouse over the rollover. The message provides further information for the user. Follow these steps to add a message to a rollover:

1. **Begin in the Layout view of a page with a completed rollover on it.**

   Any rollover will do. This is easy.

2. **Choose Window⇨Inspector or undock the Inspector by clicking the Inspector tab at the side of the screen.**

   The Inspector appears on your page.

3. **Select the rollover image by clicking it in the Layout view of the Document window.**

   The Inspector becomes the Rollover Inspector.

4. **Choose Window⇨Actions to open the Actions palette.**

   The Actions palette appears. In the left pane, you can see some of the mouse actions that you can use. In the upper-right portion of the Actions palette, look for plus (+) and minus (–) buttons.

5. **Select Mouse Exit in the Events list and then click the plus (+) button in the Actions palette.**

   In the Actions pane, an icon with a question mark (?) appears with the word *None* next to it. In the bottom half of the Actions palette, an Action button with a question mark appears (? Action) next to the Actions pull-down menu.

6. **Click the Action button and choose Message⇨Open Alert Window from the pulldown Action menu.**

   The Message Alert icon appears next to the Action button. Below the Action button is a Message window. (That's where your message to the World Wide Web goes.)

7. **In the Message window, type a message that you want to appear in the Alert box when your mouse exits the rollover.**

   Use any message you want. In some cases, the graphic on the rollover may be a clue to the nature of the message. For example, an Information button developed for your site could be the spot where users go to get certain types of information that pops up on an Alert box. Sometimes the Alert box pops up right on top of your rollover and hides the rollover. That's one reason to select the Mouse exit event so as not to cover up the rollover.

Making Things Move on Your Web Pages

Actions *can* be events triggered by the Web surfer moving or clicking the mouse, but mouse movement isn't the only thing that can get your Web page jumping and jiving. Actions such as the appearance of a prompt or alert box can also be set off automatically when you load or unload a page. (Alert: "Are you sure you want to exit?") Other actions can be fired by key presses (press K for "Kabloee!"), and still other actions can be orchestrated sequentially with the help of the TimeLine editor.

I discuss the intricacies of the TimeLine editor in Chapter 16, so if you're interested in time-controlled actions for your page, you may want to skip a few chapters ahead. The next sections in this chapter concentrate on setting off actions automatically on loading or unloading a page and on triggering actions with the help of various mouse and key actions supplied by the viewer.

It's all in your head

Actions can be set off when a page opens or closes. For example, you may want to load a sound to play or a welcoming message to pop up when the page opens. Perhaps your domain name has changed, and you want your old domain to forward your page to your new domain automatically.

To trigger an event that sets off an action, GoLive provides Action Headitems, which work in ways similar to rollover actions. GoLive targets the head area because the head area of an HTML page always loads first, making available the JavaScript functions, CSS definitions, and other information your page can use as soon as the body of the program is loaded. For example, if you want all of your rollover images preloaded before the rest of the page is, you can have that done in the head. Then, when the user first encounters a rollover, she need not wait while the images for the over and click functions load. I find calling up popup message windows helpful when a page loads as well. Here's how to set up one for your page:

1. **Begin in the Layout view of the Document window.**

2. **Choose Window⇨Inspector or undock the Inspector by clicking the Inspector tab at the side of the screen.**

    The Inspector appears on your page.

3. **Choose Window⇨Objects or undock the Objects palette.**

    The Objects palette appears on the page.

4. **Click the Smart tab on the Objects palette.**

    The Smart tab is the second tab on the palette. Eight icons appear on the Smart tab.

5. **Open the Head window of the Layout view by clicking the down arrow to the left of the Page icon right below the Layout tab.**

   The Head window opens and you see tag icons for code in the Head area of the page.

6. **Click and drag the Head Action icon (eighth from the left) from the Smart tab of the Objects palette to the Head window.**

   Figure 14-2 shows where the Head Action icon should be placed on the page.

Drag the Head Action icon to the Head window

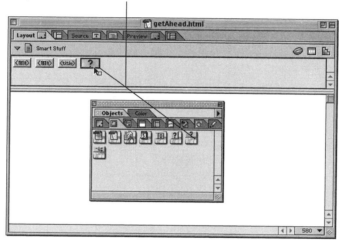

Figure 14-2:
The Head Action icon moves to the Head window.

7. **Click the Head Action icon in the Head window.**

   The Inspector becomes the Action Inspector, as shown in Figure 14-3. You see an Exec. pull-down menu near the top of the Inspector and an Action button and pull-down menu beneath the Exec. menu.

8. **OnLoad is the default option in the Exec. pull-down menu in the Action Inspector so you need not open the menu by clicking it.**

   Leave the Name window blank. GoLive generates a name (more like an ID code) for you. If you use the OnParse selection, pretty much the same thing happens, only OnParse loads the message a little sooner. (The code is loaded as soon as the browser reads it in the Head of the script — that's what parse means in this context.) If you had selected OnUnload, the message would appear when you left the page for another link.

9. **Choose Message⇨Open Alert Window from the Action pull-down menu, as shown in Figure 14-3.**

   The Head Action icon turns into a message icon, and the message window appears on the Action Inspector.

10. **Type a message in the message window.**

   The operation brings up an Alert box message as soon as the page opens. When the user encounters the popup message in the Alert box, he reads it and then clicks OK to make it disappear without affecting the page.

Because the message appears when a user opens the page, this is a good place to send out a welcome to the viewer. For e-commerce, the message could announce a special sale or new items available.

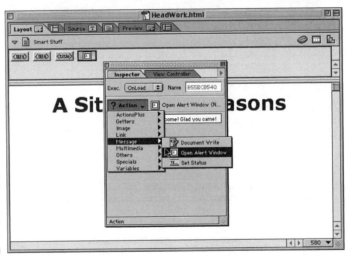

Figure 14-3:
The Action Inspector provides a wide selection of actions for the Head Action.

You can't get there from here

Sometimes when you create a new site, you place it in a new URL. However, a lot of people still know the old URL and it may even be linked from another site. Instead of forcing Web surfers to start at one page and click to another page, you can set up an automatic transfer to the new URL, and the Web surfer is none the wiser. The process is similar to forwarding mail to a new address. Follow these steps to set up automatic transfer:

1. **Begin in the Layout view of the Document window.**

2. **Choose Window⊏>Inspector or undock the Inspector by clicking the Inspector tab at the side of the screen.**

   The Inspector appears on your page.

3. **Choose Window⊏>Objects or undock the Objects palette.**

   The Objects palette appears on the page.

4. **Click the Smart tab on the Objects palette.**

   The Smart tab is the second tab on the palette. Eight icons appear on the Smart tab.

5. **Click and drag the Head Action icon from the Smart tab on the Objects palette to the Head window arrow right next to the Page icon in the Layout window.**

   The Head window drops down as soon as you drag the Head Action icon onto the Head window arrow. Drop the Head Action icon in the open Head window.

6. **Click the Head Action icon in the Head window.**

   The Inspector becomes the Action Inspector.

7. **Choose OnParse from the Exec. pull-down menu in the Action Inspector.**

   The OnParse selection parses the action from the Head area of the page and gets it up a little faster than OnLoad. OnLoad waits for the page to load, and that takes a little more time.

8. **Choose Link⊏>Goto Link from the Action pull-down menu.**

   The Inspector provides a Link and Target window.

9. **Type the URL in the Link window for the new site address and a target for a specific frame or window if you want to specify one.**

   As soon as the page loads, it redirects the viewer to the new address. The visitor to your site won't even realize she's been sent to another address.

When you set up your page to redirect traffic to your new site, be sure to let people know that you have a new domain name and URL. That way, you don't have to worry about maintaining the old page as well as keeping a reminder page.

Speeding up rollovers

When you use a rollover, the rollover effect may not appear until the user runs the pointer across the rollover several times. The delay happens because the second image takes time to load. At one quick passover, the pointer is off the hotspot before the image has a chance to make an appearance. The answer to the problem is to use a Head Action to preload the image. Here's how:

1. **Begin in the Layout view of the Document window with at least one rollover on the page and with the Site window open.**

2. **Choose Window⇨Inspector or undock the Inspector by clicking the Inspector tab at the side of the screen.**

   The Inspector appears on your page.

3. **Choose Window⇨Objects or undock the Objects palette.**

   The Objects palette appears on the page.

4. **Click the Smart tab on the Objects palette.**

   The Smart tab is the second tab on the palette. Eight icons appear on the Smart tab.

5. **Open the Head window of the Layout view by clicking the Head window arrow icon next to the Page icon below the Layout tab.**

   The Head window drops down with tag icons showing, plus any head items you've already put there.

6. **Drag the Head Action icon from the Smart tab on the Objects palette to the head section.**

   The Head Action icon is the seventh from the left. Be careful selecting it because it's right next to the Body icon that looks similar.

7. **Click the Head Action icon in the head section.**

   The Inspector becomes the Action Inspector.

8. **Choose OnLoad from the Exec. pull-down menu in the Action Inspector.**

9. **Choose Image⇨ Preload Image from the Action pull-down menu.**

   The Action Inspector provides a link window where you can use the Browse button, Point-and-Shoot button, or type in the addresses of the images you want to preload. Figure 14-4 shows the rollover images being selected from the Site window. Repeat Steps 4 through 9 for each image that is swapped into a main image's position. Then, the first time a viewer activates your rollover, they'll perform as promised.

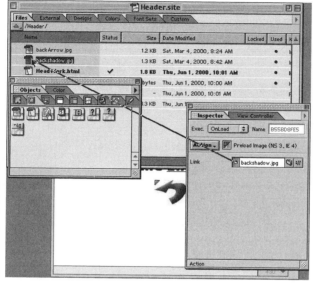

Figure 14-4:
Select
rollover
images
to be
preloaded.

Setting Up Actions with the Mouse

Actions set off by a mouse trigger are inherently interactive. The user directly initiates an action by doing something with the mouse, whether it's a click, double-click, or positioning the pointer somewhere on the page.

Clicking form buttons is just dandy for initiating different actions, but you have to create a JavaScript function first in the head of your page. Then, in the button tag, you need to input an event handler code to tell the form element button when to fire the function. Elegant, to be sure, but just a bit tricky. So, if you see a page that uses a form button to initiate an action, you'll know that it's because the designer dropped in a JavaScript function she wrote (or had GoLive 5 write it for her).

Adding a small window

A Web page has distinct advantages over a paper page in certain areas. One advantage is that a Web page is capable of showing a series of small images or a small bit of text and then letting the viewer open another window to show a larger view of an image or elaboration on the text. In that way, a single screen can reveal far more information than a paper page. This next feature of actions shows how to superimpose a little information window on top of your main window.

You can put this space-saving feature (the small added window) to work for you by doing the following:

1. **Choose File⇨New Site⇨Blank from the menu bar.**

   The New Blank Site dialog box appears.

2. **Type a name for the site in the New Site text field; then type a folder name in the In Folder text field. Click OK.**

3. **When the Site window appears, click the Files tab.**

   A new Site window appears in the Files view with a single new page titled index.html.

4. **Choose Window⇨Objects from the menu bar.**

   The Objects palette appears.

5. **Click the Site tab on the Objects palette and drag the Page icon (first on the left) to the Files view of the Site window.**

   An untitled page appears in the Site window. You can rename it by double-clicking it and typing in a new name if you want or leave it untitled. (Untitled, unloved, and neglected — for now at least.)

6. **Double-click the index.html file in the Files view of the Site window.**

   A blank page opens in the Layout view of the Document window.

7. **Choose Window⇨Inspector or undock the Inspector by clicking the Inspector tab at the side of the screen.**

   The Inspector appears on your page.

8. **Type some text in the Layout view of the Document window, select it, and then click the Link icon on the toolbar.**

   The Inspector becomes the Text Inspector and the text is underlined.

9. **In the Link tab of the Text Inspector, type a pound sign (#) in the URL window.**

   The pound sign is a false link, but it creates a hotspot in the selected text.

10. **Choose Window⇨Action.**

    The Action palette appears.

11. **Select Mouse Click in the Events column.**

12. **Click the plus (+) Action button.**

    An Action pull-down menu appears below the Events column.

13. **Click and hold on the Action menu to open it and choose Link⇨Open Window.**

    The Actions palette now shows several options for opening the new window, as shown in Figure 14-5. Options include whether the window scrolls, if it has a URL window, and how big you want it to be on the screen. (The context-sensitive Actions palette has more secret windows than a castle.)

Figure 14-5:
The Open
Window
action in the
Actions
palette
provides
several
parameters
you can set
to open the
window.

Figure 14-5:
The Open
Window
action in the
Actions
palette
provides
several
parameters
you can set
to open the
window.

14. **In the Link window in the Actions palette, enter the name of the file you want to open in the new window.**

    You can enter the file either by clicking the Browse button or by using the Point-and-Shoot button. Just drag the Point-and-Shoot line to the Select Window icon on the Toolbar to bring up the Site window. Then select the file from the Files view of the Site window.

15. **In the two Size windows in the Actions palette, enter the horizontal and vertical dimensions of the window you want to open.**

    Pick a size that provides just enough room for the content of the window (refer to Figure 14-6 to see the results).

16. **Check the boxes for Scroll, Menu, Dir. and other features you want to appear in the window, leave unchecked those features you do not want, and type in the horizontal and vertical dimensions.**

    Because the window is supposed to take up minimal space, the fewer boxes checked, the better. Notice that in Figure 14-5, only three boxes are checked. All of the check boxes represent options for the browser. I leave Resize checked in case the user wants to make the window larger or smaller and the location window open so that she can see where she is, but otherwise the window options are not needed. Added windows such as these can be used for showing the full size of a thumbnail image or for creating a floating menu, among many other uses in the designer's imagination. Figure 14-6 shows the page opened in a browser.

Figure 14-6:
A small
window
opens by
the action in
the link text.

User-controlled color

In addition to triggering actions using linked text, you can also use linked images to create actions as well. One of the more enjoyable actions is to change the background color. Here's how you do it:

1. **Open the Layout view of the Document window.**

   Start off with a nice blank page.

2. **Choose Window⇨Inspector or undock the Inspector by clicking the Inspector tab at the side of the screen.**

   The Inspector appears on your page.

3. **Drag an image to the page from its directory on your computer.**

   The Inspector becomes the Image Inspector.

4. **On the Link tab of the Image Inspector, type a pound sign (#) in the URL.**

   The pound sign is just filler for an actual URL, but it does make the selected image a hotspot.

5. **Choose Window⇨Action from the menu bar.**

   The Action palette appears.

6. **Scroll down the Events column of the Action palette until you find Mouse Up and then select it.**

   You must first press down the mouse button and then release it before the action launches when using the Mouse Up event handler.

7. **Click the plus (+) Actions button.**

   An Action pull-down menu appears below the Events column.

8. **Pull down the Action menu by clicking and holding the pulldown menu arrow and choose Others➪Set BackColor.**

   A color well appears in the Actions palette.

9. **Click the color well in the Actions palette to bring up the Color palette.**

   The Color palette appears.

10. **Select a background color from the Color palette.**

    When you select a color on the Color palette, the color appears in the color well on the Actions palette. As soon as you see the color you want in the color well, you're all finished. Save your page, give it a test drive in a browser, and see whether you like it.

If you want to surprise a viewer, use a text color the same shade as the background color. Then do a background color switch and the text hidden in the background suddenly appears on the screen.

Chapter 15

World Wide Web Movies

● ●

In This Chapter

▶ Inserting the movie on your page

▶ Working with the TimeLine window

▶ Adding sound to movies

▶ Adding special effects

▶ Integrating text in titles and credits

▶ Adding chapters to movies

● ●

*T*his chapter begins an exploration of integrating QuickTime movies into a Web Page made with GoLive. As you may expect, there's far more to creating, editing, and delivering movies over the Web than I can possibly cover in this chapter; however, GoLive can make working with movies relatively easy (and everyone knows that adding movies adds a lot of fun to your site). With the help of GoLive 5, you can add special effects or text to your video creations, as well as add neat transition effects between scenes (just like the pros in Hollywood). GoLive can't shoot the film for you, so you need either a digital video camera or the necessary hardware and software to convert analog video (tape) into digital format. However, if you do take the time to shoot the video, make format conversions (if necessary), spruce up your video with the editing tools GoLive 5 offers, and add it to your Web page, you could have a worldwide theatre to screen your masterpieces!

Putting QuickTime Movies on Your Page

GoLive makes putting QuickTime movies on your Web page easy. Putting a movie on your Web page is similar to putting anything else on your page with GoLive, and most of the same rules apply. First, you should put all of your files in the root folder; this applies to your QuickTime movies just as much as it applies to the graphic and text files you want for your site. If you follow that rule, the rest comes rather easily.

All of your work will be for naught if you don't use the correct plug-in. The QuickTime (QT) plug-ins for both Microsoft Internet Explorer and Netscape Navigator and for both Windows and Macintosh OS are available for download for free at `www.apple.com`. No plug-in. No movie. That's because the plug-in adds the movie-running capacity to the browser. Once you have the QuickTime plug-in ready on your hard drive, follow these steps to put a QuickTime movie on your page:

1. **Choose File⇨New Site⇨Blank from the menu bar.**

    The New Blank Site dialog box appears.

2. **Type a name for the site in the New Site text field; then enter a folder destination in the In Folder text field. Click OK.**

3. **When the Site window appears, click the File tab.**

    A new Site window appears in the File view with a single new page titled "index.html."

4. **Choose Site⇨Finder⇨Add Files... and select the QuickTime movie files you want on your page.**

    You import QuickTime movie files (.mov) just like any other file you want on your page. When you add files to a site, a directory dialog box appears and you select the drive, folder, and any subfolder until you find the file you want. Select it and click OK. Okay?

5. **Open the index.html page by double-clicking it in the Files tab of the Site Window.**

    The page opens in the Layout view of the Document window. (Good old index.html is the default page that GoLive generates when you create a new site.)

6. **Choose Window⇨Inspector or undock the Inspector by clicking the Inspector tab at the side of the screen.**

    The Inspector appears on the screen.

7. **Choose Window⇨Objects or undock the Objects palette by clicking the Objects tab at the side of the screen.**

    The Objects palette appears on the screen.

8. **Click the Basic tab of the Objects palette and drag the QuickTime icon onto the page.**

    The QuickTime icon is the eighth from the left (the one with the QT logo on it). The Inspector becomes the Plug-in Inspector.

9. **Select the QuickTime Movie file for your page either by pulling the point-and-shoot line in the Plug-in Inspector to the file in the Site window or by clicking the Browse button to navigate through folders until you find the file you want.**

If the Site window is not visible when using point-and-shoot, first pull the line to the Select Window icon on the toolbar to bring the Site window forward. The Plug-in placeholder on your page now shows the name of your movie without the .mov extension and the first frame of the movie, as shown in Figure 15-1.

Figure 15-1:
A QuickTime movie appears on a page in the Layout view of the Document window.

Save your page as soon as you have the movie in it. Movie files tend to be large and can crash your computer easily. If you plan to do a lot with movies, get some additional RAM and permanent storage as well. You'll need it! A minimum amount would be about 64 megabytes, but 128mg would be preferable. (You can't be too thin or too rich, and you can't have enough RAM or mass storage space.)

Working in the TimeLine Window

After you have your QT (that's Hollywood talk for QuickTime) movie embedded in the Plug-in icon on your page, you're ready to do some work with GoLive's TimeLine window. Follow these steps:

1. **Begin with your movie page loaded in the Layout view of the Document window.**

   With GoLive 5 you can actually see the initial frame of the movie.

2. **Choose Window⇨Inspector or undock the Inspector by clicking the Inspector tab at the side of the screen.**

   The Inspector appears on the screen. If you have the movie icon selected, the Plug-in Inspector is on the set...er...screen.

3. **Double-click the Plug-in icon showing on your Web page or click the Open Movie button in the QuickTime tab of the Plug-in Inspector.**

   The QuickTime movie appears in a separate window. After your movie is in your page, the Inspector becomes the Movie Inspector. The toolbar changes to the QuickTime toolbar. The Basic tab of the Movie Inspector keeps track of important information about your movie, such as duration and data size. The information changes as you make changes to your movie. One of the big problems with movies on the Web is that they take up a lot of space relative to other files. The Basic tab you see in Figure 15-2 makes this abundantly clear, showing that about 15 seconds of movie takes up almost a half megabyte of hard drive space.

4. **Choose Movie⇨Show TimeLine from the menu bar or click the ShowTimeLine Window button (second button from the left) on the QuickTime toolbar.**

   The TimeLine Window opens. Typically, when the TimeLine Window opens you see one or two tracks. One track is for the video and the other is for sound. You can add more tracks (as well as special effects provided by GoLive).

Figure 15-2:
The Movie Inspector keeps track of your movie's size.

As you make changes to your movie in GoLive, the movie's size changes. Look at the Movie Inspector periodically to make sure you're not making too big a movie.

Keeping Track of Your Tracks

After you have your movie on the screen in the QuickTime window and your TimeLine window open, you have several options. Each track on the editor contains a single movie element such as the video or sound. However, all of the tracks share a common time track and cursor. When the time cursor passes over a certain point, all of the tracks active at that point will fire. For example, sound and video on separate tracks display the position of the film and the sound they share at the point of the cursor. If the sound track falls beyond the video track, sound keeps playing as the time cursor passes over the video track even though no video is left to view. Figure 15-3 shows a TimeLine window with the following four tracks:

- ✔ **Video Track 1:** The basic movie goes on this track. All materials on the tracks can be moved on the timeline to accommodate introductions, titles, or other media that the designer wants to include.

- ✔ **Sound Track 1:** The first sound track is usually the voice track associated with the video, but it could be any sound track.

- ✔ **Sound Track 2 (Renamed Music):** A second sound track has been added for a little music. With this setup, two sound tracks can play simultaneously. You can add a second sound track for music to accompany a voiceover or dialog on the first sound track. In this particular example, a music clip was put into a sound track. GoLive also has a music track that works for MIDI (Musical Instruments Digital Interface) files, but because the music clip in the example is in AIFF (Audio Interchange File Format), I had to use the sound track icon. The popular WAV format (Windows WAVE) also works on the Sound track instead of the music track.

- ✔ **One Source Filter Track:** The Filter Track is a special effect track added in GoLive. For example, you can apply a sepia tone or black and white to your movie, as well as faux film damage to make it look like an old film. The associated Samples track with the One Source Filter specifies the nature of the filter. In Figure 15-3, the Film Noise Filter is selected.

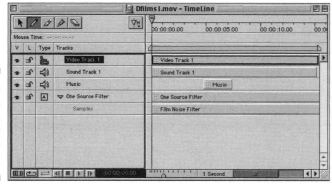

Figure 15-3: The TimeLine window shows four tracks.

The GoLive TimeLine window can create special effects and transitions with your movies, but certain basic cropping duties (such as cutting out unwanted footage) need to be done before you export your QT movie to a .mov file. If your movie has several segments, however, don't join the segments together just yet. Hold off until you can open the segments into the TimeLine window; then you can take advantage of the transition effects tools of the TimeLine Window to join everything together.

TimeLine window tools

The TimeLine window has a small but useful toolkit. You do most of the work with the TimeLine window in conjunction with the various Inspectors that come alive when you select a track. However, certain tools are only in the TimeLine window, including the following:

- **Time Cursor:** The vertical line capped with a blue triangle shows you where you are on the time track. You can drag it manually anywhere on the time track or let it run left to right automatically as you run a movie.

- **Time Scale Slider:** Use this slider to change the perspective of the tracks. It's located at the bottom of the TimeLine window, right next to the timer. The Track bars that show duration and timing of the elements in the movie can extend beyond the right side of the TimeLine window. If that happens, change the slider so that you can see all the bars in a single window in the TimeLine window.

- **Loop button:** This feature (in the bottom-left corner of the TimeLine window) looks a little like a racetrack. Press it and your movie goes into an endless loop, where it repeats itself over and over again. (If used to create an endless bouncing onscreen, it can annoy your viewers.)

- **Palindrome control:** The double-arrow icon to the left of the Loop button marks the spot for the Palindrome control. Click this button with the Loop button selected and the Time cursor (along with the film) runs forward and then backward. By using this feature, you can run a short special effects movie backward and forward perpetually on a page. That's a trick for creating the illusion of a long movie with a small file.

- **Playback controls:** Next to the Palindrome control button you see the kind of Rewind, Stop, Play, or Fast Forward buttons you'd find on any VCR or tape recorder. You can make your way through your movie by using these controls. Although you can find the same buttons in the QuickTime window, it's nice to have them close at hand in the TimeLine window when you're fiddling around with the tracks.

Inspecting a video track

When you select a track in the TimeLine window, the Track Inspector appears. Depending on the track selected, you may also see the Video Track Inspector, Sound Track Inspector, Text Track Inspector, or one of the other Inspectors associated with a particular special effect. Each particular Inspector comes with its own set of options; the Video Track Inspector shown in Figure 15-4, for example, comes with the following set of options:

- **Title:** If you use several segments of a video, type in a name that best describes the clip.

- **Start Time/Duration.** The start time indicates where on the TimeLine the movie starts. The duration is the length of the movie.

- **Position:** If you leave the placement setting at the default of 0, the video window stays where you place it in the Layout view. Use the Layout tab of the Movie Viewer to see adjustments. The 0,0 position is where the movie is originally and changing position values will move the movie in the Layout view from the upper left-hand corner of the Movie Viewer window in horizontal and vertical pixel values.

- **Size:** Generally, leave the Constrain Proportions checked if you want to change these dimensions. Constraining the proportions means that if you resize the video, the height and width proportions are maintained. Otherwise, you might get a misshapen file with a long narrow width and a short fat height.

- **Mode:** Experiment with the Graphics Mode pull-down menu. The Transparent and Blend modes enable you to change colors in the video by using the color well. For example, if you want to give your video a jealous tint, you can select magenta or some other reddish color to Blend to give it a green tint. The other choices are *alpha channel modes,* which determine how opaque the layers you place on the video are.

If you want to jump the time cursor to the beginning of the movie, press Ctrl+Left Arrow (Windows) or Cmd-Left Arrow (Macintosh). You perform the same action to jump to the end of the movie, except you press the right arrow instead.

Figure 15-4:
Video Track
Inspector is
used for
setting the
name of the
track, its
position and
size, and its
mode.

Keeping track of time

The TimeLine window can be a little confusing when mixed in with the various Inspectors that have time elements. Here's a list that describes what the features of the TimeLine window actually do:

✔ **Start Time:** The start time is relative to the time line. If the track sample begins at 00:00:00, it means that it begins at the very start of the movie. If it begins at 00:01:00, then it begins 1 second after the beginning of the TimeLine. The Time cursor (that vertical line that moves as the movie plays) position is actually a time position that can be read in the Mouse Time timer right above the Track list.

✔ **Duration:** The duration is a constant that describes how long the clip on the track lasts. A sound clip might last 2 seconds (00:02:00) but not begin until 00:05:15. The start time is variable but the duration is a constant.

✔ **Timers:** On the TimeLine window you can find two timers with identical times linked to the position of the Time cursor. The Mouse Time timer is at the top of the Track list and the other (unnamed) timer is at the bottom between the Playback controls and the Time Scale timer.

✔ **Time Scale:** The Time scale (the ruler-like scale at the bottom right of the TimeLine window) shows track bars relative to a changing time scale. If the unit of measurement is one frame, the bars are quite long, but if the measurement units are seconds, the bars are shorter. The smaller the time unit, the more precisely you can set elements in your movie, and the larger the units, the more you can see because the bars are shorter and will fit in the TimeLine window.

Getting the FX

In Hollywood lingo, FX means special effects. GoLive provides several special effects for making your movies more interesting on the Web. Figure 15-5 shows a digital film that looks like an old celluloid movie with lines and scratches on it. When the movie runs, the effect makes the movie look like an old film damaged from use over the years. (For good measure, the effect also turns the video black and white.)

Figure 15-5:
Special effects created in GoLive TimeLine window.

You can create the "scratchy film" effect as well as a number of other effects by using the One Source Filter feature of GoLive 5. Before we get started, though, you need to know about the Sample Tools and how to use them to work on the movie tracks. (A *sample* is whatever you put on your tracks — a video sample, a music sample, or a special effects sample are different types.) All of the following tools are located in the upper-left-hand corner of the TimeLine window:

- ✔ **Inspect/Move/Copy Sample:** The arrow icon is used to select tracks and move the tracks or elements in the tracks.

- ✔ **Create Sample:** The pencil icon initially traces the area where the effect goes in the TimeLine.

- ✔ **Divide Sample:** Cut a long sample into smaller parts and then move the parts to different locations on the track.

- ✔ **Glue Samples:** When two samples are adjacent, the Glue Samples tool joins them together. You can achieve a seamless connection by using this tool.

- ✔ **Delete Sample:** The eraser icon removes an unwanted sample. However, it doesn't remove the track. So if you don't want your sample to stick around but you want to keep the track, use the Delete Sample tool.

After you're familiar with GoLive's the various tools to add special effects to your movie, follow these steps to add special effects:

1. **From the Site Window, open the movie you want to edit by double-clicking it in the Files tab.**

   Your QuickTime movie appears, along with the Movie toolbar.

2. **Choose Window⇨Inspector or undock the Inspector by clicking the Inspector tab at the side of the screen.**

   The Inspector palette appears on the screen.

3. **Choose Window⇨Objects or undock the Objects palette by clicking the Objects tab at the side of the screen.**

   The Objects palette appears on the screen.

4. **Click the Show TimeLine Window button (second from left) in the Movie toolbar.**

   The TimeLine Window appears, displaying the existing tracks.

5. **Click the QuickTime tab of the Objects palette**

   The QT tab is the eighth from the left (or second from the right). It has 16 different icons on it.

6. **Drag the One Source Filter Track icon from the QuickTime tab of the Objects palette to the Track List column of the TimeLine Window.**

   The fourth icon from the left with a black "A" on a yellow background is the icon you want.

7. **Click the downward pointing arrow on the One Source Filter Track icon to open the sample track.**

   A new row appears with a dimmed label denoting "Samples."

8. **Click the Create Sample icon (the one that looks like a pencil) in the upper-left corner of the TimeLine window and outline a sample in the sample track below the One Source Filter Track by tracing (dragging with the mouse) a rectangle.**

   As you trace on the track, a blue sample bar appears. Try to make it roughly the same length as the video track. Note that a duplicate sample appears in the One Source Filter Track.

9. **Select the One Source Filter Track by clicking it.**

   The One Source Filter Inspector is now on the screen. Note the Source pull-down menu at the bottom.

10. **Click to open the Source pull-down menu at the bottom of the One Source Filter Track Inspector and select the video track where you want the filter to create the special effect.**

    When you pull down the Source menu, you will see only those tracks you've placed in the TimeLine. This is a crucial step and one that you can overlook easily. (Experience speaking here.) If you miss this step, your movie won't work correctly.

11. **Click the Inspect Sample arrow icon and then click on the Samples track beneath the One Source Filter track.**

    Now the One Source Filter *Sample* Inspector appears. Note the Select button beneath the Effects window.

12. **Click the Select Effect button on the One Source Filter Sample Inspector.**

    The Select Effect window appears. A large "A" icon resides in the bottom left-hand corner. It shows a preview of the effect.

13. **Choose the effect you want from the menu.**

    Notice in Figure 15-5 that among the 14 possible effects (including lens flare, emboss, and blur), I selected "Film Noise." Watch the effect of your choices in the preview block in the bottom left corner where the "A" icon sits.

14. **Make any wanted adjustments to the attribute values of the effect.**

    When you select an effect, you can change the values of the effect's attributes. In the Film Noise example, you can change hair density and length, scratch density, duration, and width by using the five separate slider bars.

15. **Click the OK button after you make your selections and adjustments.**

    If you want to reuse a special effect with the adjustments you just put in, click the Save button and save it to your disk.

That should do it. Now run your movie and see how it looks with this new look.

Adding Text, Titles, and Credit

Now that your movie looks like it came out of an old film vault, you'll want to give credit (or blame) where it's due in the closing credits. Don't expect to get the titling effects of a James Bond movie (your budget probably isn't so extensive), but you can still get the basics across with the help of a few wisely chosen text additions. Here's how:

1. **From the Site Window, open the movie you want to edit by double-clicking it in the Files tab.**

    Your movie appears and begins playing. Stop it by clicking the stop button.

2. **Choose Window⇨Inspector or undock the Inspector by clicking the Inspector tab at the side of the screen.**

    The Movie Inspector appears on your screen.

3. **Choose Window⇨Objects or undock the Objects palette by clicking the Objects tab at the side of the screen.**

   The Objects palette appears.

4. **Click the Show TimeLine Window (second from left) button on the Movie toolbar.**

   The TimeLine Window appears.

5. **Select the QuickTime tab of the Objects palette.**

   The QT tab is the eighth from the left (or second from the right).

6. **Drag the Text icon from the QuickTime tab of the Objects palette to the Track List column of the TimeLine Window.**

   The Text icon is the twelfth from the left.

7. **Click the Create Sample pencil icon from the top of the TimeLine Window and click the downward-pointing arrow on the Text track .**

   The Text Sample track appears.

8. **Draw an area on the Text Sample track in the area of the TimeLine just beyond the end of the Video track movie by using the Create sample pencil.**

   Just make a relatively small rectangle. It's easier if you set the Time cursor at the end of the Video track sample. The Text *Sample* Inspector appears and the Text track duplicates the rectangle. Note the text window in the middle of the Text Sample Inspector. That's where you enter your title, credits, and subtitles.

9. **Type the credits for your movie in the large text box right below the End Time setting in the Text tab of the Text Sample Inspector.**

   After you type everything you want, select an alignment and click Apply. (See Figure 15-6.)

10. **Click the Properties tab of the Text Sample Inspector.**

    You see several display, scroll, and highlight options in the Text Sample Inspector. Select any that you like and then run your movie to test your selections. You can deselect whatever you don't like and select more. If you select a highlight color, be sure to include a begin and end value. The *begin* value is the character number to begin with and the *end* value is the last character affected by the highlight. For example, if your first text is "Starring" you would begin at "0" and end at "8." For some reason, the beginning value begins with "0" and the ending number is the number of characters in the word. (I like the scroll in option — it looks like a real movie credit roller.)

11. Click the Layout tab of the Text Sample Inspector.

The Layout tab provides margin width and height options, a background color well, and Drop Shadow, Anti-alias, and Transparent options. The anti-alias blurs the edges so that you don't get that jagged edged look. (They are called "jaggies.") If your text is scrolling over the Video track, select the Transparent option for the text to scroll over the actions. Generally I select anti-alias to smooth out the text, but the Drop Shadow may clutter things up too much.

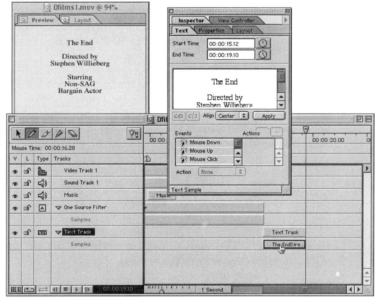

Figure 15-6: Use the Text tab of the Text Track Sample Inspector to add credits to your movie.

After you add text in the Text Track Inspector and adjust timing, you're ready to make final adjustments to your movie by using the TimeLine window. Here's how you do it:

1. Adjust the Scale Bar at the bottom of the TimeLine Window so that you can see the entire timeline from beginning to end. Make adjustments by sliding (dragging) the pointer in the Time Scale slider at the bottom of the TimeLine window.

2. Move the Track bars (samples) for all the tracks so that your titles and credits don't overlap your video track by using the Inspect/Move/Copy Sample tool to drag them.

In some cases, you may want the Text Track bar to overlap the Video Track bar as a way to superimpose text over your video image, but I chose not to do that in the current example. Remember, you can always make further adjustments in the duration by going back to the Text Track Sample Inspector.

Finding Sound Effects

What Hollywood producer would make a film without sound effects? GoLive 5's QuickTime TimeLine window enables you to add all the sound effects you want in your movie and lets you put them exactly where you want them.

Apple Computer, Inc. has sound effects you can download for free from the iMovie section of their Web site (www.apple.com/imovie/freestuff). Check out the different categories, from Animals to Drama and Action to Planes, Trains, and Cars for a wide range of sound effects. The Apple site uses the AIFF format for its files, a format compatible with the Macintosh OS. If you'd prefer WAV files, a preferred sound file for Windows, check out WAV Central (www.wavcentral.com) for lots of sound files you can download at no cost.

Go to the TimeLine window to add a separate Sound Track for sound effects. Just follow these steps:

1. **From the Site window, open the movie you want to edit by double-clicking its file in the Files tab.**

   Your movie appears along with the Movie toolbar.

2. **Choose Window➪Inspector or undock the Inspector by clicking the Inspector tab at the side of the screen.**

   The Movie Inspector makes an entrance.

3. **Choose Window➪Objects or undock the Objects palette by clicking the Objects tab at the side of the screen.**

   The trusty Objects palette appears.

4. **Click the Show TimeLine Window button (second from left) in the Movie toolbar.**

   The TimeLine window opens up.

5. **Click the QuickTime tab of the Objects palette.**

   The QT tab is the eighth from the left (or second from the right).

6. **Drag the Sound icon from the QuickTime tab of the Objects palette to the Track List column of the TimeLine window.**

   The Sound icon is the thirteenth icon from the left. (It's got a speaker on it to make it easy to spot.) As soon as you attempt to drop the Sound icon into the Track list, a browse directory appears. Select the sound file you want from the appropriate drive and folder in the directory window. The Inspector becomes the Sound Track Inspector. Most movies already have at least one sound track when you begin work on them.

7. Drag the Sound Track bar to the left or right to change its Start time.

Notice that, on the Sound Track Inspector, none of the values can be changed in the Inspector itself except for the name of the track. Provide a clear name. My file was a trumpet fanfare so I named the track Trumpets. The Start time can only be changed by dragging the Sound Track bar to the left and right in the TimeLine window.

Special effects, text, and sound all add to the file size of the QuickTime movie. Be sure to check your QuickTime movie size before you put it on a server. (Just look at the file size of the movie in the Files tab of the Site Window. You did remember to put your sound and movie files in the root directory, didn't you?) Otherwise, you may find that your Web page has the "forever load." Remember, your QuickTime movies may be just part of the page, and the page itself has a load weight as well.

Music, please

In addition to adding sound effects, you can add music as well. To add music, follow the same steps for adding sound except drag the Music icon rather than the Sound icon from the QuickTime tab of the Objects palette to the TimeLine window. Standard MIDI(Musical Instruments Digital Interface.) files run on the Music tracks. (See www.midiweb.com for good information on this format.) However, non-MIDI files, such as AIFF and WAV files, only run on the Sound track, even if they contain music instead of sound effects or voice. Please note that

- ✔ Music files take up a lot of memory.
- ✔ Music is likely to be copyrighted. Even samples of sounds that virtually all online music sites give away for free are subject to copyright laws. (Check out www.cdnow.com or www.amazon.com for lots of free music samples, but be careful about putting them on the Web without permission.)

Chapter and Verse

The final adjustment to your QuickTime movie involves partitioning it so that different parts are easy to find. GoLive enables you to place a pull-down menu at the bottom of your movie so that viewers can jump to any point in the movie they choose. Most QuickTime Web movies may be no more than 30 seconds or less because of the bandwidth they devour. However, in some applications where precise segments may tell a different story, it's convenient for the user to jump wherever she wants in the film. The segments are called *chapters.* Like so many other aspects of GoLive moviemaking, dividing your movie into chapters is done by using the TimeLine Window. Here's how:

1. **From the Site Window, open the movie you want to edit by double-clicking its file in the Files tab.**

   Your movie appears along with the Movie toolbar.

2. **Choose Window⇨Inspector or undock the Inspector by clicking the Inspector tab at the side of the screen.**

   The Movie Inspector makes an entrance.

3. **Choose Window⇨Objects or undock the Objects palette by clicking the Objects tab at the side of the screen.**

   The trusty Objects palette appears.

4. **Click the Show TimeLine Window (second from left) button in the Movie toolbar.**

   The TimeLine window opens up.

5. **Click the QuickTime tab of the Objects palette.**

   The QT tab is the eighth from the left (or second from the right).

6. **Drag the Chapter Track icon from the QuickTime tab of the Objects palette to the Track List column of the TimeLine window.**

   The Chapter Track icon is the eleventh from the left. It has little up/down arrows on it to indicate that you use it like a pull-down menu.

7. **Select the Chapter Track in the TimeLine window.**

   The Inspector becomes the Chapter Track Inspector. In the Track list, the Chapter Track has a little arrow next to it.

8. **In the Chapter Track Inspector, select the track you want to provide chapters for in the Act As Chapter Track For pull-down menu.**

   The pull-down menu has a list of tracks that are on your TimeLine window. Select one. I usually choose a video track because everything is connected to the video.

9. **Click the arrow on the Chapter Track.**

   A Sample track opens. The Chapter Track Sample Inspector appears when you select the Chapter Sample Track. It contains a Label window.

10. **Select the Create Sample pencil icon from the top of the TimeLine window and draw sample bars on the Chapter Samples track.**

    Instead of drawing a single bar, draw a bar for each chapter, as shown in Figure 15-7. As you draw each bar, provide a label for it in the Chapter Track Sample Inspector. Label each one clearly and descriptively. For example, near the front you might use "Introduction" and "Credits" at the end where the credit text rolls.

11. **Click the Layout tab of the Movie window and click on the movie image.**

    The Text Track Inspector appears. Even if you have the Chapter Track selected, the Text Track Inspector appears when you click on the video image.

12. **In the Size window of the Inspector (see Step 10), type 275 or more.**

    Be sure the Constrain Proportion box is checked. You need to have the video at least 275 pixels wide so that there is room to see the pulldown menu.

13. **Save your page by choosing File⇨ Save from the menu bar or by using Ctrl+S (Windows)or Cmd+S (Macintosh).**

    When you run your page on a browser, you will see the pulldown menu.

By putting in chapters, you allow the viewer to go over any part she needs to see simply by activating the pull-down menu and selecting the portion she wants to view without having to wait for the video to reach the desired part.

Figure 15-7:
The Chapter Tracks in the TimeLine window and pull-down chapter menus in your movie.

Chapter 16

Getting Dynamic with DHTML

• •

• •

*M*aking a Web page more interesting requires both talent and tools. One of the most interesting tools in Dynamic HTML's bag of trick is the *floating box.* Static boxes like tables and forms can do some interesting tricks, but they cannot fly around the page, change position and depth, and make themselves invisible or visible. This chapter introduces you to the truly dynamic world of Dynamic HTML and shows you how easily you can use GoLive 5 to put Dynamic HTML to work.

About Floating Boxes

Dynamic HTML (DHTML) gets its name in large part by helping Web designers add mobile features such as floating boxes to a page. In addition to Cascading Style Sheets and some JavaScript to move the floating boxes, DHTML provides the designer (that's you) with the power to make animated, viewer-activated pages. (For example, imagine that a Web surfer moves the mouse and causes a floating box to fly across your page.) Floating boxes are so called because they float on top of the Web page, appearing on top of other windows and even changing position if set up for that option. You control several attributes of floating boxes by using JavaScript, and GoLive 5 has been nice enough to figure out how to write all the JavaScript you'll ever need for creating a DHTML page with floating boxes.

The following list gives you a needed look at some key characteristics of floating boxes.

- ✔ **Visibility:** Floating boxes and their contents can be made to appear or disappear.

- ✔ **Position:** Floating boxes can change position. The boxes' distance (measured in pixels) from the top and left side of a Web page defines their position.

- ✔ **Background color and graphic:** Floating boxes can have their own background color or graphic, just like a Web page or window.

- ✔ **Text and Graphic Containment:** Floating boxes can contain either text or graphics. Whatever happens to the floating box also happens to the contents. That is, when the floating box moves or disappears, the contents of the box move or disappear right along with it.

- ✔ **Layer Level:** Floating boxes can appear on top of or underneath other boxes. The layer level is known as *depth*. When moved, a box can glide over or under another floating box.

About the only down side of floating boxes is that some versions of some browsers do not work well with them (or work in unexpected ways). Again, GoLive comes to the rescue by churning out code that maximizes the utility of floating boxes for different versions of different browsers. But just in case you do not have at least Version 4.0 of either Netscape Navigator or Internet Explorer, go out and get one now. Netscape Communicator is available at www.netscape.com, and Internet Explorer is available at www.microsoft.com. (Remember, the browsers are free, and at the time of this writing Netscape has a Beta Version 6 of Navigator and Explorer is in Version 5. If you have a version prior to version 3 of either browser, DHTML simply will not work. So Update Your Browsers!)

GoLive generates a good deal of JavaScript code when you start moving around or doing other tricks with your floating boxes. The JavaScript code often makes up the majority of the script in the Source view of your Web page in the Document window or Source palette. The following steps show you how to send all the JavaScript code from your Web page to a separate file.

1. **Choose Edit⇨Preferences from the menu bar.**

   The Preferences dialog box appears.

2. **Click the Script Library icon.**

   A JavaScript preferences pane appears on the right side of the Preferences dialog box.

3. **In the Preferences dialog box you can now click the Import the GoLive Script Library radio button.**

4. **Click OK to save this setting.**

   You do not need a file name. The next time you load GoLive 5, the settings are retained.

After you redirect your JavaScript code to a file separate from your Web page, you can more clearly see what's going on in your page's Source view. And you'll find other benefits to having your JavaScript separate: When your code is saved in a separate file, it is placed in your root folder so that you won't lose it. Finally, if you have several Web pages that use the same operations — and therefore use the same JavaScript code — you can save space by keeping one code file for use with all pages.

Set Your Boxes

When using floating boxes, the first order of business is getting a floating box on your Web page. You need not use the grid for this operation because the floating boxes can be placed and move wherever you want.

1. **Create a new Web site and open the Index page (index.html) in the Layout view of the Document window.**

   This sample site has a single Web page, so you can use the automatically generated index.html. You will want to have your graphics available in the root folder, and GoLive will generate a CSSscriptLib.js file (also in the root folder) for your external JavaScript code.

2. **Choose Window⇨Inspector from the menu bar or undock the Inspector by clicking the Inspector tab at the side of the screen.**

   The Inspector palette appears on your screen.

3. **Choose Window⇨Floating Boxes from the menu bar or undock the Floating Boxes palette by clicking the Floating Boxes tab at the side of the screen.**

   The Floating Boxes palette appears on the screen.

4. **Choose Window⇨Objects from the menu bar or undock the Objects palette by clicking the Objects tab at the side of the screen.**

   The Objects palette appears.

5. **Click the Basic tab of the Objects palette.**

   Twenty icons appear in the Basic tab of the Objects palette.

6. **Drag the Floating Box icon (the third icon from the left) from the Objects palette to your Web page.**

   A square box appears on the page and a yellow icon slips to the upper-left corner of the page. The Inspector becomes the Floating Box Inspector. In the Floating Box palette, the word *Layer* appears next to the eye and pencil icons. I suggest that you change the name *Layer* to something that better represents what the floating box is to be used for. In Figure 16-1, the Floating Box Inspector shows that I changed the name *Layer* to *wordPros*.

7. **Move the mouse pointer over the box until you see a Hand icon and then click the mouse button.**

   The floating box is now selected. Several pull points appear on the sides of the box to indicate its selection.

8. **With the Hand icon showing on the side of the floating box, drag the box to any position on the page.**

   You can move the floating box anywhere on the page; when you find just the right place for it, release the mouse button and the box stays put. The little yellow square, however, remains in the upper-left corner of the page window.

   When you drag the floating box to a different position on your Web page, notice that the values for the Left and Top positions in the Floating Box Inspector change accordingly. You can move the floating box to different positions on the page to get a clear idea of what values correspond to several locations on the page. If you change the Left and Top values in the Floating Box Inspector and press Enter/Return, the floating box jumps to that location. In the example shown in Figure 16-1, the values are both set at 100.

The process of adding a floating box to your Web page involves little more than dragging an icon onto the page, but the benefits are enormous. The rest of the chapter tells you how floating boxes can provide your pages with dramatic and dynamic possibilities.

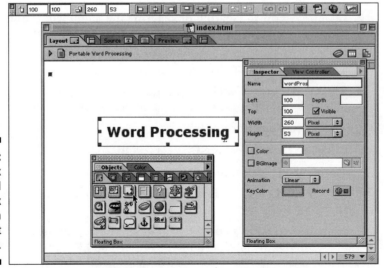

Figure 16-1:
Floating Box palette and floating box on a page in the Layout View.

Adding Text to the Box

After you have your floating box set where you want it on the page, you can add some text to it. It's easy.

1. **In the Layout view of the Document window, place the mouse pointer arrow over the floating box and click the mouse button.**

   You should see the I-beam cursor that shows you where to start typing.

2. **Type your text in the floating box.**

   Notice that the floating box expands to accept the text. In the Floating Box Inspector, you can see the dimensions of the box change from the default 100 by 100 pixels to the size necessary to contain the text. You format text in a floating box just as you would were it on a Web page — by using either the Type menu on the menu bar or the Text toolbar.

3. **Select the floating box so that you can see the pull points on the side.**

   Little blue pull points or handles should be in the corners and on each side.

4. **Place the mouse pointer — now shaped as an arrowhead — over the lower-left pull point on the side of the floating box and push it up and to the left until it will not go further.**

   With this step, you remove the extra space between the text and the box wall so that the floating box perfectly fits the text.

Putting text into floating boxes is pretty much like putting it on a Web page. GoLive 5 generally uses the same tools for different aspects of the page, and in this case, you don't have to figure out a whole new way of getting text where you want it.

Floating Graphics

Placing graphics into floating boxes is very similar to putting graphics into a table cell or directly on a page. So get your site set up, open your Document window to the Layout view, and proceed with the following steps.

1. **Choose Window➪Inspector from the menu bar or undock the Inspector by clicking the Inspector tab at the side of the screen.**

   The Inspector palette appears on your screen.

2. **Choose Window➪Floating Boxes from the menu bar or undock the Floating Boxes palette by clicking the Floating Boxes tab at the side of the screen.**

   The Floating Boxes palette appears on the screen.

3. **Choose Window⇨Objects from the menu bar or undock the Objects palette by clicking the Objects tab at the side of the screen.**

   The Objects palette appears.

4. **Click the Basic tab of the Objects palette.**

   Twenty icons appear in the Basic tab of the Objects palette.

5. **Drag the Floating Box icon (the third icon from the left) from the Objects palette to the Layout view of the Document window.**

   The floating box gravitates to the upper left of the page.

6. **Drag the Image icon (fifth from the left) from the Objects palette and place it inside the floating box.**

   The Floating Box Inspector becomes the Image Inspector as soon as you drop the Image icon into the floating box.

7. **Pull the point-and-shoot line from the Image Inspector to the Select Window icon on the toolbar to bring up the Site window and select the graphic file from the Files tab of the Site window.**

   As always, if you worry about the steadiness of your hand, you can also use the Browse button in the Image Inspector to select a graphic file. The image now appears in the floating box and stays there no matter where you move the box.

8. **In the Floating Box Inspector, replace the name *Layer* in the Name text field with a name that better reflects the graphic you added to the floating box.**

   The new name then appears in the Floating Box palette. (I named mine *Ink*. Originality is not required.)

Whenever you move a floating box with an image in it, watch the Hand cursor. If the Hand cursor appears, the whole floating box and image in it will move together. However, if the arrowhead cursor with the box next to it appears, that means it is on the graphic alone. If you attempt to move the floating box at this point, you'll pull the image out of the box instead.

Hide and Go Seek Boxes

You can create dramatic effects with floating boxes by controlling their visibility. When a floating box is hidden, all its contents are hidden as well. You can create conditions to make boxes appear and disappear. The conditions can be automatic (based on a timing, for example) or triggered by a certain action taking place (such as a mouse click). To initially hide a floating box, simply deselect the Visible check box in the Floating Box Inspector, as shown in Figure16-2.

Figure 16-2:
The Floating
Box
Inspector
indicates a
hidden box
when the
Visible
check box
is not
selected.

After you have hidden a box, making it reappear is simply a matter of creating an action to make it happen. For example, you can make a button, add it to your Web page, and set it up so that clicking the button toggles the visibility on and off.

Begin with a floating box you have hidden by deselecting the Visible check box in the Floating Box Inspector. (See Figure 16-2.) Before starting this operation, create or download a graphic image that can be used as a button. Any graphic will do. Put the graphic in the root folder of the site. With your page and site open, continue with the following steps:

1. **Choose Window⇨Inspector from the menu bar or undock the Inspector by clicking the Inspector tab at the side of the screen.**

   The Inspector palette appears on your screen.

2. **Choose Window⇨Objects from the menu bar or undock the Objects palette by clicking the Objects tab at the side of the screen.**

   The Objects palette appears.

3. **Choose Window⇨Floating Boxes from the menu bar or undock the Floating Boxes palette by clicking the Floating Boxes tab at the side of the screen.**

   The Floating Boxes palette appears on the screen.

4. **Drag the button graphic image from the Site window to any position on the page in the Layout view.**

   The Inspector becomes the Image Inspector. Keep the button selected for the next step.

5. **Click the Link tab of the Image Inspector and click the Link icon (the chain link) on the Link tab.**

   The (Empty Reference!) message appears in the URL window.

6. **Type a pound sign (#) to replace the (Empty Reference!) message.**

   The pound sign is a stand-in for the URL, but it effectively makes the graphic a hot spot. That means you can add an action to it.

7. **Select Window⇨Actions from the menu bar.**

   The Actions palette appears on the screen.

8. **Select the Mouse Click item in the Events column.**

   The action is set up to occur when a mouse click takes place.

9. **Click the Plus (+) sign under Action.**

   The palette is now set to add an action from the Action pulldown menu.

10. **Choose Action⇨Multimedia⇨ShowHide from the Action pulldown menu.**

    The Multimedia menu includes control over floating box visibility. On the right side of the Actions palette, two pulldown menus appear, named Floating Box and Mode.

11. **From the Actions palette pulldown menu named Floating Box choose the name of the floating box that you want to be visible and invisible.**

    You will see the name of your floating box, or the name *layer*. However, if you have several floating boxes on your page, you'll wish you had renamed them to something more descriptive.

13. **From the Action palette, choose Mode⇨Toggle.**

    You could have selected Hide or Show instead of Toggle. Hide can only hide the floating box, and Show can only reveal a hidden floating box. But Toggle does both. (See Figure 16-3 for the final settings.)

Your Web page now has a button that lets the viewer toggle between showing and hiding the floating box.

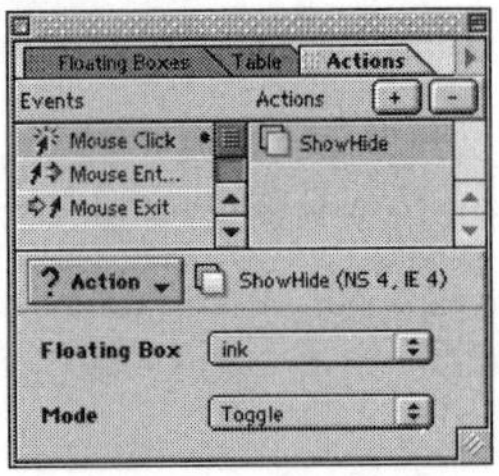

Figure 16-3:
The Actions palette set up for visibility toggle for the Floating box named "ink."

Instead of going nuts trying to remember where you put your hidden floating boxes when working in the Layout view, use the Floating Box palette to make them visible during development. To do so, choose Window➪Floating Box to get the Floating Box palette on-screen. Click the pencil icon in the Floating Box palette next to the name of the floating box. The box appears on your screen, and the eye in the Floating Box palette turns red, indicating that the box is really hidden (or that it's been keeping too many late nights).

Make the Floating Boxes Fly

You can make any or all your floating boxes move around on your Web page. Movement can begin when your page opens or when a person viewing the Web page clicks or rolls over a hotspot that's connected to an action. One of the better features in GoLive is the Record button in the Floating Box Inspector. Using this button makes adding movement to your floating boxes simple and intuitive.

1. **Begin in the Layout view with a visible floating box containing text and/or a graphic image in place.**

   I created a floating box with the word *Fly* in it.

2. **Choose Window➪Inspector from the menu bar or undock the Inspector by clicking the Inspector tab at the side of the screen.**

   The Inspector appears on your screen.

3. **Choose Window➪Floating Boxes from the menu bar or undock the Floating Boxes palette by clicking the Floating Boxes tab at the side of the screen.**

   The Floating Boxes palette appears on-screen.

4. **Select the floating box by clicking the box's outline.**

   The Inspector becomes the Floating Box Inspector.

5. **In the Animation pulldown menu at the bottom of the Floating Box Inspector choose Curve.**

   Linear is the default that you will see in the pulldown menu's bar. By selecting Curve, the movement of your floating box is smoother.

6. **Click the Record button so that it is in the *on* position and can record the movement of your floating box.**

   When the Record button is on, it appears to be indented.

7. **Drag the floating box over the path you want it to travel.**

   Make the path as convoluted as you like — GoLive writes all the code for you.

8. **When you reach the ending position for your Flying Box, release the mouse button.**

The Record button pops to the *off* position. You see a gray line tracing the path that your floating box just took, as shown in Figure 16-4.

When you load your page into a browser, you can see your floating box follow the path you made for it. A floating box flying on your page gets the viewer's attention and, if done judiciously, can make a dramatic and interesting beginning for an index page. (You can also watch the flight of your floating box by viewing your Web page in the Preview mode.)

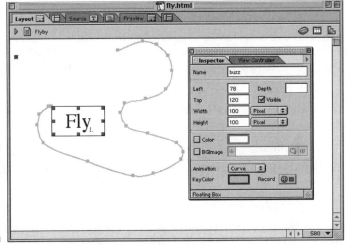

Figure 16-4:
The Path of
a floating
box from the
Layout view.

Get on the TimeLine

You may not think that much of anything happens when a Web browser launches a standard Web page. You type in the URL address, hit Enter, and the Web page appears. Take the time to think about it, however, and you can see that, when a standard Web page is launched, its elements meet certain preset conditions. For example, perhaps all elements are meant to be visible and to stay put on the page.

To put it another way, *being visible* and *staying put on the page* are the default conditions applied to a standard Web page. But everyone knows that defaults are there to be changed; nothing on a Web page is set in stone. If you change the conditions (from *being visible* to *being invisible,* and from *staying put on the page* to *jumping all over the page*), you add the distinctive dynamism of Dynamic HTML to your Web page.

You can set up the timing for a change in the default conditions of your Web page with the help of the GoLive TimeLine Editor. The TimeLine Editor uses *keyframes* placed on a timeline as triggers for changing certain conditions and enables you to see and control every step of animations, visibility, and depth. The keyframes are those frames associated with a position on the Web page or an action. (Those dots on the trail of the floating box in Figure 16-4 indicate where a keyframe is located.)

You open the TimeLine Editor from Layout view by clicking the icon that looks like a piece of film — between the JavaBean and CSS icon — in the upper-right corner of the Document window.

Pages with floating box movement paths (see Figure 16-4) are shown in sequential, linear arrangement in the TimeLine Editor. Each little dot on the movement path is a keyframe on the timeline. (See Figure 16-5.) The following are key elements in the TimeLine Editor. (The TimeLine Editor in this chapter and the TimeLine window in Chapter 15 are different and should not be confused. Other than each being a time line with tracks, they are not very similar.)

- ✔ **Time track:** Each floating box has its own Time track. Time tracks make up the rows in the TimeLine Editor. An arrow appears in the left column of the Time track for the currently selected floating box.

- ✔ **Time cursor:** The Time cursor looks like a vertical line topped by a triangle. This line extends from top to bottom through the Time tracks, and you can drag it from left to right across the screen. As you drag the Time cursor left and right, you can watch the Layout view window and see what your objects are doing. At the bottom of the TimeLine Editor are the playback buttons; pressing the Play button moves the Time cursor from left to right in the correct time proportions.

- ✔ **Frame:** Each hash mark in the timeline at the top of the TimeLine Editor represents a frame. Think of each frame as a frame in a movie. At the bottom of the TimeLine Editor, you see the default speed set to 15 FPS — that's 15 frames per second. You can change this default setting to speed up or slow down the actions.

- ✔ **Keyframes:** A *keyframe* is a frame that marks a change in direction or status of a property of the floating box. Properties include position, depth, and visibility. All those little marks on the path line in Figure 16-4, for example, represent keyframes. The TimeLine Editor helps you keep track of all the keyframes for a floating box by marking keyframes in the time line as little boxes with circles in them. (See Figure 16-5.)

- ✔ **Actions track:** The row above the Time tracks is the Actions track. Different built-in actions can be placed on the Actions track to effect changes to properties associated with the page. For example, you might want to insert an action to change the background color of the page temporarily.

✔ **Scenes:** When your page opens, you may want to have all the objects on your page perform a particular set of actions, such as appearing and moving around the screen. However, at another point, you may want your objects to do a completely different set of activities, such as moving behind another floating box where they're hidden from view.

If you think of all the visual happenings you create for your Web page as a short movie, you can imagine that one set of activities becomes one scene of your movie and the next set of activities becomes the next scene. GoLive 5 thinks in such film terms, too. The Scenes button appears in the upper-left corner of the TimeLine Editor and shows the image of both a film reel and a single frame of film. Clicking the down arrow on this button opens the Scenes popup menu, where you can name and add all the scenes you want.

✔ **Loop and Palindrome Controls:** In the lower-left corner of the TimeLine Editor screen you can see two buttons graced with the images of a) a racetrack arrow and b) two opposing arrows. The race track arrow is the Loop button. When it is selected, the movement on the page repeats itself continuously. The opposing arrows represent the palindrome button, and when selected in conjunction with the loop button the actions run backwards and forward. The default condition is *not* a loop.

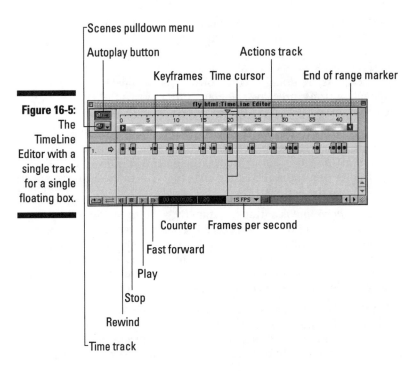

Scenes pulldown menu

Autoplay button

Actions track

Keyframes Time cursor

End of range marker

Figure 16-5:
The
TimeLine
Editor with a
single track
for a single
floating box.

Counter Frames per second

Fast forward

Play

Stop

Rewind

Time track

Adding Actions in Movement

The TimeLine Editor's many features may seem overwhelming at first, but with practice, you'll soon get the hang of using it. A concrete example of how to use it never hurts, either. Suppose that you want an invisible floating box to appear at a certain time after the page initially loads. If you coordinate the sudden appearance of your floating box with the action of another object, you can create the impression that the action of one object causes the appearance of the other.

Figure 16-5 shows the path of a floating box that contains the word *Processing.* Another floating box contains the image of an inkbottle and is initially hidden on the page. When the Processing box hits the area with the hidden inkbottle, the inkbottle box "magically" becomes visible. The following steps show how the magic works (it's all a matter of timing and using the TimeLine Editor):

1. **Begin in the Layout view with two floating boxes on your open Web Page.**

    Make sure that you have a visible floating box and an invisible one. Each floating box should contain text and/or a graphic image. See the preceding sections for instructions on how to create floating boxes with contents and changeable visibility.

2. **Choose Window⇨Inspector from the menu bar or undock the Inspector by clicking the Inspector tab at the side of the screen.**

    The Inspector appears on your screen.

3. **Choose Window⇨Floating Boxes from the menu bar or undock the Floating Boxes palette by clicking the Floating Boxes tab at the side of the screen.**

    The Floating Boxes palette appears on-screen. Be sure that the invisible floating box icon has a "red eye" in the Floating Boxes palette. If it does not, you will not be able to see the invisible floating box! Just select the invisible floating box by clicking its name in the Floating Box palette and then click the eye next to it on the palette.

4. **Open the TimeLine Editor by clicking the TimeLine icon in the upper-right corner of the Layout view window.**

    The TimeLine icon looks like a few frames of film and is located between the JavaScript bean and the Style Sheet icon. The TimeLine Editor appears on your page.

5. **Select the visible floating box and choose Curve from the Animation pulldown menu of the Floating Box Inspector.**

6. **Click the Record button in the Floating Box Inspector and then drag the visible floating box to make a movement path that touches the invisible floating box.**

   In the TimeLine Editor, you see a number of keyframes created in the Time track of the object for which you just created a path.

7. **Drag the Time cursor back and forth until the Layout view of the Document window shows the visible floating box just touching the invisible floating box.**

   You can see where they intersect in the Layout view. If the corners overlap a little, you'll be sure that they intersect.

8. **Select the invisible floating box by clicking its name in the Floating Box palette.**

   Make sure that the Pencil icon in the Floating Box palette is selected and active. (If it is not, it locks the floating box and doesn't allow you to make changes.) The Time track of the selected floating box has an arrow in the leftmost column of the track, as shown in Figure 16-6.

9. **On the Time track for the selected (invisible) floating box, insert a keyframe at the Time cursor position you set in Step 7 by placing the mouse pointer on the Time cursor position and pressing Ctrl+single-click (Windows) or Command+single-click (Macintosh).**

   A keyframe appears in the Time track for the invisible floating box, as shown in Figure 16-6. The little box icon below the new keyframe is the temporary cursor that appears while you're inserting the keyframe. The cursor indicates that you have taken the correct steps up to this point.

10. **Immediately above the new keyframe on the Actions track, enter a Ctrl+single-click (Windows) or Command+single-click (Macintosh).**

    A question mark icon appears on the Actions track indicating the keyframe is ready to accept an action. The Inspector becomes the Actions Inspector, and an Actions pulldown menu icon appears near the top of the Actions Inspector.

11. **Choose Multimedia⇨ShowHide from the Actions pulldown menu in the Actions Inspector.**

    A Show/Hide icon appears on the Actions track. The Actions Inspector shows two pulldown menus, one for Floating Box and the other for the Mode. The modes in Show/Hide are Show, Hide, and Toggle.

12. **In the Floating Box menu, select the name of the invisible floating box that you want to show. In the Mode menu, choose Show.**

    As soon as the floating box reaches the keyframe on the timeline in the Actions track where the Actions icon appears, the event is launched. In this case, the event causes the invisible floating box to become visible (that is, to Show).

With these steps, you place a marker on the Actions track so that when the visible floating box comes to the Action marker in the TimeLine (which is invisible on a Web page) the property of the selected object changes the visibility from invisible floating box to visible. Figure 16-6 shows what the page and TimeLine Editor look like when the combination of elements comes together. The effect is something like a magic wand as the moving floating box touches the invisible floating box. Presto! It becomes visible.

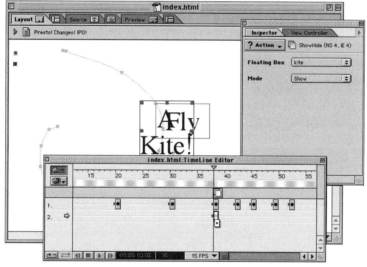

Figure 16-6:
TimeLine
Editor,
keyframes,
and action
on Action
Track.

By using a similar set of steps, you can change any other feature of a floating box in the Floating Box Inspector. For example, you can change the depth of a floating box so that it passes on top of instead of underneath another floating box.

You can achieve a fun, eyeball-grabbing effect by changing background colors to reveal a hidden message on your Web page. Just type in some message (like *Wow!*) in the same color as your original background color. When you change the background color to contrast with the message color, the words jump out. Changing back to the original background color hides the message again.

Part V
The Part of Tens

The 5th Wave   By Rich Tennant

In this part . . .

Are you ready to create a dazzling Web page but find you can't decide on the right look? Do you want to uncover the best features of GoLive 5 and take advantage of them quickly? Well, look no further, my friend, for you're about to enter The Part of Tens. This traditional element of all *For Dummies* books spells out what I consider the best tips on designing a Web page.

In this part, you find out the do's and don'ts of good Web page design, such as don't use camouflage as a background image on your page if you want people to be able to read your text! This part gets you thinking ahead of time about the common mistakes Web page designers make, such as using so many fonts that their pages look like a kaleidoscope. Cluttering the background is another common mistake Web page designers make. Some folks just don't think about those kinds of things and fill the background of their pages with cute little teddy bears. They don't realize that e-mail and other contact information is lost amongst those critters.

Part V also tells you why GoLive 5 is the best thing since sliced bread. I identify what I consider the best ways to use ten fantastic GoLive features to create classy-looking Web pages. It's the kind of information that inquiring minds want and need to know, and it's all right here in The Part of Tens. Don't hesitate. Don't think twice! Get wise and get smart.

Chapter 17

Ten Best Features of GoLive 5

*T*he most difficult part of writing this book is narrowing down GoLive 5's best features to ten. I like virtually every feature, but an endless list isn't much help to you. When I first began using GoLive, I was struck by a number of features I hadn't seen before in other HTML page development tools, and a number of these features make my top ten.

Keeping Control with a Grid

My first and still-favorite GoLive feature is the grid. Using a grid eases the process of putting together a Web page so much that I shudder at the thought of going back to either watching all the parts of my page flying all over the place or trying to get them to behave by creating my own tables for the bit and pieces.

Whatever you do with GoLive, don't neglect using the grid! You need to use the grid to take advantage of the Align palette. With objects all over the grid, you can align, space, and place your page components quickly by using the Align palette in the grid. (All right, so I sneak in the Align palette as another favorite, but it does compliment the grid.)

Seeing the Big Site Map Picture

GoLive 5 makes you think *site* and not just *page*. It gets you started with a broader attitude by providing different ways you can look at your site. The tools included to see and develop your site include the Navigation and Links view windows, the Site Design window, and the In & Out Links Inspector. All of these tools, along with the Site window and all its views, make life a breeze when you seriously have to make a Web site. By providing a graphical view of your site as well as its links, you can better decide which alternatives in your design work the best. The thumbnail or icon images with lines showing the links between pages puts the site designer in a position to better visualize whether the site design goals have been accomplished and all the pages and links that need to be in the site are where they belong. (You can also see if some of the pages or links need to be removed.)

Painless FTP

GoLive's file transfer options help you get your sites on and off the Web host without going crazy. By integrating the FTP (File Transfer Protocol) into the Site window, transferring files no longer requires guesswork. By design, GoLive 5 uses the Site window to show all the files in the root folder. Since the site has been developed in the Site window, transferring sites to a host server is simply a matter of clicking a button on the toolbar to send the site as a whole to the server. Because GoLive treats your work as a *site* instead of a collection of loose pages, all of the relative links are maintained during transfer. So when you tweak a page to improve it, your whole site doesn't collapse when you send in your modified page.

Divvying up the Work with WebDAV

If you are working on a group project, the WebDAV feature (short for *Web-based Distributed Authoring and Versioning*) lets you synchronize and work with a group on a site, so when it's time to put the site on the Web, nobody is surprised by what they see! WebDAV is a great way to bring together everyone's contribution to a project while at the same time keeping tabs on what revisions have been made. All in all, its a great addition to GoLive 5.

Keeping Organized with Point-and-Shoot

At first I thought point-and-shoot was just a fun way to make links to pages, graphics and other media. However, using point-and-shoot forces me to pay attention to all the elements in my site. If my page or other media isn't in the Site window, the point-and-shoot doesn't work. (The point-and-shoot line just sort of wobbles and returns to the button when the target isn't where it belongs.) Intuitively, point-and-shoot establishes a link between the Web page and other pages and media located in the root folder. Because the point-and-shoot procedure *only* works with pages and media in the root folder, you're more likely to spot a problem right at the point in developing the site where the problem resides. Later, you do not need to fumble through all the pages and media in your site to locate a problem. I know of no other tool that has a point-and-shoot feature, and I like it.

Cloning Your Features

You put a lot of work into getting a navigation system, a design element, or some other page component just right. "Cloning" a feature and using it on all the pages of your site is a blessing indeed! Few people discuss the component feature when they talk about GoLive, but I find it's a real time-saver. For site work, it's best to get an element right the first time and then use the component on all the pages you want.

Matching Those Web Colors

When I found that I could drag the mouse pointer from the Color palette across the page and match a color with a graphic on the page, I was sold! Without a doubt, the color-matching feature of the Color palette is worth the price of the application. Combined with the color wells, drop-down swatches, and site color collections, GoLive 5 is unparalleled when it comes to handling colors.

In addition to all the other color features of GoLive 5, a little-used Custom palette is available on the Palettes color tab of the Color palette. Put your favorite color combinations in your own Custom palette once, and GoLive 5 stores them permanently.

Previewing Before You Post

Another favorite feature in GoLive 5 is the Preview view in the Document window. Not only does this feature save you time galloping between GoLive and the browsers, you can view your page as it appears on different platforms and different browsers and browser versions. If you've ever created a page on a Macintosh and then viewed it on a Window's platform, you may have been surprised by "BIG text" or some other formatting that wasn't quite what you had in mind. Likewise, a page in Microsoft Internet Explorer can look very different in Netscape Navigator. By having a preview of both different platforms and browsers, GoLive 5 saves you the time of browser and platform jumping. It's a simple, elegant, and incredibly useful tool.

Making the Objects Palette Your Pal

To be honest, when I first started using the Objects palette, I wasn't quite comfortable with it. However, now I find it a practical and simple way to organize a huge number of features that you can put on your pages or your site. Instead of fishing through menus, sub-menus, and sub-sub-menus to find the features you need, the Objects palette provides a well organized collection of them at your mouse-tip. (That's like a mouse's fingertip.) Familiarizing yourself with the icons is easy because they show up on the palette.

Changing the Inspector to Just What You Need

I swear, the Inspector is magic. As a context-sensitive tool, there's nothing to look up or dig up. No matter what part of the page or site you are working with, the Inspector knows what's what and presents you with all the options for a currently selected object. The page can get a little crowded with different palettes, but the Inspector keeps changing into different tools, including ones that have their own subset of tabs. It's like a very bright golf caddy who hands you *just the right club* when you need it.

Chapter 18

Ten Best Design Tips

*N*ot coming from an artistic or design background, I have had to struggle to get my Web pages looking good. The most important realization that I had was that good design doesn't happen by chance or because you know computers. I read everything I can on design and I use every tip I can. Moreover, the learning never ends.

Planning Twice and Publishing Once

I have one thing to say to those who think they can make up a design as they go along. *Forget about it!* Creating a design on the fly is like trying to get dressed on the drive to work. The time you spend planning pays you back tenfold compared to the time you take undoing a poor design. If you carefully plan your design (and GoLive 5 provides you with plenty of design tools) prior to launching your site, you'll have a better looking site and spend less time making it so. After you have a good design and design components, GoLive helps you duplicate those design elements throughout your site. In this way, you do it right the first time rather than wasting time undoing a rush job.

Talent Borrows, Genius Steals!

If you see a Web design that you like, *copy it!* You don't have to duplicate it exactly, but study it carefully and use the navigation system, the page design, or the color scheme that appeals to you. Chances are that some of the best Web sites in the World Wide Web snaked more than a few ideas themselves! All good designers flatter fellow designers by pilfering ideas. It's part of a very elaborate moral code. (Hey, I don't make the rules. I just follow them.)

Designing Good Navigation

An important element of design in Web sites is a good navigational system. Working on your own Web site, it's easy to become so familiar with all the nooks and crannies that you may forget that a Web surfer who views your site may not have a clue how to find pages. It's important that a user always knows where she is in a site and how to get to a home or core page. A clear exit point is another important feature of good navigation. If a user feels trapped in your site, she won't come back. Therefore, be sure to provide a clearly marked exit page with a fond farewell and some final goodies or tips.

Another important element of good navigational design is consistency. If one page has one navigational system and another has a different one, the user could quickly come to believe she has left your site. Use GoLive components to help maintain navigational consistency.

Considering Your Audience

Good design is good communication, and so be aware of your audience. Design your page so that it communicates who you are and that you under-stand who they are. If the group you're addressing is a group with whom you're familiar, such as a club or civic organization or a certain type of busi-ness, design your communication so that you address them the same way you would at a conference or convention. Speak the audience's language and if you don't know their primary interests and concerns, find out. In some cases, you may even want to consider a bilingual or multilingual site if your audience speaks more than a single language. Remember it's literally a *World Wide* Web, and so is your potential audience.

Keeping a Simple Elegance

Some of the best designs are simplicity exemplified. In all things, simplicity is clarity, beauty, and intelligence. Ironically, it probably takes more time to design a simple site than a complex one. If you (or your client) want everything "up front" where the Web surfer can see them, no one may see anything. A simple "front door" page with an intriguing invitation to enter the site is a far better design than a cluttered one where disparate messages call the viewer's attention in all directions at once and there's no focus.

Choosing Your Colors

Two important considerations should guide your choice of colors. First, you need to understand (or at least consider) the relationship between colors and what your Web site represents. On a more obvious level, if your client's corporate colors are blue (as in Big Blue—IBM) and your client's competition sports red, then you probably don't want to generate too much red in your site. Culturally, colors have different meanings, as well. Japan associates the color white with funerals, whereas Americans associate white with weddings. (Yes! There *is* a difference.)

A second consideration in choice of colors has to do with color schemes. Some excellent books exist on color combinations, and if you're taking site design seriously, you need to read them. If you see a Web site with an attractive color scheme, use GoLive's ability to borrow the color set for your site. If you haven't worked with color schemes and don't yet know much about them, educate yourself.

Ruling Out the Rules

Rarely do you need horizontal rules on your Web page. (That's the <HR> tag for you code jockeys.) Rules separate a page a bit too much. If you have a lot of items on a single page and you want to separate them by using rules, why put them on the same page? The world won't have a silicon shortage because you use an extra page. Use paragraph indents or double spaces instead of rules because rules extinguish continuity and connection in a page. (I'm not even going to tell you where GoLive keeps them. You'll have to dig it up yourself.)

Setting the Tone with Fonts

How you use fonts is one of the most important elements of design. Fonts themselves are designs. Look at pages in books, magazines, and (especially) at the beginning titles in movies. Fonts are everywhere. They convey every emotion humans experience and in an instant fonts tell the viewer the feeling of a page. Choose your fonts carefully, and rarely use more than two fonts on a page. As a general rule, use the sans serif fonts such as Arial, Helvetica, and Verdana for headers and the serif fonts like Times, Georgia, New York, and Palatino for body font. (Verdana is a good, general-purpose font for the Web because it was designed for Web pages.) Because the Web has so few reliable fonts (ones you can be sure all computers see the same way), don't shy away from using graphic fonts for headers. If you need an art deco font for a header on your page, don't risk 95 percent of the computers on the Internet not seeing it correctly— put it in a graphic.

Beautifying Your Page with Balance

A well-balanced page hides its balance, while an unbalanced page advertises its imbalance. When you drive your car on balanced and properly-aligned tires, you feel nothing. But if your tires are out of balance, your car wobbles noticeably. I've seen enough wobbly pages to make me carsick. *Balance* in a Web page refers to the positioning of its elements in a harmonious relationship with one another. Moving a large child forward on a teeter-totter achieves balance when a large child and a small child ride together. The same can be said for a well-balanced Web page. Position large items at the bottom and toward the center, and put smaller items upward and outward. As with considering other elements of design, balance is a quality that needs study and practice.

Lining up everything in the middle of the page and centering your text *is not* balance. Just thought you'd want to know.

Getting to the Core

I try to use a core page consistently in Web pages. Like a home page, the core page resides beyond the primary page in a Web site. It is a Web site's nerve center with an overview and window upon the whole site. Flanked by entry tunnels of pages that lure the viewer to the site and exit tunnels of pages to escort the viewer out, the core page links to all pages or major divisions that make up the site. In a single eyespan, the viewer knows where he is and where to go next in the core page. The core page introduces the navigation, design, and general feel of the site. Each page in the site has a link to the core so that no matter where the Web surfer is in the site, he can easily jump to the core for a reorientation to the site or an easy exit.

Chapter 19

Ten Most Common Web Page Mistakes

*W*eb pages and sites can be a minefield of booby traps if you don't navigate them carefully. Not only must you be aware of technological limitations; you need to consider design and navigational elements of a page. This chapter describes my little shop of horrors for Web sites and pages.

Dancing Baloney

The first rule in designing Web pages is Do Not Annoy The Viewer. Dancing baloney describes the animated pests that inhabit a Web page and draw the viewer's attention away from the content. Usually a dancing baloney page designer is a rank amateur who puts up his first animated GIF innocently and is as pleased as punch with his technological breakthrough. Pesky ads that blink at you while you're trying to find content on a page are common now. (Those ads pay the bills!) However, a grown-up Web page designer putting blinking graphics or text on a page is akin to moving into a cheap hotel room with a neon sign forever announcing its presence. Animated elements on a page draw attention, and if you must use animated materials on your page, slow it down so that the viewer doesn't beat a hasty retreat to another, calmer site.

Big Fat Graphics

The larger a file, the more time it takes to load. The more time it takes to load, the more likely the Web surfer will boogie off to a faster site. Assume that the viewer has the slowest modem speed during peak Internet use hours, and you're safe. If a graphics file is larger than 50K, think about reducing both its size and weight by using any tool you can. After all, what good is a big fat graphic when no one stays around to look at it? (The same goes for a bunch of little graphic files.)

A Web Page Is Not a Book

You're now reading a book. A Web page is not a book. Scientists using Canadian rats found that it takes the rats three times as long to read a Web page as it does a book page. (And even less than that to eat the page.) If your page scrolls on for several screens, the viewer won't be amused and you won't get your content across. As a general rule, I don't like to make my pages any more than two screen scrolls long for a page viewed on a 14-inch monitor. Instead of using the long scroll, use a good navigation system. (Add some graphics to that long page, and you've got a long, long load.)

Lost in the Background

I once saw a Web page that used camouflage for a background. I never found out what the page was about because I couldn't read the text. Another site was so sweet that I got a cavity. It used a bed of roses for a background. Further, by using a pink font, the designer made sure that no one got her message. It astounds me that people use those types of backgrounds and expect people to be able to guess what the page is all about. What's even more dumbfounding is that software companies that sell Web-design tools happily provide these backgrounds free. One of my favorites is a gritty sandpaper or a high-relief wood background that you can get with just about any Web page development program. That background does a great job making text disappear. *Use your head.* If you can't make out a single word on your gravel-encrusted background, nobody else can, either. Use background graphics on your pages judiciously and remember you probably really don't need a graphic background.

This Looks Like a Ransom Note

Just because you have numerous fonts available doesn't mean you have to use them all on your page. Your figuring out that choosing Type⇨Font from the menu bar in GoLive 5 unleashes all the fonts in your computer doesn't mean you have to employ the riches of your fontdom. First, only a handful of fonts show up on everyone's computer, and second, your page is probably really ugly. As a general rule, stick to two, possibly three, fonts. Use the same font set consistently on both your pages and sites.

No Indents Please: I'm a Web Page

One of the most useful ways to separate paragraphs is by using a simple indent. However, few Web pages contain this graceful, yet effective demarcation. Page designers usually prefer either the horizontal rule or a thumping double space. Truly consider using paragraph indents in your body text. The indent provides the information that a new paragraph has begun, but it does not separate it from the preceding paragraph. It provides continuity and uncoupling at the same moment.

Uh, They Changed the Address and Didn't Tell Us

Want to send a Web surfer scurrying? Hook him up to a nonexistent page. One Web-page designer responsibility is periodically checking to make sure that a link still exists. If a link no longer exists, remove the link or change it.

Often, and wisely so, a page design calls for a frame set. A frame set enables a designer to send viewers to an external link and use one of the frames for a navigation tool to keep the user in her own site. When a broken link occurs in a frame set, it looks like something is wrong with your own site and may turn off users.

Who Cut the Graphics with a Chain Saw?

When using graphics, especially transparent GIFs, watch out for jagged edges. Well-designed sites can look awful if the edges of the graphics (especially on curves and angles) appear to have been ripped from a page. Most software applications that prepare graphics for the Web nowadays have an *anti-aliasing* feature. Anti-aliasing smoothes off the edges by blurring them a bit. The blurs are nowhere near as noticeable as the jagged sides of the graphic images. Be acutely aware of using graphic fonts that have not been anti-aliased.

But It Works on My Browser!

If a page looks great on one browser, it may not look so great on another. You must consider two things as far as browsers are concerned. First, and most obvious, look at your site with both Netscape Navigator and Internet Explorer. If a tasteful marquee scrolling your message across the screen is a major feature of your site, you'll be delighted with it in Internet Explorer. However, in Netscape Navigator, the scrolling marquee is stuck like a duck on a frozen pond. Some features work in one browser but not in the other. Second, different versions of the browsers work differently. Newer versions generally pick up the older versions of HTML and JavaScript in Web pages. However, if your pages are involved in some fancy footwork with the latest CSS and JavaScript, you better check them out on some older browsers. This way, you're aware of what minimum version the user needs.

Gee, It Looked Fine on My Computer

On your computer with a 48-inch monitor, a dedicated T3 line, and processor measured in Gigahertz, your pages all look great and load in a blink. However, you have to be realistic if you want to extend your Web reach beyond your own office. Most users still have 14- or 15-inch monitors (including all iMacs) and use phone lines rather than high-speed links. GoLive lets you prepare for different monitor sizes and even how the page looks like on another platform. If you want to reach the widest possible audience, create pages that can be read on their systems, not yours.

Index

Notes

Notes

Notes

IDG BOOKS WORLDWIDE BOOK REGISTRATION

Register This Book and Win!

We want to hear from you!

Visit **http://my2cents.dummies.com** to register this book and tell us how you liked it!

- ✔ Get entered in our monthly prize giveaway.
- ✔ Give us feedback about this book — tell us what you like best, what you like least, or maybe what you'd like to ask the author and us to change!
- ✔ Let us know any other *For Dummies*® topics that interest you.

Your feedback helps us determine what books to publish, tells us what coverage to add as we revise our books, and lets us know whether we're meeting your needs as a *For Dummies* reader. You're our most valuable resource, and what you have to say is important to us!

Not on the Web yet? It's easy to get started with *Dummies 101*®: *The Internet For Windows*® *98* or *The Internet For Dummies*® at local retailers everywhere.

Or let us know what you think by sending us a letter at the following address:

For Dummies Book Registration
Dummies Press
10475 Crosspoint Blvd.
Indianapolis, IN 46256

FOR DUMMIES™

BESTSELLING
BOOK SERIES